D0848843

Rationality in Action

The Jean Nicod Lectures
François Recanati, editor

Rationality in Action

John R. Searle

A Bradford Book
The MIT Press
Cambridge, Massachusetts
London, England

This book was set in Palatino in 3B2 by Asco Typesetters, Hong Kong and was printed and bound in the United States of America.

Library of Congress Cataloging-in-Publication Data

Searle, John R.
  Rationality in action / John R. Searle.
    p.   cm. — (The Jean Nicod lectures)
  "A Bradford book."
  Includes bibliographical references and index.
  ISBN 0-262-19463-5 (hc : alk. paper)
  1. Reasoning. I. Title. II. Series.
BC177 .S42   2001
128'.33—dc21   2001030166

For Dagmar

Contents

Series Foreword

The Jean Nicod Lectures are delivered annually in Paris by a leading philosopher of mind or philosophically oriented cognitive scientist. The 1993 inaugural lectures marked the centenary of the birth of the French philosopher and logician Jean Nicod (1893–1931). The lectures are sponsored by the Centre National de la Recherche Scientifique (CNRS) and are organized in cooperation with the Fondation Maison des Sciences de l'Homme (MSH Foundation). The series hosts the texts of the lectures or the monographs they inspire.

Jacques Bouveresse, President of the Jean Nicod Committee
François Recanati, Secretary of the Jean Nicod Committee and Editor of the Series

Jean Nicod Committee

Mario Borillo
Jean-Pierre Changeux
Jean-Gabriel Ganascia
André Holley
Michel Imbert

Pierre Jacob
Jacques Mehler
Elisabeth Pacherie
Philippe de Rouilhan
Dan Sperber

Acknowledgments

Paul Valéry says somewhere: A poem is never finished, it is abandoned in despair. The same can be said of some works of philosophy. I have more than once, when I have finished a book and finally sent it off to the publisher, had the feeling: "If only I could rewrite it from the beginning, now that I know how it should be done!" Well with this book I actually did rewrite it from the beginning. Some years ago I had finished the draft and had it accepted for publication, but then I decided to rewrite the whole thing. I eliminated some chapters altogether, added others, and rewrote several of those that remained. Now that it is going off to the publisher I still have the same feeling: "If only I could rewrite it from the beginning...."

In part because of this extensive history I have had more helpful comments on this material than is usual, and I am even more indebted than usual to my students and other critics. This material has been the subject of seminars I gave in Berkeley as well as many lectures in North America, Europe, South America, and Asia. It was the subject of a symposium at the Wittgenstein conference in Kirchberg, Austria in 2000, and four of the chapters were presented as the Nicod lectures in Paris, and as the Tasan

Memorial Lectures in Seoul, Korea. An earlier version of
this draft, incorporating most of the first seven chapters,
was the recipient of the Jovellanos International Prize in
Spain and was published in Spanish as *Razones Para
Actuar* by Ediciones Nobel in 2000. I owe a special debt of
gratitude to my Spanish translator, Luis Valdes. Work on
this material actually began over fifteen years ago when
Michael Bratman invited me to address a conference on
practical reason. I am indebted to Michael and the other
conferees for their criticisms. I am grateful to Chris Co-
well for preparing the index, and to the many people
who read and commented on portions of the manuscript,
especially Robert Audi, Guido Bacciagaluppi, Berit Bro-
gaard-Pedersen, Winston Chiong, Alan Code, Boudewijn
de Bruin, Jennifer Hudin, Christine Korsgaard, Josef
Moural, Thomas Nagel, Jessica Samuels, Barry Smith,
Mariam Thalos, Bernard Williams, Leo Zaibert, and most
of all to my wife, Dagmar Searle, to whom this book is
dedicated.

Introduction

This book offers what with some qualification is a theory of practical reason. The main qualification is that the subject is so vast and complex that in a book of this scope I can only deal with certain central problems.

I sometimes work better when I can make a contrast between the view I am presenting and the views I am opposing. Philosophy often proceeds by debate. In this case, the opposing view is a conception of rationality that I was brought up on and that I believe is the dominant conception in our intellectual culture. I call this view, I hope not unfairly, "the Classical Model."

In criticizing the Classical Model, I am criticizing a very powerful tradition in Western philosophy. In this book I point out some of its limitations and try to overcome them. But it may seem excessively critical to be attacking a model of rationality that is in many respects correct, and which emphasizes the role of rationality and intelligence in decision making and in life in general, at a time when there are systematic attacks on the very idea of rationality. Various forms of relativism, sometimes under the label of "postmodernism," have attacked the idea of rationality as such. Rationality is supposed to be essentially oppressive, hegemonic, culturally relative, etc. Why do I criticize a pretty good theory of rationality when rationality as such is under attack? I am as appalled as anyone by these attacks, but I do not bother to answer them because I do not believe they can even be made intelligible. For example, I have sometimes been challenged, "What is your argument for rationality?"—a nonsensical challenge, because the notion of "argument" presupposes standards of rationality. This book is not a defense of rationality, because the idea of a "defense" in the form of argument, reasons, etc. presupposes constraints of rationality, and hence the demand for such a defense is nonsensical. Constraints of rationality are universal and built into the structure of mind and language, specifically into the structures of intentionality and speech acts. One can describe the operation of those contraints, as I try to do in this book, and one can criticize other such descriptions, as I also do, but rationality as such neither requires nor even admits of a justification, because all thought and language, and hence all argument, presupposes rationality. One can intelligibly debate theories of rationality, but not rationality.

This book is a discussion within the tradition of philosophical accounts of rationality and an attempt to improve on the dominant view of the tradition.

In reactions to public lectures on these topics, I have found two persistent mistakes that intelligent people make about what can be expected from a theory of rationality, and I want to block those mistakes at the very beginning. First, many people believe that a theory of rationality should provide them with an algorithm for rational decision making. They think they would not be getting their money's worth out of a book on rationality unless it gave them a concrete method for deciding whether or not to divorce their spouse, which investments to make in the stock market, and which candidate to vote for in the next election. For reasons that are implicit in the analysis that I provide, no theory of rationality will provide an algorithm for making the right decisions. The aim of such a theory is not to tell you how to decide hard issues, but to explain certain structural features of rational decision making. Just as a theory of truth will not give you an algorithm for discovering which propositions are true, so a theory of rationality will not give you an algorithm for making the most rational decisions.

A second mistake that people make about rationality is to suppose that if standards of rationality were universal and if we were all perfectly rational agents, then we would have no disagreements. Consequently, they suppose that the persistence of disagreements among apparently informed and rational agents shows that rationality is somehow relative to cultures and individuals. But all of this is mistaken. Standards of rationality, like standards of truth, are indeed universally valid across individuals and cultures. But given universal standards of rationality and rational deliberation by agents, massive disagreements are still possible, indeed inevitable. Assume universally valid and accepted standards of rationality, assume perfectly rational agents operating with perfect information, and you find that rational disagreement will still occur; because, for example, the rational agents are likely to have different and inconsistent values and interests, each of which may be rationally acceptable. One of the deepest mistakes in our social background assumptions is the idea that unresolvable conflicts are a sign that someone must be behaving irrationally or worse still, that rationality itself is in question.

Many of the issues discussed in this book are traditionally thought of as part of philosophical ethics, in the sense that they are the sorts of issues talked about in university courses on "ethical theory." I have very little to say about ethics as such or about the implication of my views for ethical theory. I am not sure that there is a well-defined branch of philosophy called "ethical theory," but to the extent that there is, its necessary presupposition is an account of rationality in decision making and acting. You cannot intelligently discuss, for example, ethical reasons for action unless first you know what an action is and what a reason is. So this book, though not directly about ethics, deals with many of the foundational issues for any ethical theory.

This investigation is a continuation of my earlier work on problems of mind, language, and social reality. Each book in that work has to stand on its own, but each is part of a much larger overall philosophical structure. To enable this book to stand on its own, I have summarized in chapter 2 some essential elements of my earlier work that will help in understanding this book.

1   The Classical Model of Rationality and Its Weaknesses

I   The Problem of Rationality

During the First World War a famous animal psychologist, Wolfgang Köhler, working on the island of Tenerife, showed that apes were capable of rational decision making. In a typical experiment he put an ape in an environment containing a box, a stick, and a bunch of bananas high up out of reach. After a while the ape figured out how to get the bananas. He moved the box under the bananas, got the stick, climbed up on the box, reached up with the stick and brought down the bananas.[1] Köhler was more interested in Gestalt psychology than in rationality, but his apes exemplified a form of rationality that has been paradigmatic in our theories. The idea is that rational decision making is a matter of selecting *means* that will enable us to achieve our *ends*. The ends are entirely a matter of what we desire. We come to the decision making situation with a prior inventory of desired ends, and rationality is entirely a matter of figuring out the means to our ends.

---

1. Wolfgang Köhler, *The Mentality of Apes*, second edition, London: Routledge and Kegan Paul, 1927. The animals were chimpanzees.

There is no question that the ape exemplifies one type of human rational decision making. But there is a very large number of other types of rational decision making that the ape did not, and presumably could not, engage in. The ape could attempt to figure out how to get bananas now, but he could not attempt to figure out how to get bananas next week. For humans, unlike the ape, much decision making is about the organization of time beyond the immediate present. Furthermore, the ape cannot consider large chunks of time terminating in his own death. Much human decision making, indeed most major decisions, such as where to live, what sort of career to pursue, what kind of family to have, whom to marry, has to do with the allocation of time prior to death. Death, one might say, is the horizon of human rationality; but thoughts about death and the ability to plan with death in mind would seem to be beyond the limitations of the ape's conceptual apparatus. A second difference between human rationality and the ape case is that humans are typically forced to choose between conflicting and incompatible ends. Sometimes that is true of animal decision making—Buridan's ass is a famous hypothetical case—but for Köhler's ape it was the box, stick, and bananas or nothing. The ape's third limitation is that he cannot consider reasons for action that are not dependent on his desires. That is, it seems that his desire to do something with the chair and the stick can be motivated only by a prior desire to eat the bananas. But in the case of human beings, it turns out we have a rather large number of reasons that are not desires. These desire-independent reasons can form the ground for desires, but their being reasons for us does not depend on their being based on desires. This is an interesting and contentious point, and I will return to it in more detail in subsequent chapters. A fourth point of difference between ourselves and the ape is that it appears that the ape has, if anything, only a very limited conception of himself as a self, that is to say, as a rational agent making decisions and capable of assuming responsibility in the future for decisions taken in the present, or responsibility in the present for decisions taken in the past. And a fifth difference, related to the fourth, is that the chimp, unlike the human, does not see his decisions as in any way expressions of, nor commitments to, general principles that apply equally to himself and to other selves.

It is customary in these discussions to say that what the ape lacks is language. The idea, apparently, is that if only we could succeed in teaching the apes the rudiments of linguistic communication, they would have the full range of rational decision making apparatus and responsibility that humans do. I very much doubt that that is the case. The simple ability to symbolize is not by itself sufficient for the full gamut of rational thought processes. Efforts to teach chimpanzees to use symbols linguistically have had, at best, only ambiguous results. But even if they have succeeded, it seems to me that the types of use of symbols purportedly taught to Washoe, Lana, and other famous experimental chimps are insufficient to account for the range of human rational capacities that come with certain special features of human linguistic abilities. The point is that the mere capacity to symbolize does not by itself yield the full range of human rationality. What is necessary, as we will see in these pages, is the capacity for certain types of linguistic representation, and for those types it seems to me we cannot make a clear distinction between the intellectual capacities that are expressed in the notation and the use of the notation itself. The key is this: animals can

deceive but they cannot lie. The ability to lie is a consequence of the more profound human ability to undertake
certain sorts of *commitments*, and those commitments are
cases where the human animal intentionally imposes *conditions of satisfaction on conditions of satisfaction*. If you do
not understand this point, don't worry; I will explain it in
the chapters to come.

Persistent philosophical problems, like the problem of
rationality, have a characteristic logical structure: How
can it be the case that *p*, given that it appears to be certainly the case that *q*, where *q* apparently makes it impossible that *p*. The classic example of this pattern is, of
course, the problem of free will. How can it be the case
that we perform free actions, given that every event has
a cause, and causal determination makes free actions
impossible? The same logical structure pervades a large
number of other problems. How can it be the case that we
have consciousness, given that we are entirely composed
of unconscious bits of matter? The same problem arises
about intentionality: how can it be the case that we have
intentional states—states that refer to objects and states of
affairs in the world beyond themselves—given that we are
made entirely of bits of matter that lack intentionality?
A similar problem arises in skepticism: how can it be
the case that we know anything, given that we can never
be sure we are not dreaming, hallucinating, or being de-
ceived by evil demons? In ethics: how can there be any
values in the world, given that the world consists entirely
of value-neutral facts? A variation on the same question:
how can we know what *ought* to be the case given that all
knowledge is about what *is in fact* the case, and we can
never derive a statement about what ought to be the case
from any set of statements about what is in fact the case?

The problem of rationality, a variant of these persistent problems, can be posed as follows. How can there be rational decision making in world where everything that occurs happens as a result of brute, blind, natural causal forces?

II The Classical Model of Rationality

In the discussion of ape rationality, I remarked that in our intellectual culture, we have a quite specific tradition of discussing rationality and practical reason, rationality in action. This tradition goes back to Aristotle's claim that deliberation is always about means, never about ends,[2] and it continues in Hume's famous claim that "Reason is and ought to be the slave of the passions," and in Kant's claim that "He who wills the end wills the means." The tradition receives its most sophisticated formulation in contemporary mathematical decision theory. The tradition is by no means unified, and I would not wish to suggest that Aristotle, Hume, and Kant share the same conception of rationality. On the contrary, there are striking differences between them. But there is a common thread, and I believe that of the classical philosophers, Hume gives the clearest statement of what I will be referring to as "the Classical Model." I have for a long time had doubts about this tradition and I am going to spend most of this first chapter exposing some of its main features and making a preliminary statement of some of my doubts. One way to describe the Classical Model is to say that it represents human rationality as a more complex version of ape rationality.

---

2. Alan Code has pointed out to me that this standard attribution may be a misunderstanding of Aristotle's actual views.

When I first learned about mathematical decision theory as an undergraduate at Oxford, it seemed to me there was an obvious problem with it: it seems to be a strict consequence of the axioms that if I value my life and I value twenty-five cents (a quarter is not very much money but it is enough to pick up off the sidewalk, for example), there must be some odds at which I would bet my life against a quarter. I thought about it, and I concluded there are no odds at which I would bet my life against a quarter, and if there were, I would not bet my child's life against a quarter. So, over the years, I argued about this with several famous decision theorists, starting with Jimmy Savage in Ann Arbor and including Isaac Levi in New York, and usually, after about half an hour of discussion, they came to the conclusion: "You're just plain irrational." Well, I am not so sure. I think maybe they have a problem with their theory of rationality. Some years later the limitations of this conception of rationality were really brought home to me (and this has some practical importance), during the Vietnam War when I went to visit a friend of mine, who was a high official of the Defense Department, in the Pentagon. I tried to argue him out of the war policy the United States was following, particularly the policy of bombing North Vietnam. He had a Ph.D. in mathematical economics. He went to the blackboard and drew the curves of traditional microeconomic analysis; and then said, "Where these two curves intersect, the marginal utility of resisting is equal to the marginal disutility of being bombed. At that point, they have to give up. All we are assuming is that they are rational. All we are assuming is that the enemy is rational!"

I knew then that we were in serious trouble, not only in our theory of rationality but in its application in practice.

It seems crazy to assume that the decision facing Ho Chih Minh and his colleagues was like a decision to buy a tube of toothpaste, strictly one of maximizing expected utility, but it is not easy to say exactly what is wrong with that assumption, and in the course of this book I want try to say exactly what is wrong with it. As a preliminary intuitive formulation we can say this much. In human rationality, as opposed to ape rationality, there is a distinction between reasons for action which are entirely matters of satisfying some desire or other and reasons which are desire independent. The basic distinction between different sorts of reasons for action is between those reasons which are matters of what you want to do or what you have to do in order to get what you want, on the one hand, and those reasons which are matters of what you have to do regardless of what you want, on the other hand.

Six Assumptions Behind the Classical Model

In this chapter I will state and discuss six assumptions that are largely constitutive of what I have been calling "the Classical Model of Rationality." I do not wish to suggest that the model is unified in the sense that if one accepts one proposition one is committed to all the others. On the contrary, some authors accept some parts and reject other parts. But I do wish to claim that the model forms a coherent whole, and it is one that I find both implicitly and explicitly influential in contemporary writings. Furthermore, the model articulates a conception of rationality that I was brought up on as a student of economics and moral philosophy at Oxford. It did not seem to me satisfactory then, and it does not seem to me satisfactory now.

1. Actions, where rational, are caused by beliefs and desires.

Beliefs and desires function both as causes and as reasons for our actions, and rationality is largely a matter of coordinating beliefs and desires so that they cause actions "in the right way."

It is important to emphasize that the sense of "cause" here is the common or Aristotelian "efficient cause" sense of the word where a cause of an event is what makes it happen. Such causes, in a particular context, are sufficient conditions for an event to occur. To say that specific beliefs and desires caused a particular action is like saying that the earthquake caused the building to collapse.

2. Rationality is a matter of obeying rules, the special rules that make the distinction between rational and irrational thought and behavior.

Our task as theoreticians is to try to make explicit the inexplicit rules of rationality that fortunately most rational people are able to follow unconsciously. Just as they can speak English without knowing the rules of grammar, or they can speak in prose without knowing that they are speaking in prose, as in the famous example of Monsieur Jourdain, so they can behave rationally without knowing the rules that determine rationality and without even being aware that they are following those rules. But we, as theorists, have as our aim to discover and formulate those rules.

3. Rationality is a separate cognitive faculty.

According to Aristotle and a distinguished tradition that he initiated, the possession of rationality is our defining trait as humans: the human being is a rational animal.

Nowadays the fashionable term for faculty is "module," but the general idea is that humans have various special cognitive capacities, one for vision, one for language, etc., and rationality is one of these special faculties, perhaps even the most distinctive of our human capacities. A recent book even speculates on the evolutionary advantages of our having this faculty.[3]

4. Apparent cases of weakness of will, what the Greeks called *akrasia*, can arise only in cases where there is something wrong with the psychological antecedents of the action.
Because rational actions are caused by beliefs and desires, and the beliefs and desires typically cause the action by first leading to the formation of an intention, apparent cases of weakness of will require a special explanation. How is it at all possible that an agent can have the right beliefs and desires, and form the right sort of intention, and still not perform the action? The standard account is that apparent cases of *akrasia* are all cases where the agent did not in fact have the right kind of antecedents to the action. Because the beliefs and desires, and derivatively the intentions, are causes, then if you stack them up rationally, the action will ensue by causal necessity. So in cases where the action does not ensue, there must have been something wrong with the causes.

Weakness of will has always been a problem for the Classical Model, and there is a lot of literature on the subject,[4] but weakness of will is always made out to be

---

3. Robert Nozick, *The Nature of Rationality*, Princeton: Princeton University Press, 1993.
4. For an anthology of earlier work, see *Weakness of Will*, edited by G. W. Mortimore, London: Macmillan St. Martin's Press, 1971.

something very strange and hard to explain, something that could only happen under odd, or bizarre, circumstances. My own view, which I will explain later, is that *akrasia* in rational beings is as common as wine in France. Anybody who has ever tried to stop smoking, lose weight, or drink less at big parties will know what I am talking about.

5. Practical reason has to start with an inventory of the agent's primary ends, including the agent's goals and fundamental desires, objectives, and purposes; and these are not themselves subject to rational constraints.
In order to engage in the activity of practical reasoning, an agent must first have a set of things that he or she wants or values, and then practical reasoning is a matter of figuring out how best to satisfy this set of desires and values. We can state this point by saying that in order for practical reasoning to have any field in which to operate, the agent must begin with a set of primary desires, where desires are construed broadly, so that the agent's evaluations, whether moral, aesthetic, or otherwise, count as desires. But unless you have some such set of desires to start with, there is no scope for reason, because reason is a matter of figuring out what else you ought to desire, given that you already desire something. And those primary desires are not themselves subject to rational constraints.

The model of practical reason is something like the following. Suppose you want to go to Paris, and you reason how best to go. You could take a ship or go by kayak or take an airplane, and finally after the exercise of practical reason, you decide to take the airplane. But if this is the only way that practical reason can operate, by figuring out "means" to "ends," two things follow: first, there can be no reasons for action that do not arise from desires, broadly construed. That is, there cannot be any desire-independent reasons for action. And second, those initial or primary desires cannot themselves be rationally evaluated. Reason is always about the means, never about the ends.

This claim—that there can be no desire-independent reasons for action—is at the heart of the Classical Model. Hume's statement that "Reason is and ought to be the slave of the passions" is usually interpreted as making this claim; and the same claim is made by many recent authors. For example, Herbert Simon writes, "Reason is wholly instrumental. It cannot tell us where to go; at best it can tell us how to get there. It is a gun for hire that can be employed in the service of any goals that we have, good or bad."[5] Bertrand Russell is even more succinct: "Reason has a perfectly clear and concise meaning. It signifies the choice of the right means to an end that you wish to achieve. It has nothing whatever to do with the choice of ends."[6]

6. The whole system of rationality works only if the set of primary desires is consistent.
A typical expression of this view is given by Jon Elster: "Beliefs and desires can hardly be reasons for action unless they are consistent. They must not involve logical, conceptual, or pragmatic contradictions."[7] It is easy to see

---

5. *Reason in Human Affairs*, Stanford, CA: Stanford University Press, 1983, pp. 7–8.
6. *Human Society in Ethics and Politics*, London: Allen and Unwin, 1954, p. viii.
7. *Sour Grapes: Studies in the Subversion of Rationality*, Cambridge: Cambridge University Press, 1983, p. 4.

why this seems plausible: if rationality is a matter of reasoning logically, there cannot be any inconsistencies or contradictions in the axioms. A contradiction implies anything, so if you had a contradiction in your initial set of desires, anything would follow, or so it seems.

Some Doubts about the Classical Model

I could continue this list, and we will have occasion to enrich the characterization of the Classical Model in the course of this book. But even this short list gives the general flavor of the concept, and I want to open the argument by giving some reasons why I think every one of these claims is false. At best they describe special cases, but they do not give a general theory of the role of rationality in thought and action.

1. Rational actions are not caused by beliefs and desires. In general only irrational and nonrational actions are caused by beliefs and desires.

Let us start, as an entering wedge, with the idea that rational actions are those that are caused by beliefs and desires. It is important to emphasize that the sense of "cause" is the ordinary "efficient cause" sense, as in: the explosion caused the building to collapse, or the earthquake caused the destruction of of the freeway. I want to say that cases of actions for which the antecedent beliefs and desires really are causally sufficient, far from being models of rationality, are in fact bizarre and typically irrational cases. These are the cases where, for example, the agent is in the grip of an obsession or an addiction and cannot do otherwise than to act upon his desire. But in a typical case of rational decision making where, for example, I am trying to decide which candidate to vote for, I have a choice and I consider various reasons for choosing among the alternatives available to me. But I can only engage in this activity if I assume that my set of beliefs and desires by itself is not causally sufficient to determine my action. The operation of rationality presupposes that there is a gap between the set of intentional states on the basis of which I make my decision, and the actual making of the decision. That is, unless I presuppose that there is a gap, I cannot get started with the process of rational decision making. To see this point you need only consider cases where there is no gap, where the belief and the desire are really causally sufficient. This is the case, for example, where the drug addict has an overpowering urge to take heroin, and he believes that this is heroin; so, compulsively, he takes it. In such a case the belief and the desire are sufficient to determine the action, because the addict cannot help himself. But that is hardly the model of rationality. Such cases seem to be outside the scope of rationality altogether.

In the normal case of rational action, we have to presuppose that the antecedent set of beliefs and desires is not causally sufficient to determine the action. This is a presupposition of the process of deliberation and is absolutely indispensable for the application of rationality. We presuppose that there is a gap between the "causes" of the action in the form of beliefs and desires and the "effect" in the form of the action. This gap has a traditional name. It is called "the freedom of the will." In order to engage in rational decision making we have to presuppose free will. Indeed, as we will see later, we have to presuppose free will in any rational activity whatever. We cannot avoid the presupposition, because even a refusal to engage in rational decision making is only intelligible to us as a refusal if we take it as an exercise of freedom. To see this, consider examples. Suppose you go into a restaurant, and the waiter brings you the menu. You have a choice between, let's say, veal chops and spaghetti; you cannot say: "Look, I am a determinist, che sarà, sarà. I will just wait and see what I order! I will wait to see what my beliefs and desires cause." This refusal to exercise your freedom is itself only intelligible to you as an exercise of freedom. Kant pointed this out a long time ago: There is no way to think away your own freedom in the process of voluntary action because the process of deliberation itself can only proceed on the presupposition of freedom, on the presupposition that there is a gap between the causes in the form of your beliefs, desires, and other reasons, and the actual decision that you make.

If we are going to speak precisely about this, I think we must say that there are (at least) three gaps. First, there is the gap of rational decision making, where you try to make up your mind what you are going to do. Here the gap is between the reasons for making up your mind, and the actual decision that you make. Second, there is a gap between the decision and the action. Just as the reasons for the decision were not causally sufficient to produce the decision, so the decision is not causally sufficient to produce the action. There comes the point, after you have made up your mind, when you actually have to do it. And once again, you cannot sit back and let the decision cause the action, any more than you can sit back and let the reasons cause the decision. For example, let us suppose you have made up your mind that you are going to vote for candidate Jones. You go into the voting booth with this decision firmly in mind, but once there you still have to do it. And sometimes, because of this second gap, you just do not do it. For a variety of possible reasons—or maybe none—you do not do the thing you have decided to do.

There is a third gap that arises for actions and activities extended in time, a gap between the initiation of the action and its continuation to completion. Suppose, for example, that you have decided to learn Portuguese, swim the English Channel, or write a book about rationality. There is first the gap between the reasons for the decision and the decision, second the gap between the decision and the initiation of the action, and third there is a gap between starting the task and its continuation to completion. Even once you have started you cannot let the causes operate by themselves; you have to make a continuous voluntary effort to keep going with the action or activity to its completion.

At this point of the discussion I want to emphasize two points: the existence of the gap(s) and the centrality of the gap(s) for the topic of rationality.

What is the argument for the existence of the gap(s)? I will develop these arguments in more detail in chapter 3; for present purposes we can say that the simplest arguments are the ones I just gave. Consider any situation of rational decision making and acting and you will see that you have a sense of alternative possibilities open to you and that your acting and deliberating make sense only on the presupposition of those alternative possibilities. Contrast these situations with those where you have no such sense of possibilities. In a situation in which you are in the grip of an overpowering rage, so that you are, as they say, totally out of control, you have no sense that you could be doing something else.

Another way to see the existence of the gap is to notice that in a decision making situation you often have several different reasons for performing an action, yet you act on one and not the others and you know without observation which one you acted on. This is a remarkable fact, and notice the curious locution we have for describing it: *you acted on* such and such a reason. Suppose for example that you had a whole bunch of reasons both for and against voting for Clinton in the presidential election. You thought he would be a better president for the economy but worse for foreign policy. You liked the fact that he went to your old college but didn't like his personal style. In the end you voted for him because he went to your old college. The reasons did not operate on you. Rather you *chose* one reason and acted on that one. You made that reason effective by *acting on it*.

This is why, incidentally, the explanation of your action and its justification may not be the same. Suppose you are asked to justify voting for Clinton; you might do so by appealing to his superior management of the economy. But it may be the case that the actual reason you acted on was that he went to your old college in Oxford, and you thought, "College loyalty comes first." And the remarkable thing about this phenomenon is: in the normal case you know without observation which reason was effective, because you made it effective. That is to say, a reason for action is an effective reason only if you make it effective.

An understanding of the gap is essential for the topic of rationality because rationality can operate only in the gap. Though the concept of freedom and the concept of rationality are quite different, the extension of rationality is exactly that of freedom. The simplest argument for this point is that rationality is possible only where irrationality is possible, and that requirement entails the possibility of choosing between various rational options as well as irrational options. The scope of that choice is the gap in question. The claim that rationality can operate only in the gap is as much true of theoretical reason as it is of practical reason, but for theoretical reason it is a more subtle point to make, so I will save it for later and concentrate on practical reason now.

I will have a great deal more to say about the gap in the course of this book, and in a sense the book is about the gap, because the problem of rationality is a problem about the gap. At this stage just two more points:

First: what fills the gap? Nothing. Nothing fills the gap: you make up your mind to do something, or you just haul off and do what you are going to do, or you carry out the decision you previously made, or you keep going, or fail to keep going, in some project that you have undertaken.

Second: even though we have all these experiences, could not the whole thing be an illusion? Yes it could. Our gappy experiences are not self-validating. On the basis of what I have said so far, free will could still be a massive illusion. The *psychological* reality of the gap does not guarantee a corresponding *neurobiological* reality. I will explore these issues in chapter 9.

2.   Rationality is not entirely or even largely a matter of following rules of rationality.

Let us turn to the second claim of the Classical Model, that rationality is a matter of rules, that we think and behave rationally only to the extent that we think and act according to these rules. When asked to justify this claim, I think most traditional theorists would simply appeal to the rules of logic. An obvious kind of case that a defender of the Classical Model might present would be, let's say, a simple modus ponens argument:

If it rains tonight, the ground will be wet.

It will rain tonight.

Therefore, the ground will be wet.

Now, if you are asked to justify this inference, the temptation is to appeal to the rule of modus ponens: p, and if p then q, together imply q.

$$(p \,\&\, (p \rightarrow q)) \rightarrow q$$

But that is a fatal mistake. When you say that, you are in the grip of the Lewis Carroll paradox.[8] I will now remind you how it goes: Achilles and the tortoise are having an argument, and Achilles says (this is not his example but it makes the same point), "If it rains tonight, the ground will be wet, it will rain tonight, therefore the ground will be wet," and the tortoise says, "Fine, write that down, write all that stuff down," And when Achilles had done so he says, "I don't see how you get from the stuff before the 'therefore' to the stuff after. What forces you to to make or even justifies you in making that move?" Achilles says, "Well that move rests on the rule of modus ponens, the rule that p, and if p then q, together imply q." "Fine," says the tortoise, "So write that down, write that down with all the rest." And when Achilles had done so the tortoise says, "Well we have all that written down, but I still don't see how you get to the conclusion, that the ground will be wet." "Well don't you see?" says Achilles, "Whenever you have p, and if p then q, and you have the rule of modus ponens that says whenever you have p, and if p then q, you can infer q, then you can infer q." "Fine," says the tortoise, "now just write all that down." And you see where this is going. We are off and running with an infinite regress.

The way to avoid an infinite regress is to refuse to make the first fatal move of supposing that the rule of modus ponens plays *any role whatever* in the validity of the inference. The derivation does not get its validity from the rule of modus ponens; rather, the inference is perfectly valid as it stands without any outside help. It would be more accurate to say that the rule of modus ponens gets its validity from the fact that it expresses a pattern of an infinite number of inferences that are independently valid. The actual argument does not get its validity from any external source: if it is valid, it can be valid only because the premises entail the conclusion. Because the meanings of the words themselves are sufficient to guarantee the validity of the inference, we can formalize a pattern that describes an infinite number of such inferences. But the inference does not derive its validity from the pattern. The so-called rule of modus ponens is just a statement of a pattern of an infinite number of such independently valid inferences. Remember: *If you think that you need a rule to infer q from p and (if p then q), then you would also need a rule to infer p from p.*

What goes for this argument goes for any valid deductive argument. Logical validity does not derive from the rules of logic.

It is important to understand this point precisely. It is usually said that the mistake of Achilles was to treat modus ponens as another premise and not as a rule. But that is wrong. Even if he writes it down as a rule and not a premise, there would still be an infinite regress. It is equally wrong (indeed it is the same mistake) to say that the derivation derives its validity from both the premises and the rule of inference.[9] The correct thing is to say that the rules of logic play no role whatever in the validity of valid inferences. The arguments, if valid, have to be valid as they stand.

We are actually blinded to this point by our very sophistication, because the achievements of proof theory have been so great, and have had such important payoffs in fields like computer science, that we think that the syntactical analogue of modus ponens is really the same thing as the "rule" of logic. But they are quite different. If you have an actual rule that says whenever you see, or your computer "sees," a symbol with this shape:

p

followed by one with this shape:

$p \rightarrow q,$

you or it writes down one with this shape:

$q,$

you have an actual rule that you can follow and that you can program into the machine so as to causally affect its operations. This is a proof-theoretical analogue of the rule of modus ponens, and it really is substantive, because the marks that this rule operates over are just meaningless

---

9. For an example of this claim see Peter Railton, "On the Hypothetical and the Non-Hypothetical in Reasoning about Belief and Action," pp. 53–79 in G. Cullity and B. Gaut, *Ethics and Practical Reason*, Oxford: Oxford University Press, 1997, esp. pp. 76–79.

symbols. The rule operates over otherwise uninterpreted formal elements.

Thus are we blinded to the fact that in real-life reasoning, the rule of modus ponens plays no justificatory role at all. We can make proof-theoretical or syntactical models, where the model exactly mirrors the substantive or contentful processes of actual human reasoning. And of course, as we all know, you can do a lot with the models. If you get the syntax right, then you can plug in the semantics at the beginning and it will go along for a free ride, and you get the right semantics out at the end because you have the right syntactical transformations.

There are certain famous problems, most famously Gödel's Theorem, but if we leave them to one side, the sophistication of our simulations in machine models of reasoning makes us forget the semantic content. But in real-life reasoning it is the semantic content that guarantees the validity of the inference, *not the syntactical rule.*

There are two important philosophical points to be made about the Lewis Carroll paradox. The first, which I have been belaboring, is that the rule plays no role whatever in the validity of the inference. The second is about the gap. *We need to distinguish between entailment and validity as logical relations on the one hand, and inferring as a voluntary human activity on the other.* In the case we considered, the premises entail the conclusion, so the inference is valid. But there is nothing that forces any actual human being to make that inference. You have the same gap for the human activity of inferring as you do for any other voluntary activity. Even if we convinced both Achilles and the Tortoise that the inference was valid as it stands and that the rule of modus ponens does not lend any validity to the inference, all the same, the tortoise might still, irrationally, refuse to make the inference. The gap applies even to logical inferences.

I am not saying that there could not be any rules to help us in rational decision making. On the contrary there are many famous such rules and even maxims. Here are some of them: "A stitch in time saves nine." "Look before you leap." "He who laughs last laughs best." And my favorite, "Le coeur a ses raisons que la raison ne connaît pas." What I am saying is that rationality is not constituted as a set of rules, and rationality in thought as well as in action is not defined by any set of rules. The structure of intentional states and the constitutive rules of speech acts already contain constraints of rationality.

3.   There is no separate faculty of rationality.

It should be implicit in what I have said that there cannot be a separate faculty of rationality distinct from such capacities as those for language, thought, perception, and the various forms of intentionality, because rational constraints are already built into, they are internal to, the structure of intentionality in general and language in particular. Once you have intentional states, once you have beliefs and desires and hopes and fears, and, especially, once you have language, then you already have the constraints of rationality. That is, if you have a beast that has the capacity for forming beliefs on the basis of its perceptions, and has the capacity for forming desires in addition to beliefs, and also has the capacity to express all this in a language, then it already has the constraints of rationality built into those structures. To make this clear with an example: there is no way you can make a statement without committing yourself regarding such questions as, "Is it true or false?" "Is it consistent, or inconsistent with other things I have said?" So, the constraints of rationality are not an extra faculty in addition to intentionality and language. Once you have intentionality and language, you already have phenomena that internally and constitutively possess the constraints of rationality.

I like to think of it this way: The constraints of rationality ought to be thought of adverbially. They are a matter of the way in which we coordinate our intentionality. They are a matter of the way in which we coordinate the relations between our beliefs, desires, hopes, fears, and perceptions, and other intentional phenomena.

That coordination presupposes the existence of the gap. It presupposes that the phenomena at any given point are not causally sufficient to fix the rational solution to a problem. And I think we can now see why the same point operates for theoretical as well as for practical reason. If I hold up my hand in front of my face, there is no gap involved in seeing my hand, because I cannot help seeing my hand in front of my face if there is sufficient light and my eyesight is good. It is not up to me. So there is no question of such a perception being either rational or irrational. But now, suppose I refuse to believe that there is a hand in front of my face, even in this situation where I cannot help seeing it. Suppose I just refuse to accept it: "You say there's a hand there but I damn well refuse to accept that claim." Now the question of rationality does arise, and I think we would say that I am being irrational in such a situation.

I want to emphasize a point I made earlier. You can only have rationality where you have the possibility of irrationality. And with just sheer, raw perceptions, you do not get rationality or irrationality. They only come into play where you have a gap, where the existence of the intentional phenomena by themselves is not sufficient to cause the outcome, and these are cases where you have to decide what you are going to do or think.

This is why people whose behavior is determined by sufficient causal conditions are removed from the scope of rational assessment. For example, not long ago I was in a committee meeting, and a person whom I had previously respected voted in the stupidest possible way. I said to him afterwards, "How could you have voted that way on that issue?" And he said, "Well, I'm just incurably politically correct. I just can't help myself." His claim amounts to saying that his decision making in this case was outside the scope of rational assessment, because the apparent irrationality was a result of the fact that he had no choice at all, that the causes were causally sufficient.

4.   Weakness of will is a common, natural form of irrationality. It is a natural consequence of the gap.
On the Classical Model, cases of weakness of will are strictly speaking impossible. If the antecedents of the action are both rational and causal, and the causes set sufficient conditions, then the action has to ensue. It follows that if you did not do the thing you set out to do, then that can only be because there was something wrong with the way you set up the antecedents of the action. Your intention was not the right kind of intention,[10] or you were not fully morally committed to the course you claimed to be committed to.[11]

---

10. Donald Davidson, "How Is Weakness of the Will Possible?" *Essays on Actions and Events*, Oxford: Clarendon Press, Oxford University Press, New York, 1980.
11. R. M. Hare, *The Language of Morals*, Oxford: Oxford University Press, 1952.

I want to say, on the contrary, that no matter how perfectly you structure the antecedents of your action, weakness of will is always possible. Here is how: at any given point in our waking lives, we are confronted with an indefinitely large range of possibilities. I can raise my right arm, or I can raise my left arm; I can put my hat on top of my head, or I can wave it around. I can drink water or not drink water. More radically, I can walk out of the room and go to Timbuktu, or join a monastery, or do any number of other things. I have an open-ended sense of possibilities. Now, of course, in real life there will be restrictions set by my Background, by my biological limitations and by the culture that I have been brought up in. The Background restricts my sense of the possibilities that are open to me at any given time. I cannot, for example, in real life, imagine doing what St. Simeon Stylites did. He spent thirty five years on top of a pillar, just sitting there on a tiny platform, all for the glory of God. That is not an option that I could seriously consider. But I still have an indefinite range of real options that I am capable of perceiving as options. Weakness of will arises simply from the fact that at any point the gap provides an indefinitely large range of choices open to me and some of them will seem attractive even if I have already made up my mind to refuse them. It does not matter how you structure the causes of the action in the form of antecedent intentional states—beliefs, desires, choices, decisions, intentions—in the case of voluntary actions, the causes still do not set sufficient conditions, and this opens the way for weakness of will.

It is an unfortunate feature of our philosophical tradition that we make weakness of will out to be something really strange, really bizarre, whereas, I have to say, I think it is very common in real life. I devote chapter 7 to this issue, so I will not say any more about it now.

5. Contrary to the Classical Model there are desire-independent reasons for action.

The fifth thesis of the Classical Model that I want to challenge has a very long history in our philosophical tradition. The idea is this: a rational act can only be motivated by a desire, where "desire" is construed broadly to include moral values that one has accepted and various sorts of evaluations that one has made. Desires need not be all egotistical, but for any rational process of deliberation there must be some desire that the agent had prior to the process, otherwise there would be nothing to reason from. There would not be any basis on which you could do your reasoning, if you did not have a set of desires in advance. Thus there can be no reasoning about ends, only about means. A sophisticated contemporary version of this view is found in the work of Bernard Williams,[12] who claims that there cannot be any "external" reasons for an agent to act. Any reason that is a reason for the agent must appeal to something "internal" to his "motivational set." This, in my terminology, amounts to saying that there cannot be any desire-independent reasons for action.

I am going to criticize this view in great detail later, but at this point I want to make only one criticism. This view

---

12. "External and Internal Reasons," reprinted in his *Moral Luck: Philosophical Papers 1973–1980* Cambridge: Cambridge University Press, 1981, pp. 101–113. Williams denies that his model is restricted to ends-means reasoning, but the other sorts of cases he considers, such as inventing alternative courses of action, do not seem to me to alter the basic ends-means structure of his model. See his "Internal Reasons and the Obscurity of Blame" reprinted in his *Making Sense of Humanity and Other Philosophical Papers*, Cambridge University Press, 1998, pp. 38–45.

has the following absurd consequence: at any given point in one's life no matter what the facts are, and no matter what one has done in the past or knows about one's future, no one can have any reason to do anything unless right then and there, there is an element of that person's motivational set, a desire broadly construed, to do that thing, or a desire for which doing that thing would be a "means" to that "end," that is, a means to satisfying that desire.

Now why is that absurd? Well, try to apply it to real-life examples. Suppose you go into a bar and order a beer. The waiter brings the beer and you drink it. Then the waiter brings you the bill and you say to him, "I have looked at my motivational set and I find no internal reason for paying for this beer. None at all. Ordering and drinking the beer is one thing, finding something in my motivational set is something else. The two are logically independent. Paying for the beer is not something I desire for its own sake, nor is it a means to an end or constitutive of some end that is represented in my motivational set. I have read Professor Williams, and I have also read Hume on this subject, and I looked carefully at my motivational set, and I cannot find any desire there to pay this bill! I just can't! And therefore, according to all the standard accounts of reasoning, I have no reason whatever to pay for this beer. It is not just that I don't have a strong enough reason, or that I have other conflicting reasons, but I have zero reason. I looked at my motivational set, I went through the entire inventory, and I found no desire that would lead by a sound deliberative route to the action of my paying for the beer."

We find this speech absurd because we understand that when you ordered the beer and drank it, if you are a sane and rational person, you were intentionally *creating* a desire-independent reason, a reason for doing something regardless of what was in your motivational set when the time came to do it. The absurdity lies in the fact that on the Classical Model the existence of a reason for an agent to act depends on the existence of a certain sort of psychological element in his motivational set, it depends on the existence of a desire, broadly construed, then and there; and in the absence of that desire the agent has no reason, regardless of all the other facts about him and his history, and regardless of what he knows. But in real life the sheer knowledge of external facts in the world, such as the fact that you ordered the beer and drank it, can be a rationally compelling reason to pay for it.

The question, how is it possible that there can be desire-independent reasons for action, is an interesting and nontrivial question. I think most of the standard accounts are mistaken. I intend to devote extensive discussion to this issue later in this book, in chapter 6, so I will not discuss it further here.

There are really two strands to this aspect of the Classical Model. First we are supposed to think that all reasoning is about means not about ends, that there are no external reasons for action. And second, we are to believe a corollary, that the primary ends in the motivational set are outside the scope of reason. Remember that Hume also says, "'Tis not contrary to the dictates of reason, to prefer the destruction of the whole world to the scratching of my little finger." The way to assess any such claim is always to bring it down to real-life cases. Suppose the president of the United States went on television and said, "I have consulted with the Cabinet and the leaders of Congress, and I have decided that there's no reason why I should prefer the scratching of my little finger to the destruction of the whole world." If he did this in real life we would feel he had, to use the terminology of Hume's era, "lost his reason." There is something fishy about Hume's claim and about the general thesis that one's fundamental ends can be anything whatever, and are totally outside the scope of rationality, that where primary desires are concerned, everything has equal status and is equally arbitrary. I think that cannot be the right way to look at these matters.

The thesis that there are no desire-independent reasons for action, that there are no external reasons, is logically closely related to Hume's doctrine that one cannot derive an "ought" from an "is." Here is the connection. "Ought" statements express reasons for action. To say that someone ought to do something is to imply that there is a reason for him to do it. So Hume's claim amounts to the claim that statements asserting the existence of reasons for action cannot be derived from statements about how things are. But how things are is a matter of how things are in the world as it exists independent of the agent's motivational set. So on this interpretation, the claim that how things are in the world cannot imply the existence of any reasons in an agent's motivational set (one cannot derive "ought" from "is") is closely related to the claim that there are no facts in the world, independent of the agent, that by themselves constitute reasons for action (there are no external reasons). Hume says, in effect, we cannot get values from facts; Williams says we cannot get motivations from external facts by themselves. The point of connection lies in the fact that the acceptance of a value is the acceptance of a motivation. However we interpret both claims, I think they are both demonstrably false, and I intend to discuss this issue in some detail in the course of this book.

6.   Inconsistent reasons for action are common and indeed inevitable. there is no rational requirement that rational decision making must start with a consistent set of desires or other primary reasons for acting.

The last point I want to take up is the question of consistency. As with the argument about weakness of will, this part of the Classical Model—the claim that the set of primary desires from which one reasons must be consistent —does not seem to me just a little bit false, but radically mistaken. It seems to me that most practical reasoning is typically about adjudicating between conflicting, inconsistent desires and other sorts of reasons. Right now, today, I very much want to be in Paris but I also want very much to be in Berkeley. And this is not a bizarre situation; rather it seems to me typical that we have an inconsistent set of ends. Given the extra premise that I know I cannot be both in Berkeley and in Paris at the same time, I have an inconsistent set of desires; and the task of rationality, the task of practical reason, is to try to find some way to adjudicate between these various inconsistent aims. Typically in practical reasoning you have to figure out how to give up on satisfying some desires in order to satisfy others. The standard way out of this problem in the literature is to say that rationality is not about desires as such but about *preferences*. Rational deliberation must begin with a well-ordered preference schedule. The problem with that answer is that in real life deliberation is largely about forming a set of preferences. A well-ordered set of preferences is typically the *result* of successful deliberation, and is not its *precondition.* Which do I prefer, to be in Berkeley or Paris? Well, I would have to think about it.

And even after you have made up your mind, you decide "OK, I'm going to Paris," that decision itself introduces all sorts of other conflicts. You want to go to Paris, but you do not want to stand in line at airports, you do not want to eat airplane food, you do not want to sit next to people who are trying to put their elbow where you are trying to put your elbow. And so on. There are just all kinds of things that you do not want to happen, which you know are going to happen once you try to carry out your decision to go to Paris and to go by plane. By satisfying one desire you frustrate other desires. The point I want to emphasize is that there is a long tradition associated with the Classical Model, whereby inconsistent reasons for action, such as inconsistent obligations, are supposed to be philosophically odd or unusual. Often people in the tradition try to fudge the inconsistencies by saying that some of the apparently inconsistent obligations are not real honest-to-john obligations, but mere "prima facie" obligations. But rational decision making is typically about choosing between conflicting reasons for action, and you only have a genuine conflict of obligations where they are all genuine obligations. There is a serious question as to how there can be logically inconsistent but equally valid reasons for action, and why practical reason must involve conflicts between such valid but logically inconsistent reasons. I will take up this issue in more detail in subsequent chapters.

The aim of this chapter has been to introduce the subject matter of this book by laying bare some of the constitutive principles of the tradition I wish to overcome, and by stating, in a preliminary way, some of my objections to the tradition. We began the chapter with Köhler's apes, so let's end with them. On the Classical Model human rationality is an extension of chimpanzee rationality. We are extremely clever, talking chimps. But I think there are some fundamental differences between human rationality and the instrumental reasoning of the chimpanzees. The greatest single difference between humans and the rest of the animal kingdom as far as rationality is concerned is our ability to create, recognize, and act on desire-independent reasons for action. I will explore this and other features of human rationality in the rest of this book.

2   The Basic Structure of Intentionality, Action, and Meaning

I said in chapter 1 that many mistakes in the discussion of practical reason derive from an adherence to a mistaken conception of rationality, a conception that I have called the "Classical Model." But there is a second reason for a number of mistakes: the authors in question seldom proceed from an adequate philosophy of intentionality and of action to start with. Trying to write about rationality without an adequate general conception of mind, language, and action is like trying to write about transportation without knowing about cars, buses, trains, and airplanes. For example, a question that is commonly asked is: what stands to action in the way that truth stands to belief? The idea is that if we could get clearer about the purpose of action the way that we can get clear about the relation of belief to truth, then somehow or other the subject of practical reason would become clearer. But the whole question is muddled. Nothing stands to action in the relation in which belief stands to truth, for reasons that will become, I hope, completely clear when I explain the intentional structure of actions.

In this chapter I present, in bare outline, a general theory of the intentional structure of human action, meaning, and institutional facts. It is impossible to understand rational action if you do not understand what an intentional action is in the first place, and it is impossible to understand reasons for action if you do not understand how humans can create commitments and other meaningful entities and thereby create reasons. But it is impossible to understand these notions without first having some understanding of intentionality in general. Unless the reader is clear about such basic notions as psychological mode, intentional content, conditions of satisfaction, direction of fit, intentional causation, causal self-referentiality, status functions, etc., he or she will not understand the argument that follows. What I say in this chapter is almost entirely a repetition of material from my other books, especially *Intentionality*[1] and *The Construction of Social Reality*.[2] For a more detailed exposition of the points made in this chapter, as well as arguments for these conclusions, the reader should consult those books. Readers familiar with the arguments of those books can read through this chapter rapidly.

I do not know how to present the material of this chapter efficiently except by laying it out, Tractatus style, as a set of numbered propositions.

1.   The definition of intentionality: intentionality is directedness.

"Intentionality," as philosophers use the word, refers to that aspect of mental states by which they are directed at, or about, or of states of affairs in the world beyond themselves. "Intentionality" has no special connection with

1. John R. Searle, *Intentionality: An Essay in the Philosophy of Mind*, Cambridge: Cambridge University Press, 1983.
2. John R. Searle, *The Construction of Social Reality*, New York: The Free Press, 1995.

"intending" in the ordinary English sense, in which, for example, I intend to go to the movies tonight. Intending is just one kind of intentionality among others. Thus, for example, beliefs, fears, hopes, desires, and intentions are all intentional states, as are the emotions such as love and hate, fear and joy, pride and shame. Any state that is directed at something beyond itself is an intentional state. So, for example, visual experiences are intentional but undirected anxieties are not.

2. Intentional states consist in a content and a psychological mode, and often the content is a whole proposition.

Intentional states typically have a structure analogous to the structure of speech acts. Just as I can order you to leave the room, ask whether you will leave the room, and predict that you will leave the room, so I can hope that you will leave the room, fear that you will leave the room, or desire that you will leave the room. In each case there is a propositional content, that you will leave the room, which comes in one or another of the various linguistic or psychological modes. In the case of language it can, for example, come in the form of a question, prediction, promise, or order. In the case of the mind it can, for example, come in the form of beliefs, fears, and desires. For this reason I will represent the general structure of intentionality as of the form

S (p)

The "S" in this formula marks the type of psychological state, and the "p" marks the propositional content of the state. It is essential to make this distinction because the same propositional content can occur in different psychological modes. For example, I can both believe that it will rain, and hope that it will rain; and of course the same psychological mode, such as belief, can accommodate a potentially infinite number of different propositional contents. I can believe all sorts of things.

Not all intentional states have an entire proposition as their intentional content. Beliefs and desires have entire propositions, but love and hate do not necessarily. One can, for example, simply love Sally or hate Harry. For this reason, some philosophers refer to intentional states with an entire propositional content as "propositional attitudes." I think this terminology is confused, because it suggests that a belief or a desire is an attitude toward a proposition, but that is not the case. If I believe that Clinton is president, my attitude is toward Clinton, the man himself, not toward the proposition. The proposition is the *content*, not the object, of my belief. So I will avoid the terminology of "propositional attitudes," and just refer to intentional states, and make a distinction within intentional states between those that have entire propositions as their contents, and those that do not. Thus the difference between believing that Clinton is president and hating Harry will be represented as follows:

Bel (Clinton is president)

Hate (Harry)

3.   Propositional intentional states typically have conditions of satisfaction and a direction of fit.
Intentional states with a propositional content can either match or fail to match reality, and the way they are supposed to match reality is determined by the psychological mode. Beliefs, for example, are true or false, depending on

whether the content of the belief matches an independently existing reality. But desires are not true or false; they are fulfilled or frustrated, depending on whether reality matches or comes to match the content of the desire. Intentions, like desires, are not true or false but are carried out or not carried out, depending on whether the behavior of the person with the intention comes to match the content of the intention. To account for these facts, we need the notions of *conditions of satisfaction* and *direction of fit*. Intentional states such as beliefs, desires, and intentions have conditions of satisfaction and directions of fit. A belief is satisfied if true, not satisfied if false. A desire will be satisfied if fulfilled, not satisfied if frustrated. An intention will be satisfied if carried out, not satisfied if not carried out.

Furthermore, these conditions of satisfaction are represented with different *directions of fit*, or different responsibilities for fitting. Thus, for example, a belief can be true or false, depending on whether or not the propositional content of the belief actually matches the way things are in the world that exists independently of the belief. For example, if I believe that it is raining, my belief will be true, hence satisfied, if and only if it is raining. Because it is the responsibility of the belief to match an independently existing state of affairs in the world, we can say that the belief has the *mind-to-world direction of fit*. It is the task of the belief, as part of the mind, to represent or fit an independently existing reality, and it will succeed or fail depending on whether or not the content of the belief in the mind actually does fit the reality in the world. Desires, on the other hand, have the opposite direction of fit from beliefs. Desires represent not how things are in the world, but how we would like them to be. It is, so to speak, the task of the world to fit the desire. Desires and intentions, unlike beliefs, have the *world-to-mind direction of fit*. If my belief is false, I can fix it up by changing the belief, but I do not in that way make things right if my desire is not satisfied by changing the desire. To fix things up, the world has to change to match the content of the desire. For that reason I say that desires and intentions, unlike beliefs, have the *world-to-mind direction of fit*.

This distinction is marked for us in ordinary language by the fact that we do not say of desires and intentions that they are true or false. We say rather that the desire is fulfilled or frustrated; and the intention is or is not carried out, depending on whether or not the world comes to match the content of the desire or the intention. The simplest rough and ready test for whether or not an intentional state has the mind-to-world direction of fit is whether or not you can literally say of it that it is true or false.

Some intentional states, such as many of the emotions, do not in this sense have a direction of fit, because they presuppose that the propositional content of the emotion is already satisfied. Thus if I am overjoyed that France won the World Cup, I simply take it for granted that France won the World Cup. My joy has as its propositional content that France won the World Cup, and I presuppose that the propositional content matches reality. It is not the point of the intentional state to represent either how I believe the world is in fact or how I want it to be; rather it is presupposed that the propositional content matches reality. In such cases I say that the intentional state has the null or zero direction of fit. We may then identify three directions of fit: mind-to-world, which is characteristic of beliefs and other cognitive states; world-to-mind, which is characteristic of intentions and desires as well as other volitive and conative states; and the null direction of fit, which is characteristic of emotions such as pride and shame, joy and despair. Though many emotions do not have a direction of fit as such, they typically contain desires and beliefs and these do have directions of fit. Thus emotions such as love and hate can play a role in practical reason because they contain desires, and these desires do have a direction of fit and thus can motivate rational actions. This feature will prove important in our discussion of motivation.

The notions of conditions of satisfaction and direction of fit apply to both mental and linguistic entities. Indeed it was because of the parallels with speech acts that I was led to many of the conclusions I came to about the nature of the mind. Statements, like beliefs, represent their conditions of satisfaction with the word-to-world (like mind-to-world) direction of fit; orders and promises, like desires and intentions represent their conditions of satisfaction with the world-to-word (like world-to-mind) direction of fit.

4. Many entities in the world that are not, strictly speaking, parts of mind or language have conditions of satisfaction and direction of fit.
The map of a territory, for example, can be accurate or inaccurate; it has the map-to-world direction of fit. The blueprints for a house to be built will either be followed or not followed; they have the world-to-blueprint direction of fit. The contractor is supposed to build the building to match the blueprint. Needs, obligations, requirements, and duties are also not in any strict sense linguistic entities, but they also have propositional contents and directions of fit. They have the same direction of fit as desires,

intentions, orders, and promises. If for example I am under an obligation to pay some money, then my obligation will be discharged (satisfied) if and only if I pay the money. Thus the obligation is satisfied if and only if the world changes to match the content of the obligation. Needs, requirements, commitments, and duties, like obligations, have a direction of fit that requires the world to change to match the need, requirement, commitment, or duty, in order that they be satisfied.

I like to use very simple metaphors, and represent phenomena such as beliefs, statements, and maps as hovering above the world, pointing down at the world they represent. So I think of the language-to-world, mind-to-world direction of fit as going downward. And I sometimes represent that direction of fit with a downward arrow. Correspondingly, desires, intentions, orders, promises, obligations, and commitments have the world-to-mind, world-to-language direction of fit. I think of that direction of fit as pointing upward, and I represent it with an upward arrow. To avoid the cumbersome locutions I will sometimes just say "downward" and "upward" respectively, or sometimes just draw a downward or upward arrow.

I cannot overestimate the importance of this rather dry discussion for the understanding of rationality. *The key to understanding rationality in action is to understand the relations of the gap to the upward direction of fit.*

5.   Intentional states often function causally by a special kind of causation, intentional causation, and some of them have causation built into their conditions of satisfaction. Such states are causally self-referential. The general notion of causation is the notion of something making something else happen. Thus in the classic example, billiard ball A hits billiard ball B, causing it to move. It is sometimes said that this sort of causation is only one kind of causation, "efficient causation" after Aristotle; and there are supposed to be at least three other kinds, also using Aristotle's terminology: formal, final, and material. I think this whole discussion is confused. There is only one kind of causation, and it is efficient causation. However, within efficient causation, there is an important subcategory having to do with mental causation. These are cases where something causes a mental state, or where a mental state causes something else. And within the subcategory of mental causation, there is yet another subcategory, that of *intentional causation*. In the case of intentional causation an intentional state either causes its conditions of satisfaction, or the conditions of satisfaction of an intentional state cause it. To put this same point in slightly different terminology, in the case of intentional causation an intentional state causes the very state of affairs it represents, or the state of affairs it represents causes it. Thus if I want to drink water, my desire to drink water may cause me to drink water, and thus I have a case of intentional causation. The desire has the content *that I drink water*, and that desire causes it to be the case *that I drink water* (though we must remember of course that there is generally a gap in such cases of voluntary action). If I see that the cat is on the mat, then the fact that the cat is on the mat causes the very visual experience, part of whose conditions of satisfaction are that the cat is on the mat. Intentional causation is any causal relation between an intentional state and its conditions of satisfaction, where the intentional state causes its conditions of satisfaction, or its conditions of satisfaction cause it.

Just as we found the notion of *direction of fit* essential for understanding the ways in which intentionality and the real world relate to each other, so it seems to me we also need the notion of *direction of causation*. If I am thirsty, and I drink water in order to satisfy my thirst, then my thirst, being among other things a desire to drink water, will have the world-to-mind (upward) direction of fit. The desire to drink, if satisfied, will be satisfied by a change in the world so that the world matches the content of the desire: the desire that I drink water. But if my desire causes me to drink the water, then the causal relation between my desire and my drinking is from mind-to-world. My desire in the mind causes me (modulo the gap, of course) to drink water in the world. The world-to-mind direction of fit, in this case, is paralleled by the mind-to-world direction of causation. In the case of visual perception, for example, the direction of fit and the direction of causation are different. If the visual experience is, as they say, *veridical*, then the visual experience will match the world, and we will have a successful mind-to-world direction of fit. But if the visual experience is truly satisfied, it must be the case that the state of affairs I am perceiving in the world causes the very visual experience by way of which I perceive that state of affairs. Thus, in this case, the mind-to-world direction of fit is paralleled by the world-to-mind direction of causation.

This example illustrates a special subclass of cases of intentional causation, where it is part of the conditions of satisfaction of the intentional state in question that it must itself function causally in producing its conditions of satisfaction, if it is to be satisfied. Thus, in the case of intentions, unlike desires, the intention is not actually carried out unless the intention itself causes the very action that is represented in the content of the intention. If the action has a different cause, then the intention is not carried out. We may say in such cases, then, that the conditions of satisfaction of the intentional state are *causally self-referential*.[3] The cases of intentional states that are causally self-referential are: perceptual experiences, memories, and intentions. Let us consider each of these in order. In the case of perceptual experience, the experience will be satisfied only if the very state of affairs that is purportedly perceived causes that very perceptual experience. Thus, for example, if I see that the cat is on the mat, the intentional content of the visual experience is

Vis. Exp. (that the cat is on the mat, and the fact that the cat is on the mat causes this Vis. Exp.).

This formula is to be read as follows: I am now having a visual experience whose conditions of satisfaction are that the cat is on the mat, and the fact that the cat is on the mat is causing this visual experience. Notice that we need to distinguish what is actually seen from the total conditions of satisfaction of the visual experience. What is actually seen is the fact that the cat is on the mat, but the total conditions of satisfaction of the visual experience include a causally self-referential component. It is important to emphasize that I do not actually see causation—I see a cat and a mat, and I see the former on the latter. But in order that I should be able to do that, there must be a causal component to the total conditions of satisfaction of the visual experience, and it is this logical feature that I am trying to capture with the formula above.

Memories are similarly causally self-referential. If I remember that I went on a picnic yesterday, then the conditions of satisfaction are both that I went on a picnic

---

3. Recognition of the phenomenon of causal self-referentiality goes back a long way. It was noticed, for example, by Kant in his discussion of the causality of the will. The terminology, as far as I know, was first used by Gilbert Harman, "Practical Reasoning," *Review of Metaphysics* 29, 1976, pp. 431–463.

yesterday, and that the fact that I went on a picnic yesterday causes this very memory. Notice that in the case of
perception and memory we have the mind-to-world
direction of fit and the world-to-mind direction of causation. In both the case of perception and memory, if I see
how the world really is, or remember how it was, and
thus achieve mind-to-world direction of fit, it can only be
because the world's being that way or having been that
way causes me to have this perceptual experience and this
memory, and thus achieve world-to-mind direction of
causation. Mind-to-world direction of fit is achieved in
virtue of successful world-to-mind direction of causation.

We also find causal self-referentiality in the structure of
intention and action. In a very simple case here is how it
works. I have a set of beliefs and desires, and by engaging
in reasoning on these beliefs and desires, I arrive at an intention. Such intentions that are formed prior to an action
I call *prior intentions*. Thus for example suppose that in
a meeting I want to vote for a motion that has been put
forward, and I believe that I can vote for the motion by
raising my right arm. I thus form the prior intention that I
raise my arm. The intentional content of the prior intention to raise my arm can be represented as follows:

p.i. (that I raise my arm and that this p.i. causes that I
raise my arm).

This formula is to be read as follows: I have a prior intention whose conditions of satisfaction are that I raise my
arm, and that this very prior intention causes that I raise
my arm.

The prior intention has to be distinguished from what I
call the *intention-in-action*. The intention-in-action is the
intention I have while I am actually performing an action.
Thus in this case, when the moment to vote comes, and

the chair says "All those in favor raise your arm," I will act on my prior intention, and thus have an intention in action whose conditions of satisfaction are that that very intention-in-action should cause the bodily movement of my arm going up. We can represent that as follows:

i.a. (my arm goes up and this i.a. causes that my arm goes up).

This formula is to be read as follows: I have an intention-in-action whose conditions of satisfaction are that my arm goes up, and that this very intention-in-action causes that my arm go up.

In ordinary English the closest word for intention-in-action is "trying." If you had an intention-in-action but failed to achieve its conditions of satisfaction, you did at least try. In a typical case, then, of a premeditated action where I act on a prior intention, such as this case where I raise my arm, the structure of the whole thing is that first I formed a prior intention (whose conditions of satisfaction are that it should cause the whole action) and then I perform the whole action, where the whole action consists of two components, the intention-in-action and the bodily movement (and the condition of satisfaction of the intention-in-action is that it should cause the bodily movement).

Of course, not all actions are premeditated. Many of the things I do, I do quite spontaneously. In such a case I have an intention-in-action but no prior intention. For example, I sometimes just get up and walk around the room when I am thinking about a philosophical problem. My walking around the room is done intentionally, even though I had no prior intention. My bodily movements in such a case are caused by an ongoing intention-in-action, but there was no prior intention.

**6. The intentional structures of cognition and volition
are mirror images of each other, with directions of fit
and directions of causation running in opposite
directions.**

If we start with action and perception we can see these
symmetries and asymmetries. Perceptions consist of two
components. In the case of vision, for example, a perception consists of a conscious visual experience, together
with a state of affairs perceived. So if I see that the cat is
on the mat, then I both have the visual experience, and
there is a corresponding state of affairs in the world, that
the cat is on the mat. Furthermore, if the visual experience
is to be satisfied, its causally self-referential component
must be satisfied: the state of affairs in the world that I am
perceiving must cause the very experience of perceiving.
Human action is exactly parallel but with opposite directions of fit and causation. Thus a successfully performed
intentional action consists of two components, an intention-
in-action, and, typically, a bodily movement. So if I raise
my arm in the performance of a human action, then there is
an intention-in-action; and it has as its conditions of satisfaction that my arm goes up, and that that very intention-
in-action causes that my arm goes up. Thus the two components of the successfully performed intentional action
are the intention-in-action and the bodily movement.

The symmetries and asymmetries of the relations
between perception and action are typical of cognition
and volition generally. We saw above that the cognitive
states of perception and memory have mind-to-world
direction of fit, and world-to-mind direction of causation.
But the prior intention and the intention-in-action have
opposite directions of fit and of causation. They have
world-to-mind direction of fit and mind-to-world direc-

tion of causation. That is just another way of saying that the intention is carried out only if the world comes to be the way the intention represents it, and the intention causes it to be that way. Thus, in order to be satisfied, the intention must achieve world-to-mind direction of fit and mind-to-world direction of causation. The intention will be satisfied only if the intention itself functions causally in achieving the world-to-mind direction of fit. In such a case we achieve upward direction of fit only in virtue of downward direction of causation. A typical pattern, then, of premeditated action, is that on the basis of beliefs and desires you form a prior intention. The prior intention is a representation of a whole action, and the whole action consists of two components—the intention-in-action and the bodily movement. If the prior intention is carried out, it will cause the intention-in-action, which in turn will cause the bodily movement. The entire formal structure of the relationships between cognition and volition is depicted in table 1.

Intentions in action may or may not be conscious. When they are conscious experiences, I call them "experiences of acting," and I believe that what I call experiences of acting is what William James called the feeling of "effort."[4]

7.   Deliberation typically leads to intentional action by way of prior intentions.

In a simple case where the only reasons are beliefs and desires, we can say: reflection on beliefs and desires, with their different directions of fit, leads to a decision, that is, the formation of a prior intention, which has upward direction of fit and downward direction of causation. The

4. William James, *The Principles of Psychology, Volume II*, chapter 26, New York: Henry Holt, 1918.

Table 1

	Cognition			Volition		
	Belief	Memory	Perception	Desire	Prior intention	Intention-in-action
Direction of fit	↓	↓	↑	↑	↑	↑
Direction of causation determined by conditions of satisfaction	none	↑	↑	none	↓	↓
Causally self-referential	No	Yes	Yes	No	Yes	Yes

prior intention has the condition of satisfaction that it cause an action. The action consists of two components, the intention-in-action and the bodily movement, and the intention-in-action has as its condition of satisfaction that it cause the bodily movement. Thus the sequence in the case of premeditated action is:

Deliberation causes prior intention, which causes intention-in-action, which in turn causes bodily movement. The total action consists of the intention-in-action and the bodily movement. The pattern, then, can be represented as follows, letting the arrows stand for the causal relation:

Deliberation on beliefs and desires → prior intention → intention-in-action → bodily movement (action = intention-in-action + bodily movement)

In the case of volition, the direction of fit of the causally self-referential states is always world-to-mind, and the direction of causation, mind-to-world. In the case of cognition, the direction of fit of the causally self-referential states is always mind-to-world, and the direction of causation is always world-to-mind. The intention will be satisfied, and thus achieve world-to-mind direction of fit, only if the intention itself functions causally to bring about that fit. Perceptions and memories will be satisfied, and thus achieve mind-to-world direction of fit, only if the world itself causes those very perceptions and memories. Thus we achieve mind-to-world direction of fit only in virtue of world-to-mind direction of causation.

8. The structure of volition contains three gaps.

Once we allow for the differences in direction of fit and direction of causation, the chief asymmetry between the

formal structure of cognition, on the one hand, and volition on the other, is that volition has gaps. "The gap" is
the general name that I have introduced for the phenomenon that we do *not* normally experience the stages of our
deliberations and voluntary actions as having causally
sufficient conditions or as setting causally sufficient conditions for the next stage. We can segment the continuous
experience of the gap, for the purposes of this book, as
follows. In the structure of deliberation and action, there
is first the gap between the deliberations and the prior
intentions that are the result of the deliberations. Thus if
I am deliberating about whether or not to vote for the
motion, there is a gap between the reasons that I have for
and against voting for the motion, and the actual decision,
the actual formation of a prior intention, to vote for the
motion. Furthermore there is a gap between the prior
intention and the intention-in-action, that is, the gap
between deciding to do something and actually trying to
do it. There is no such gap between the intention-in-action
and the bodily movement. If I am actually trying to do
something, and if I succeed, my trying has to be causally
sufficient for the success. The third gap is in the structure
of temporally extended intentions-in-action. Where I have
an intention-in-action to engage in some complex pattern of activity such as writing a book or swimming the
English Channel, the initiation of the original intention-in-
action is not by itself sufficient to guarantee the continuation of that intention-in-action through the completion of
the activity. Thus at any stage of the carrying out of an
intention-in-action there is a third gap. Furthermore, if it is
some lengthy act such as swimming the English Channel
or writing a book, my prior intention continues to be
causally effective throughout the entire operation. That is,

I have to keep making an effort to carry out to completion the pattern of action that I originally planned in the formation of the prior intention.[5]

9. Complex actions have an internal structure whereby the agent intends to do one thing by means of doing something else, or he intends to do one thing by way of doing something else. These two relations are causal and constitutive, respectively.

I have been talking as if one simply performed an action, so to speak, just like that. But except for such simple actions as raising one's arm, human actions are more complex and have a complex internal structure. Normally one does one thing by-way-of or by-means-of doing something else. One turns on the light by means of moving the switch, one fires the gun by means of pulling the trigger, for example. Even in the simple example I gave, one votes by way of raising one's arm. There are not two actions, raising one's arm and voting, but only one action: voting by way of raising one's arm. The internal structure of action is very important for the topic of practical reason, because often the decision is a matter of choosing the by-means-of relation or the by-way-of relation for achieving one's goal. In the simple ape example that we discussed in chapter 1, the ape got the bananas by means of poking at them with the stick. The two most important structural forms in the internal structure of actions are the causal by-means-of relation and the constitutive by-way-

---

5. I did not see this point when I wrote *Intentionality*. In that book I represent the prior intention as ceasing to exist once the intention-in-action begins. But that is a mistake. The prior intention can continue to be effective throughout the performance of an act. This mistake was pointed out to me by Brian O'Shaughnessy.

of relation. If I fire the gun by means of pulling the trigger, the relationship is causal. Pulling the trigger causes the gun to fire. If I vote by way of raising my arm, the relation is constitutive. In that context raising my arm constitutes voting. In the case of the by-means-of relation, the relation between the components of the action is one of causation: flipping the switch causes the light to go on, and when I turned on the light by means of flipping the switch, I had a complex intention-in-action, that this intention-in-action should cause the flipping of the switch, which in turn would cause the light to go on. But when I raised my arm in order to vote, my arm's going up did not cause me to vote; rather my arm going up *constituted* my voting. In that context the bodily movement constituted or counted as the action in question. For complex actions, extending over long periods of time, these relations become quite complex. Consider writing this book. I work on it by sitting at my computer and typing my thoughts. These acts do not cause the writing of the book, but they are constitutive of its stages. When I hit the keys of the computer, on the other hand, my actions cause the text of the book to appear on the screen.

Another idealization I have been employing is to talk as if all actions were cases of intentions-in-action causing bodily movements. But of course there are also mental actions, for example, doing addition in one's head. And there are negative actions, for example, refraining from smoking. There are also, as I mentioned above, extended actions such as writing a book or training for a ski race. I believe the account I have given, with its distinctions between prior intentions and intentions-in-action, and its distinction between the causal by-means-of relations and the constitutive by-way-of relations in the inner structure, will account for all of these cases as well.

10. Meaning is a matter of the intentional imposition of conditions of satisfaction on conditions of satisfaction.

If, for example, a speaker says, "It is raining," and means by that utterance that it is raining, then the conditions of satisfaction of his intention-in-action are first, that the intention-in-action should cause the utterance of a sentence, "It is raining," and second, that the utterance should itself have the condition of satisfaction with downward direction of fit, that it is raining. In the case of speaker meaning, the speaker creates a form of intentionality by intentionally imposing conditions of satisfaction on something that he has produced intentionally, such as sounds from his mouth or marks on paper. He produces an utterance intentionally, and he produces the utterance with the additional intention that that utterance should itself have conditions of satisfaction.

This procedure in a natural human language is made possible by the fact that the words in the sentences of the language have a form of intentionality that is itself derived from the intrinsic or observer-independent intentionality of human agents. And that leads to my next point:

11. We need to distinguish between observer-independent and observer-dependent intentionality.

I have been talking about the intentionality of the human mind. But there are intentional ascriptions to things other than the mind that are literally true, where the intentionality depends on the intrinsic or observer-independent intentionality of the mind. Most obviously in the case of language, words and sentences can be said to have meaning, and meaning is a form of intentionality. This is the difference between my saying "I am hungry," which literally ascribes intentionality to me, and my saying, "The French sentence 'J'ai faim' means I am hungry." By ascribing meaning to the sentence, I have ascribed a form of intentionality to it. But the intentionality of the French sentence is not, so to speak, intrinsic; it is derived from the intentionality of French speakers. Thus I will say that there is a distinction between the *observer-independent* intentionality of my mental state of hunger, and the *observer-dependent* or *observer-relative* intentionality of words and sentences in French, English, and other languages. There is a third form of intentional ascriptions, which is neither observer-independent nor observer-relative, and which is not literal at all. I am thinking of such things as when we ascribe memory to a computer or desire to a plant. This is a harmless manner of speaking. If I say, "My plants are thirsty for water," no one will be confused into thinking that I am literally ascribing intentionality to them. These ascriptions I will call metaphorical or "as-if" ascriptions of intentionality. But I am not ascribing a third kind of intentionality; rather plants, computers, and lots of other things behave as if they had intentionality; and thus we can make these metaphorical, as-if ascriptions to them, even though they do not, literally speaking, have any intentionality.

12. The distinction between objectivity and subjectivity is really a conflation of two distinctions, one ontological, and one epistemic.

We can use the distinction between observer-relative and observer-independent forms of intentionality to make a further distinction that is important for the subsequent argument of this book. The notion of *objectivity* and the contrast between *objectivity* and *subjectivity* figure large in our intellectual culture. We seek scientific truths that are "objective." But there is a massive confusion in these notions, which we need to sort out. We need to distinguish between *ontological objectivity and subjectivity* on the one hand, and *epistemic objectivity and subjectivity* on the other. Examples will make the distinction clear. If I say I have a pain, I ascribe to myself a subjective experience. That subjective experience has a subjective ontology because it exists only when it is experienced by a conscious subject. In that respect pains, tickles, and itches differ from mountains, molecules, and glaciers; because mountains, etc. have an objective existence, or an objective ontology. The distinction between ontological subjectivity and objectivity is not at all the same as the distinction between epistemic subjectivity and objectivity. If I say, "Rembrandt spent his entire life in the Netherlands," that statement is epistemically objective because we can ascertain its truth or falsity without reference to the attitudes and feelings of observers. But if I say, "Rembrandt was the greatest painter that ever lived in Amsterdam"; well, that is, as they say, a matter of opinion. It is epistemically subjective because its truth cannot be settled independently of the subjective attitudes of the admirers and detractors of the works of Rembrandt and other Amsterdam painters. We can say, in light of this distinction, that all observer-relative phenomena contain an element of ontological subjectivity. The fact that something means something as a sentence of French is dependent on the ontologically subjective attitudes of French speakers. But, and this is the crucial point, ontological subjectivity does not necessarily imply epistemic subjectivity. We can have epistemically objective knowledge about the meanings of sentences in French and other languages, even though those meanings are ontologically subjective. This distinction will prove crucial to us later on when we discover that many of the features of the world that motivate rational actions are similarly ontologically subjective but epistemically objective.

13. Collective intentionality enables the creation of institutional facts. Institutional facts are created in accordance with constitutive rules of the form "X counts as Y in C."

Intentionality can be not only individual, as in "I intend to go to the movies," but also collective, as in "We intend to go to the movies." Collective intentionality enables groups of people to create common institutional facts, such as those involving money, property, marriage, government, and above all, language. In such cases, the existence of the institution enables individuals or groups of individuals to impose on objects functions that the objects cannot perform in virtue of their physical structure alone, but only in virtue of the collective recognition of the object as having a certain status, and with that status, a special function. I call these *status functions*, and they typically take the form "X counts as Y in C." Thus, such and such a sequence of words counts as a sentence of English, such and such a piece of paper counts as a ten dollar bill in the United States, such and such a position counts as checkmate in chess, a person who satisfies such and such conditions counts as the President of the United States. These status functions differ from physical functions because an object such as a screwdriver performs its physical function in virtue of its physical structure, whereas English sentences, checkmates, money, and presidents can perform their functions only if they are collectively recognized as having a certain status and with that status a function.

The combination of institutional reality, itself created by the imposition of status functions according to the constitutive rule "X counts as Y in C," together with a special form of status function, namely the imposition of meaning, enables individual human beings to create certain forms of desire-independent reasons for action. We will explore this phenomenon in detail in chapter 6. At this point I just want to emphasize the following. We have seen that meaning is a matter of the imposition of conditions of satisfaction on conditions of satisfaction (point 10); and that fact is combined with the fact that institutional facts are created within institutional systems, whereby an agent imposes a function on an entity where the entity cannot perform that function without some sort of collective acceptance or recognition of that function. These two factors together enable us to see how, in the performance of a speech act such as making an assertion or giving a promise, the speaker creates a new set of conditions of satisfaction, and this new set of conditions of satisfaction is the result of the creation of an institutional fact, for example, the fact that the speaker has made an assertion to the hearer or made a promise to the hearer.

14. Intentionality functions only to determine conditions of satisfaction against a pre-intentional or nonintentional Background of abilities.

In addition to the intentional structure of cognition and volition we need to explain that the entire system of intentionality functions, that intentional states determine conditions of satisfaction, only against a Background of abilities, capacities, tendencies, and dispositions that human beings and animals have, and that do not themselves consist in intentional states. In order that I can form the intention to walk across the room or brush my teeth or write a book, I have to be able to walk across the room, brush my teeth, or write a book, or at least I have to presuppose that I am able to do these things. But my abilities do not themselves consist in further intentional states, though the abilities are capable of generating intentional states. Think of my abilities, capacities, tendencies, and dispositions ontologically speaking as a set of brain structures. Those brain structures enable me to activate the system of intentionality and to make it function, but the capacities realized in the brain structures do not themselves consist in intentional states.

The Background is important for understanding the structure of rationality in many ways that go beyond the scope of this book. Apparent cases of cultural relativity of rationality are usually due to different cultural Backgrounds. Rationality as such is universal. At this point in the argument, I just want to call attention to the fact that the system of intentionality is not so to speak fully intentional right down to the ground. In addition to the system of intentionality we have to suppose that agents have a set of abilities that do not themselves consist in further intentional states. And these sets of abilities I am labeling, by fiat and with a capital letter, "the Background."

15.   Intentionality-with-a-t must be distinguished from intensionality-with-an-s.

Intentionality-with-a-t is that property of the mind, and derivatively of language, by which mental states and speech acts are about, or of, objects and states of affairs.

Intensionality-with-an-s is that property of statements, and other sorts of representations, by which they fail certain tests for extensionality. The two favorite tests are the substitutability of coreferring expressions without loss or change of truth value (sometimes called Leibniz's Law) and existential generalization. For example, the statement "Oedipus wants to marry Jocasta" fails the substitutability test, because together with the statement "Jocasta is identical with his mother" it does not permit the inference: "Oedipus wants to marry his mother." The statement is intensional with respect to substitutability. Statements that fail the substitutability test are sometimes called *referentially opaque*. The statement "Oedipus is looking for the lost city of Atlantis" does not permit the existential inference "There exists a lost city of Atlantis," for Oedipus may be looking, even if the thing he is looking for does not exist. So the statement fails the test of existential generalization. Intensionality is important for the subject of practical reason, because, among other reasons, statements of reasons for action are typically intensional-with-an-s.

Conclusion

I apologize to the reader for the dryness as well as the swiftness of this discussion. I am going to need this apparatus in the subsequent chapters, and I cannot in good conscience tell my readers to first go and read all of my other books. So I have summarized enough to give you the weaponry to cope with the chapters that follow. Already we have enough material to see that the quest, common in writings on practical reason, to find an analogue that stands to intentional action in the way that truth stands to belief, is hopeless from the beginning. Belief is an intentional state with conditions of satisfaction. If these conditions are satisfied, the belief is said to be true. Beliefs have the mind-to-world direction of fit. But intentional action consists of two components, an intention-in-action and a bodily movement. Actions, as such, do not have conditions of satisfaction. Rather, each intention-in-action has a condition of satisfaction, and if satisfied it will cause the bodily movement or other phenomenon that constitutes the rest of the action. So the action will be successfully performed if and only if the intention-in-action is satisfied. But in addition to that condition of satisfaction, there is no further condition of satisfaction for actions as such. Where the action is premeditated, that is, where there is a prior intention, the occurrence of the action itself, as caused by the prior intention, will constitute the conditions of satisfaction of the prior intention. Both the prior intention and the intention-in-action have the world-to-mind direction of fit. Actions are indeed the conditions of satisfaction of prior intentions, just as bodily movements are the conditions of satisfaction of intentions-in-action. But as I mentioned earlier, not all actions require a prior intention because not all actions are premeditated. All actions do require an intention-in-action, and indeed we may define a human action as any complex event that contains an intention-in-action as one of its components. In subsequent chapters we will be concerned to see how rational agents can organize their intentional contents as well as their representations of facts in the world so as to form rationally motivated prior intentions and intentions-in-action.

3 The Gap: Of Time and the Self

I Widening the Gap

The existence of the gap leaves us with a number of questions. Here is one: In explaining actions by giving reasons, we do not normally cite causally sufficient conditions. But if that is so, then how can the explanation really explain anything? If the causal antecedents are insufficient to determine the action, then how can citing them explain why this action occurred rather than some other action that was also possible, given the same set of antecedent causes? The answer to that question has deep implications, and I am going to try to work out some of them in the course of this chapter.

My first objective will be to try to establish beyond any reasonable doubt that there really is a phenomenon of the gap of the sort I have been talking about. To do that I have to give a more precise definition of the gap and say more about its geography. My second objective will be to answer the question I just posed and to draw out some of the implications of the answer. I will argue that in order to account for the phenomena of the gap we have to presuppose a non-Humean, irreducible notion of the self, and we have to presuppose certain special relations between the self and time, as far as practical reason is concerned.

The Definition of the Gap

The gap can be given two equivalent descriptions, one forward-looking, one backward. Forward: the gap is that feature of our conscious decision making and acting where we sense alternative future decisions and actions as causally open to us. Backward: the gap is that feature of conscious decision making and acting whereby the reasons preceding the decisions and the actions are not experienced by the agent as setting causally sufficient conditions for the decisions and actions. As far as our conscious experiences are concerned, the gap occurs when the beliefs, desires, and other reasons are not experienced as causally sufficient conditions for a decision (the formation of a prior intention); the gap also occurs when the prior intention does not set a causally sufficient condition for an intentional action; and it also occurs when the initiation of an intentional project does not set sufficient conditions for its continuation or completion.

The Geography of the Gap

These three manifestations of the gap illustrate its basic geography. First, when one is making rational decisions, there is a gap between the deliberative process and the decision itself, where the decision consists in the formation of a prior intention. Second, once one has made up one's mind to do something, that is, one has formed a prior intention, there is a gap between the prior intention and the actual initiation of the action in the onset of an intention-in-action. And third, whenever one is in the course of some extended pattern of activity, such as I am in now while writing this book, there is a gap between the causes in the form of the prior intention to perform the action and the intention-in-action on the one hand, and the actual carrying out of the complex activity to its completion, on the other. Where extended actions are concerned, even given your prior intentions and the initiation of the action in the intention-in-action, you still have to keep trying; you have to keep going on your own. All three gaps can be seen as different aspects of the same feature of consciousness, that feature whereby our conscious experiences of making up our minds and our conscious experiences of acting (the exercise of the will, the conscious feeling of effort—these are all names for the same thing) are not experienced as having psychologically sufficient causal conditions that make them happen.

II Arguments for the Existence of the Gap

There are, it seems to me, three sorts of skepticism that one might have about the gap. First, maybe I have misdescribed the consciousness in question. Perhaps there is no such gap. Second, even if there is, maybe the unconscious psychology overrides the conscious experience of freedom in every case. The psychological causes may be sufficient to determine all our actions, even if we are not conscious of these causes. Third, even if we are free psychologically, this freedom might be epiphenomenal. The underlying neurobiology might determine all of our actions. There are, after all, no gaps in the brain. In this chapter I answer the first, and in chapter 9 I discuss the third. I have nothing to say about the second, because I do not take it seriously. There are indeed some cases where our actions are fixed by unconscious pyschological causes —hypnosis cases for example—but it seems incredible that all our actions are like acting in a hypnotic trance. I discuss this issue briefly in another book,[1] and I will say nothing further about it here.

The simplest proof of what I am describing as the special causal and volitional elements of the gap is in the following thought experiment, based on the research of Wilder Penfield.[2] He found that by stimulating the motor cortex of his patients with a microelectrode he could cause bodily movements. When asked, the patients invariably said, "I did not do that, you did it" (p. 76). So the patient's experience, for example, of having his arm raised by Penfield's stimulation of the brain is quite different from his experience of voluntarily raising his arm. What is the difference? Well, to answer that, let us imagine the Penfield cases on a grand scale. Imagine that all of my bodily movements over a certain period of time are caused by a brain scientist sending electromagnetic rays into my motor cortex. Now clearly the experience would be totally different from normal conscious voluntary action. In this case, as in perception, I *observe* what is happening to me. In the normal case, I *make it happen*. There are two features of the normal case. First, I cause the bodily movement by trying to raise my arm. The trying is sufficient to cause the arm to move; but second, the reasons for the action are not sufficient causes to force the trying.

---

1. *Minds, Brains, and Science,* Cambridge, MA: Harvard University Press, 1984. See chap. 6.
2. *The Mystery of the Mind,* Princeton: Princeton University Press, 1975, pp. 76–77.

If we put this under the magnifying glass we find that the action consists of the two components I described in chapter 2, the intention-in-action (the trying), which, when conscious, is a conscious experience of acting, and the bodily movement. The intention-in-action is causally sufficient for the bodily movement. So, if I raise my arm, the intention-in-action causes the arm to go up. But in a normal case of voluntary action, the intention-in-action does not itself have psychologically causally sufficient antecedent conditions, and when I say the whole action lacks sufficient conditions it is because the intention-in-action lacks them. That is a manifestation of the gap of human freedom. In the normal case, the experience of acting will cause the initiation of movement by sufficient conditions, but that experience itself (the experience of trying, what William James called the feeling of "effort") does not have sufficient pychological causal conditions in the free and voluntary cases.

In the first chapter I briefly mentioned a second argument: I believe the most dramatic manifestation of the gap in real life comes out in the fact that when one has several reasons for performing an action, or for choosing an action, one may act on only one of them; one may select which reason one acts on. For example, suppose I have several reasons for voting for a particular political candidate. All the same, I may not vote for the candidate for all of those reasons. I may vote for the candidate for one reason and not for any of the others. In such a case, I may know without observation that I voted for the candidate for one particular reason and not for any of the others, even though I know that I also had those other reasons for voting for him. Now, this is an amazing fact and we ought to ponder it. There are several reasons operating on me, but only one of these is actually effective and *I select which one will be effective*. That is, as far as my awareness of my own actions is concerned, my various beliefs and desires don't *cause* me to behave in a particular way. Rather, I select which desire I act on. I decide, in short, which of the many causes will be effective. This suggests a fascinating hypothesis that will also come up in later chapters. If we think of the reasons I act on as the reasons that are *effective*, then it emerges that where free rational action is concerned, *all effective reasons are made effective by the agent*, insofar as he chooses which ones he will act on.

When I say that we "select" which reasons to act on, or that we "make" reasons effective, I do not mean that there are any separate acts of selecting and making going on. If there were, we could quickly construct vicious-infinite-regress arguments about making the makings and selecting the selectings.[3] I just mean that when you freely act on a reason you have thereby, in that act, selected that reason and made it effective.

A third, more indirect way to argue for the existence of the gap is to note that rationality is only possible where irrationality is possible. But the possibility of each requires freedom. So in order to behave rationally I can do so only if I am free to make any of a number of possible choices and have open the possibility of behaving irrationally. Paradoxically, the alleged ideal of a perfectly rational machine, the computer, is not an example of rationality at all, because a computer is outside the scope of rationality altogether. A computer is neither rational nor irrational,

---

3. Gilbert Ryle is known for these types of regress arguments against traditional action theory. See his *The Concept of Mind*, New York: Harper and Row, 1949.

because its behavior is entirely determined by its program and the structure of its hardware. The only sense in which a computer can be said to be rational is observer-relative.

III   Causation and the Gap

In order to explore the relation of the gap to causation, let us focus on the gap embedded in the actual structure of voluntary actions. When we perform conscious voluntary actions, we typically have a sense of alternative possibilities. For example, I am right now sitting at a computer, typing words that appear on the screen. But I could be doing a host of other things. I could get up and walk around, read a book, or type words other than these. You are, let us suppose, reading this while seated in a chair. Unless something is radically unusual about your situation—you are, for example, strapped into the chair or paralyzed—you also have the sense that you could be doing a host of other things. You could read something else, call up an old friend on the phone, or go out for a beer, to mention just a few possibilities. This sense of alternative possibilities is built right into the structure of ordinary human actions, and it gives us the conviction—or perhaps the illusion—of freedom. We do not know what conscious life is like for animals, but the neurophysiology of the higher animals is so close to ours that we have to assume that the experiences typical of human voluntary action are shared by many other species.

If we had the life of conscious trees or stones, able to perceive our surroundings but unable to initiate any actions of our own, we would not have the experiences that give us the conviction of our own free will. Not every experience, not even the experiences of our own movements, contains this sense of freedom. If we act while in the grip of a powerful emotion, in a total rage for example, we do not have the sense that we could be doing something else. Worse yet, if things are totally out of our control, if we have fallen off a building, or if our body is held immobile, we do not have the sense of alternative possibilities, at least not alternative possibilities of physical movement.

In perception, as opposed to action, we have nothing like this sense of alternative possibilities open to us. On the contrary, we take it for granted that our perceptual experiences are fixed by the combination of how the world is and how we are. For example, if I look down at the computer keys, it is not up to me what I see. Though there is a voluntaristic element in perception (for example, in Gestalt switching perceptions I can freely choose to see a figure now as a duck, now as a rabbit), in a case such as this I take it that the visual experiences I have are entirely determined by such things as the structure of the keyboard, the lighting conditions, and my perceptual apparatus. Of course I can always turn my head, but that is a voluntary action, not an act of perception. Note the contrast between the freedom of action and the determined nature of perception. The letters I am now putting on the computer screen are up to me to produce here and now and I can produce others at will, whereas the letters I see on the keyboard are fixed by the physics of the machinery. But what does it mean to say that we have a sense of freedom? What are the implications of such a sense?

Another pervasive feature of our experiences is the experience of causation. In conscious action and conscious perception we often experience our relations to the world as causal in their very structure. In action we experience ourselves acting causally on things outside us, and in perception we experience things in the world acting causally on us. Now here is the anomaly introduced by the experience of voluntary action: The sense of freedom in voluntary action is a sense that the causes of the action, though effective and real in the form of the reasons for the action, are insufficient to determine that the action will occur. I can tell you why I am doing what I am now doing, but in telling you why, I am not trying to give a causally sufficient explanation of my behavior, because if I were, the explanation would be hopelessly incomplete. It could only be a *partial* causal explanation of my behavior, because in specifying these causes, I do not give you what I take to be causally sufficient conditions. If you ask me, "Why are you writing this argument?" I will answer, "I want to explain some peculiar features of voluntary action." That answer, which is complete and adequate as an explanation of my behavior, could only be part of a *causal explanation* of my present behavior, because it does not specify a cause that is sufficient to *determine* my present actions. Even if I filled in all the details of my beliefs and desires to explain what I am doing, even given this total set of causes, my behavior would still not be completely determined, and I would still have the feeling that I could be doing something else. The consequence of this is that the explanation of our own behavior has a peculiar feature: The explanations we typically give when we state the reasons for our actions are *not sufficient* causal explanations. They do not show that what happened had to happen.

As we saw in chapter 1, it is commonly said that actions are caused by beliefs and desires; but if "cause" is meant to imply "causally sufficient," then as far as our ordinary *but notice that the action isn't (merely?) undeterministically produced by my reasons, me, or both.*

experience of voluntary action is concerned, this statement is just false. In *Intentionality*,[4] I tried to explain some of the striking parallels between the intentional structure of cognitive phenomena such as belief, memory, and perception on the one hand, and volitive phenomena such as desire, prior intention, and intentional action on the other. I summarized some of these basic features of the structure of intentionality in chapter 2 of this book. What that chapter shows is that as far as the formal structure of intentionality, including intentional causation, is concerned, cognition and volition are mirror images of each other. These relations are illustrated on the chart in chapter 2. I think the parallels are exact, but right now I want to call attention to a difference: volition typically contains the gap in a way that cognition does not.

IV The Experiential Gap, the Logical Gap, and the Unavoidable Gap

Let us suppose that I am right so far: there is an experienced gap, and it is defined in relation to intentional causation, but the experience is one of the absence of sufficient causal conditions. It seems to me someone might just say, "So what? You have these experiences but so far no reason is given why we should care about them or why they might not be systematic illusions. We also have color experiences but some people think that physics has shown that color is an illusion. It is an illusion we cannot help having, but it is an illusion all the same. Why should the gap be any different?"

---

4. John R. Searle, *Intentionality: An Essay in the Philosophy of Mind*, Cambridge: Cambridge University Press, 1983. See chapter 3, esp. p. 79.

As far as anything I have said so far is concerned, the gap might be an illusion, but unlike the belief in the ontologically objective existence of colors, it is not a belief we can give up. The interest of the discussion is not mere "phenomenology." We have to presuppose that there really is a gap, that the phenomenology corresponds to a reality, whenever we engage in choosing and deciding, and we cannot avoid choosing and deciding. I can intelligibly give up my belief in the reality and the objective existence of colors as something in addition to light reflectances, but I cannot in that way give up my belief in the reality of the gap.

I am advancing three theses here.

1. We have experiences of the gap of the sort I have described.

2. We have to presuppose the gap. We have to presuppose that the psychological antecedents of many of our decisions and actions do not set causally sufficient conditions for those decisions and actions.

3. In normal conscious life one cannot avoid choosing and deciding.

Here is the argument for 2 and 3: If I really thought that the beliefs and desires were sufficient to cause the action then I could just sit back and watch the action unfold in the same way as I do when I sit back and watch the action unfold on a movie screen. But I cannot do that when I am engaging in rational decision making and acting. I have to presuppose that the antecedent set of psychological conditions was not causally sufficient. Furthermore, here is an additional argument for point 3: even if I became convinced of the falsity of the thesis of the gap, all the same I would still have to engage in actions and thus exercise my own freedom no matter what. Suppose I become convinced that there is no gap; all the same I still have to do something, and in doing something I am exercising my own freedom, at least as far as my experience of the gap is concerned. As we saw in chapter 1, even the refusal to exercise freedom is intelligible to me as an agent only if I take it to be an exercise of freedom.

For example, there is a kind of practical inconsistency in maintaining the following two theses:

1. I am now trying to make up my mind whom to vote for in the next election.

2. I take the existing psychological causes operating on me right now to be causally sufficient to determine whom I am going to vote for.

The inconsistency comes out in the fact that if I really believe (2), then there seems no point in making the effort involved in (1). The situation would be like taking a pill that I am sure will cure my headache by itself, and then trying to add some further psychological effort to the effects of the pill. If I really believe the pill is enough, then the rational thing to do is to sit back and let it take effect.

Suppose I believe the doctrine that rational actions are caused by beliefs and desires. Suppose, as a science-fiction fantasy, that there are pills that induce beliefs and desires. Now suppose I want someone to do something rationally. I want him to vote for the Democratic candidate for a reason, so I give him the red pills that give him a desire to vote for the candidate whom he thinks would be best for the economy and I give him the blue pills that convince him that the Democratic candidate is best for the economy.

Now can I just sit back and watch the causes work? Is it just like putting dynamite under a bridge, lighting the fuse, and watching the bridge blow up? No. Even in this case it is not like that, for suppose I wish to induce myself to vote for the Democrats, so I take both the red and the blue pills. After a couple of weeks I might think, well the pills have worked. I have come to believe that the Democrat is better for the economy and I have come to want a candidate who will be good for the economy. But this is still not sufficient. I still have to decide whom I am going to vote for, and that presupposes that the causes are not sufficient.

To summarize these points: We have the experience of freedom, we must presuppose freedom whenever we make decisions and perform actions, and we cannot avoid making decisions and carrying out actions.

V   From the Gap to the Self

In the case of voluntary action, the psychological causes do not necessitate the effect. Then what does? At the psychological level: nothing. The effect is not necessary, it is voluntary. What makes the action a psychologically free action is precisely that the antecedent psychological causes were not sufficient to cause it. Perhaps at some different level of description, perhaps at the level of synapses and neurotransmitters, the causes were sufficient for the bodily movements, but at the level of description of intentional action, the definition of a free (voluntary, rational, conscious) action is that it does not have causally sufficient psychological antecedents. The mistake is to think we must find something that necessitates the effect. That is wrong. The effect is the conscious intention-in-action, that is, the experience of acting.

But what does it mean to say the effect is voluntary and not necessary? What could it mean? In the examples we have been considering, we suppose that I am making up my mind to do something and then doing it. The reasons for the action are not causally sufficient, and I am operating under the presupposition that they are not causally sufficient. How then are we to describe what is going on? How does the action come about if nothing fills the gap? *The intelligibility of our operation in the gap requires an irreducible notion of the self.*

This is an important claim for the subsequent argument of this book and I want to try to clarify and justify it. To start with, let us again make the contrast with perception. When I see something, I don't actually have to do anything. Assuming my perceptual apparatus is intact and I am appropriately situated, I just have perceptual experiences. My sequence of experiences includes one that was not there previously. But that is all. Now suppose that I am trying to decide what to do. I can't just wait and observe what happens. I actually have to do something, even if it is only to make up my mind. When I open up my closet to see if my shirt is there, I don't have to do anything except look; the rest takes care of itself. But to put the shirt on I actually have to make an effort. I have to have an intention-in-action. The intelligibility of that process together with its outcome requires the postulation of an entity that is not required for perception. Why? Well, I have to do it, it won't just happen on its own.

We need to distinguish:

1. The act just happens.
2. I do the act.

(1) is not a correct description of voluntary human action. Such action does not just happen. Rather, (2) is right: I have to do the act for it to happen. But is (2) not a causal claim? For every causal claim, always ask, "What exactly causes what?" And in this case there is no answer to that question. Was there some feature of me that together with my beliefs and desires was sufficient to bring about the action? Maybe so, but if so that is not part of the experience of acting, for I cannot sit back and let the feature do its job. I have to, as they say, make up my mind and then do the act. The fact that I make the decision and perform the act does not mean there was some event in me that together with my reasons was causally sufficient for the decision and the action.

VI Hume's Skeptical Account of the Self

I am now going to explore these issues in some detail. With the greatest reluctance I have come to the conclusion that we cannot make sense of the gap, of reasoning, of human action and of rationality generally, without an irreducible, that is, non-Humean, notion of the self. I now turn to the issue of the self, and since the argument needs to be developed carefully I will say a little about the traditional problem of the self in philosophy and about the neo-Humean conception, which is more or less accepted in our philosophical tradition and, until recently, even by me.

The self is one of the most scandalous notions in philosophy. There is nothing wrong with the notion of the self as it occurs in ordinary speech. When we say, for example, "I have just cut myself" or "Self-pity is a vice," the concept of the "self" is just short for the appropriate personal pronouns and other expressions referring to people and animals. It carries no metaphysical weight. But in philosophy the notion has been used to do a number of quite weighty tasks, and not all of them can be justified. Among the metaphysical concepts of the self in philosophy are:

1. The self is the bearer of personal identity through time. I am the same person at time t_2 that I was at t_1 because the self is the same. Identity of self accounts for identity of person.

2. The self is really the same as the soul. Therefore, because the soul is different from the body, the self can survive the destruction of the body. My body is one thing, my soul or self is something else. The body is mortal, the soul or self is immortal.

3. Related to (1), the self is what makes me into the person that I am. There is a certain entity within me that constitutes my identity as a person and distinguishes me from all other people, and that is my self. On this conception, the self is constitutive of my character and personality.

4. The self is the bearer of all my mental properties. In addition to my thoughts, feelings, etc. there is a self that has all these thoughts and feelings.

No doubt there are other jobs done by the self. But many philosophers, and I am one, could never find sufficient reason to postulate the existence of a self as something in addition to the sequence of experiences and the body in which they occur. This sort of skepticism about the self is inspired by Hume. As he pointed out, when I turn my attention inward, I find particular thoughts and feelings but nothing in addition by way of the self. The self, according to Hume, is just a bundle of experiences and nothing more. Hume's point, I take it, is not just that as a matter of fact I do not find a self when I turn my attention inward, but rather that nothing could count as the experience of the self, for any experience I had would just be another experience. Suppose I had a constant experience that accompanied all my other experiences. Suppose I had a continuous experience of a yellow spot in my visual field. Suppose it lasted my entire life. Is that a self? No, it is just a yellow spot. Not only is there no experience of the self, but there could not be one, because nothing could logically satisfy the constraints placed on the metaphysical notion of the self.

Hume's account of the self as just a bundle of perceptions needs revision in at least one respect, in order to account for an objection made by Kant. All of my experiences at any given point in time come to me as part of a unified conscious field. My conscious life has what Kant, with his usual gift for catchy phrases, called "the transcendental unity of apperception." What I believe he meant is this: I do not just have the feeling of the shirt on my back and the taste of beer in my mouth, but I have them both as part of a single unified conscious field. Hume thought of each perception as separate and distinct, but that cannot be right; because then we could not distinguish between one consciousness having ten experiences —the feeling of the shirt, the taste of the beer, the sight of the sky, etc.—and ten different consciousnesses each with one experience. So we have to insist that at any given point in time, all of one's experiences are united into a single conscious field. But the conscious field does not give us a self in addition to the conscious field. There is just the continuously developing unified conscious field, flowing through time, and each time-slice of the conscious field is a unity of all of its different components. Some of these conscious states within the conscious field will be memories of earlier events in the life-history of the sequence of conscious states. Some will even be feelings that, in my case, I would describe as the feeling of what it is like to be me. But we still can locate no self in addition to the sequence of experiences.

I would want to add to this revised Humean conception of the self the claim that the body is essential to my having the sequence of conscious experiences. We need not worry at this stage about whether the requirement of a body is an empirical requirement or a matter of logic. The point at this stage is merely that the sequence of conscious states has to have some physical realization. Even if I am a brain in a vat, still there has to be a physical brain at a bare minimum, and if I am to have experiences of the world, then my brain must be in some kind of causal interaction with the world.

This then is the updated neo-Humean account of the self: I am an embodied brain in causal contact with the world. That brain is capable of causing and sustaining unified conscious fields, and these states within the fields will include memory experiences of earlier conscious experiences. It is true that there is something that it feels like to be me, but that is just a feeling like any other and it carries no metaphysical weight. The existence of such feelings does not by itself guarantee any identity through time, and for all I know there may be a large number of other people who have type-identical feelings with my feelings of what it is like to be me. In summary the "self" is entirely reducible to simpler elements. It consists of conscious feelings, including memories and a sense of "me-ness." (No doubt it also includes a lot of false beliefs about the self.) These are caused by and are realized in a continuously existing physical system, my embodied brain. On the neo-Humean view, *in addition to all of that there simply is no such thing as the self.* End of the story about the self.

VII   An Argument for the Existence of an Irreducible, Non-Humean Self

For the moment let us put all our Humean considerations to one side and reflect on how human beings make decisions and carry out actions in the gap. Let us suppose that I am in a meeting and the chairman says, "All those in favor of the motion, raise your right arm." I raise my arm. I perform the action of voting for the motion by way of raising my right arm. Now what caused me to perform the action of raising my right arm? I can give a partial causal explanation by giving the reason for my action. I wanted to vote for the motion because I was in favor of it and I believed that in raising my right arm I was voting for it. In that context, raising my arm constituted voting for it.

So far so good, but as we have seen over and over, the reasons did not constitute causally sufficient conditions. So how do we get over the gap from my reasons in the form of psychological causes to the actual performance of the action? Here are the two possibilities I mentioned earlier, more completely described:

1. The action does not have a sufficient explanation of any kind. The action just happened. It did not have causally sufficient antecedent psychological causes, so as a psychological event, it was just an arbitrary or random occurrence.

2. The action does have an adequate psychological explanation even if it lacks causally sufficient antecedent psychological conditions. I *performed* the action for a reason. I did it for a reason, even though the reason does not fix an antecedently sufficient cause.

Thesis (1) cannot be right. The action was not a random or arbitrary event that just happened out of the blue. Indeed, the threat of (1) is what many compatibilists, including Hume by the way, use as an argument for determinism. Unless the act was determined, they say, it must have been a random or arbitrary occurrence, something for which I am in no way responsible. But the action was neither arbitrary nor determined. We have already seen reasons to reject psychological determinism. We need also to reject its apparent alternative, randomness and arbitrariness.

So (2) must be right. But what does it mean? There are really two questions. First, assuming that the thesis of the gap is correct, what does it mean to say that I, a person, performed an action for a reason? What is the logical form of the claim that S performed action A for reason R? To put the question in its old-fashioned form: what fact corresponds to the claim that S performed A because R? And second, how can a claim of this form, which specifies the reason I performed the action, ever be an adequate explanation if the reason does not determine the action? What kind of an explanation is it if it has a big hole in it? It seems any adequate answer to the first question must provide an answer to the second.

Much of my debate with the Classical Model concentrates at precisely this point. On the classical model there can be no gap. The explanation of action requires us to quantify only over events and to state causal relations between them: the event of action A was caused by the events B and D, the beliefs and desires of the agent. (By the way, the fact that beliefs and desires are not events is an embarrassment that is often glossed over by saying that the real causes are the *onsets* of the beliefs and desires, or the events that caused the beliefs and desires.)[5] Many philosophers who reject various aspects of the Classical Model are still in its grip over precisely this question. Thus Thomas Nagel, one of the most powerful critics of certain aspects of the Classical Model, argues that if we accept the gap, then the absence of causally sufficient conditions in the determination of an action would force us to the conclusion that there is an element of randomness in the performance of free actions, and our explanations would fail to explain, because they fail to cite sufficient conditions. As Nagel puts it, such an explanation "cannot explain precisely what it is supposed to explain, *why I did what I did rather than the alternative that was causally open to me*."[6] One answer to these questions

---

5. Donald Davidson, "Actions, reasons, and causes," reprinted in *Essays on Actions and Events*, New York: Oxford University Press, 1980, pp. 3–19.

6. Thomas Nagel, *The View from Nowhere*, New York: Oxford University Press, 1986, pp. 116–117. Similar worries have been expressed by Galen Strawson, "Libertarianism, Action, and Self-Determination," reprinted in T. O'Connor (ed.), *Agents, Causes, and Events: Essays on Indeterminism and Free Will*, New York: Oxford University Press, 1995, pp. 13–32.

has been proposed by a lot of good philosophers,[7] but it is wrong. Here it is: The cause of the action is *me*. I, the person who performs the action, am its cause. So there is no causal gap. The person is the cause. In some versions, we are to think of such personal causation, ("agent causation," "immanent causation") as a very special kind of causation. On Chisholm's account we need to distinguish agent causation, what he calls "immanent causation," from ordinary event causation, "transeunt causation." In other accounts we are just to think that the person is a cause like any other cause. But in both versions the causal gap is filled by a person acting as cause.

I believe this answer is worse than mistaken philosophy, it is bad English. It is a constraint on the notion of causation that wherever some object x is cited as a cause, there must be some feature or property of x or some event involving x that functions causally. It makes no sense to say, *tout court*, that object x caused such and such an event. So, for example, if I say, "Bill caused the fire," that is shorthand for something such as, for example, "Bill's lighting the match caused the fire," or "Bill's carelessness caused the fire." The original, "Bill caused the fire," is intelligible only if I see it as subject to some such completion. But what is the completion supposed to be in "I caused my action of raising my arm"? Notice that it makes perfectly good sense to say in answer to "What caused your arm to go up?" to say "I caused it to go up." Because in this case we hear that as short for "I caused it to go up

---

7. For example, Christine Korsgaard, *The Sources of Normativity*, Cambridge: Cambridge University Press, 1996, and Roderick Chisholm, "Human Freedom and the Self," in Gary Watson (ed.), *Free Will: Oxford Readings in Philosophy*, Oxford: Oxford University Press, 1982, pp. 24–35. I believe Chisholm later abandoned this view.

by raising it." In such a case it is my intention-in-action that functions causally to make my arm go up. Also it makes perfectly good sense to say, "My desire to vote for the motion caused me to raise my arm." But that is just to cite a reason, and it leaves us with the same gap we have been unsuccessfully trying to plug.

So what is the correct interpretation of (2)? *The first step in understanding (2) is to see that for its understanding we require a very special notion of agency.* The Humean bundle, even if unified and embodied, is not enough. You have to have an animal agent. Something is an agent in this sense if and only if it is a conscious entity that has the capacity to initiate and carry out actions under the presupposition of freedom. That sounds trivial, as it should, but it is not innocuous, because it implies that a bundle is not enough for agency. An agent is more than a bundle. On the Humean conception the bundle is just a sequence of natural phenomena, part of the sequence of efficient causes and effects in the world. But an agent in this sense requires more than being a bundle or being a part of the bundle. Why? Because the intention-in-action is not just an event that occurs by itself. It can occur only if an agent is actually doing something, or at least trying to do something. *Agency requires an entity that can consciously try to do something.*

But so far we still have not explained how or why we can or should accept nonsufficient causal explanations. So let us go to the next step. Because the agent has to be able to make decisions and perform actions on the basis of reasons, the same entity that acts as agent must be capable of perception, belief, desire, memory, and reasoning. To use the old-time jargon, the notion of agency was introduced to account for *volition*, but the same entity that has volition must also have *conation* and *cognition*. The agent must in short be a self. Just as agency has to be added to the bundle to account for how embodied bundles can engage in free actions, so selfhood has to be added to agency to account for how agents can act rationally.

The reason that we can rationally accept explanations that do not cite sufficient conditions in these cases is that we understand that the explanations are about rational selves in their capacity as agents. Thus the following three sentences look similar in surface syntax, but their underlying semantics, as we understand them given our Background presuppositions, reveals important differences.

(1)   I raised my arm because I wanted to vote for the motion.

(2)   I got a stomachache because I wanted to vote for the motion.

(3)   The building collapsed because the earthquake damaged the foundation.

(1) is perfectly acceptable as an explanation even though it does not cite sufficient conditions, because we understand it against the Background presupposition of the existence of rational selves, acting on reasons, under the presupposition of freedom. To see this point contrast (1) with (2). Given our Background presuppositions, (2) is interpreted like (3). It works as an explanation because, in context, it gives causally sufficient conditions, and rationality and freedom are not in the picture at all. Getting a stomachache is not a case of acting on a reason.

But why should we accept explanations of form (1) if they do not cite causally sufficient conditions? If there is a gap in the explanation, then it seems the event had an element of randomness. No reason has been given why that event occurred as opposed to some other event. How do we answer Nagel's objection? The key to the answer is to see that the question, "Why did you do it?" asks for a totally different sort of answer from the question, "Why did it happen?" I now want to explain the difference. The first step is this: always look at phenomena such as rational behavior and its explanation from the first-person point of view, because they have a first-person ontology. They only exist from the first-person point of view. And from that point of view there is no question that it is both the case that the reasons were not causally determining, and yet the explanation is perfectly adequate as it stands. It explains both why I did what I did, and why I did that rather than an alternative that was causally open to me. It is adequate because it cites the reason that I, as a rational self, made effective by acting on it. It gives a perfectly adequate answer to the question "Why did you do it?" without implying "It is causally impossible that anything else could have happened." It gives an adequate answer to the question because it precisely answers the questions "Why?" and "Why did you do that and not something else?" And it is not a requirement on such an answer that the answer give determining causal conditions. *The causal gap does not imply an explanatory gap.* The question, "Why did you do that?" does not ask: what causes were sufficient to determine your action? but rather it asks: what reason(s) did you, as a rational self, act on? And the answer to that question explains not by showing how the act as a natural event was inevitable given the antecedent causes, but by *showing how a rational self operated in the gap.* In a Wittgensteinian tone of voice one wants to say: this is how the language game of explaining actions is played, and don't suppose it must be played according to the rules of the language game of explanations in classical mechanics. The reason the language game of explaining actions by giving reasons is played differently is that the actual facts recorded by statements made in this language game have a different logical form from ordinary causal statements.

Nagel's requirement as stated is actually ambiguous. The requirement that I explain why I did the act rather than some other act that was open to me can mean either (a) I state what reason I acted on; in which case I state a reason that explains this action and excludes others that were causally open to me. Or it could mean (b) I state the causes of an event, my action, which explain why that event had to occur and no other event could have occurred. Nagel's objection raises a problem only if we suppose that requirement (b) must be satisfied if there is to be an explanation. But that would be a mistake. The question "Why did you do it?" in the relevant sense, asks me to state *the reason(s) I acted on.*

Of course, as Nagel points out, giving a reason does not by itself answer why I acted on that reason and not on some other reason available to me. But that is a different question. "Why did you do it?" asks initially for the reason(s) I acted on. One can always continue the line of questioning. "Why was that reason adequate for you?" And such lines of questioning will reveal more gaps, but explanation has to come to an end somewhere. And it does not show an inadequacy in my answer to the first question, that it admits of further questions.

The requirement that I state the reasons I acted on requires a reference to a self. The truth conditions of sentences of the form "X performed act A for reason R" require not just the existence of events, psychological states, and causal relations between them, they require a self (which is something more than an agent) that makes a reason effective by acting on it. Various philosophers, perhaps most notably Korsgaard, have claimed that in voluntary actions we *create* our selves. If so, this is a totally different notion of the self from the one I am now expounding. They must mean we create our character and personality. The point I am making now is not that action creates a self, but that action *presupposes* a self.

On the classical model the explanation of action requires only quantification over events. Thus the logical form of "*S* did *A* because of his belief and desire" comes out as:

There is some x such that x is a doing of A by S and there is some y such that y is a belief and there is some z such that z is a desire and (the onsets of) y and z caused x.

The apparent reference to a self is only a means to identify a token event.

On the account I am proposing the logical form of "*S* performed *A* because of reason *R*" is pretty much what it appears to be on its face:

There is an x such that $x =$ self S, and there is a y such that $y =$ action token A, and there is some z such that $z =$ reason R, and x performed y and in the performance of y, x acted on z.

Notice that the reference to a self is ineliminable. I have not yet explained what is a "reason for action" and what it means to act on a reason. That comes in the next chapter. We are going one step at a time, and in this chapter I am just trying to make it clear that the form of rational action explanations is not one of causation between events, but requires an irreducible notion of the self.

What shows that my analysis is better than the Classical Model? There are a number of arguments, but the one we are considering at this point has two premises. Grant me:

1. Reason explanations typically do not cite causally sufficient conditions.

2. In normal cases, they are perfectly adequate as they stand.

We know that (2) is true from considering first-person examples. I can tell you exactly why I voted for Clinton, even though the reasons I cite did not compel me to do it. In order to explain (2), given (1), we have to introduce the notion of acting on a reason. The special feature of reason explanations is this:

3. The request for a reason explanation of an action is a request for a statement of the reason that the agent acted on.

On the basis of (3) we can conclude (4):

4. Such explanations require the notion of an agent capable of acting on a reason, and any such agent is a self, in the sense I am trying to elucidate.

The fact that we are inclined to suppose that all explanations must fit a preconceived model of billiard ball causation is a limitation on our Background sensibility that I am now trying to overcome. I am trying to explain the conditions of the particular form of intelligibility of this language game.

Let us now turn to the next step in the argument.

Only for a self can something be a reason for an action.
So far we have identified an experiential gap and a self
that operates in that gap. But the self operates in that gap
on the basis of reasons. So the question arises: what is
a reason and what fact makes something into a reason?
I will have more to say about reasons in the next two
chapters, but at this point it is clear that in order that
something be a reason that can function in deliberation
and action, it must be a reason for an agent. The point has
to be stated precisely. There are lots of reasons for doing
things that no one knows about. For example, people had
a reason for eating whole wheat bread—it prevents beri
beri—without knowing that they had a such a reason. But
such a reason cannot have a role in deliberation. In deliberation a reason must be in the possession of an agent in
order to function as a reason. This is an additional feature
of the self, as well as being an argument for the existence
of the self. Furthermore, since reasons can be cognitive
—beliefs and perceptions, for example—the self must
involve more than agency, more than just volition. One
and the same entity must be capable of operating with
cognitive reasons as well as deciding and acting on the
basis of those reasons.

Given all of this we can now take the next step. If
we assume the existence of an irreducible conscious self
acting on the basis of reasons under the constraints of
rationality and on the presupposition of freedom we can
now make sense of *responsibility* and all of its attendant
notions. *Because the self operates in the gap on the basis of
reasons to make decisions and perform actions, it is the locus of
responsibility.*

This is a separate argument for the existence of an irreducible self. In order that we can assign responsibility,

there must be an entity capable of assuming, exercising, and accepting responsibility. We will understand this point better if we introduce the notion of time. The notion of responsibility makes sense only if we can now assign responsibility for actions that occurred in the past. I am held responsible now for things I did in the distant past. But that only makes sense if there is some entity that is both the agent of the action in the past and me now. That entity is what I have been calling "the self." Notice that I am not in that way responsible for my perceptions. Perceptions affect me but I am not accountable for them in the way I am accountable for my actions.

Only of a self, in the sense explained, can we say that he or she is responsible, guilty, to blame, to get credit, is deserving of reward or punishment. These attributions are different from "is good looking," "is in pain," or "sees the oncoming car." The former set require an irreducible notion of the self for their intelligibility. The latter do not.

Reasoning is a process of the self in time, and, for practical reason, reasoning is essentially concerned with time.

The introduction of the notion of time enables us to see that rationality in action is always a matter of an agent consciously reasoning in time, under the presupposition of freedom, about what to do now or in the future. In the case of theoretical reason, it is a matter of what to accept, conclude, or believe; in the case of practical reason, it is a matter of what actions to perform. There is thus a sense in which all reasoning is practical, because it all issues in doing something. In the case of theoretical reason, the doing is typically a matter of *accepting* a conclusion or hypothesis on the basis of argument or evidence. Theoretical reason is, thus, a special case of practical reason. The difference between theoretical and practical reason is in the direction of fit of the conclusion: mind-to-world, in the case of drawing a conclusion from evidence or premises, and world-to-mind, in the case of forming a decision and hence an intention on the basis of considerations. This has important further consequences: practical reasoning is not just something that occurs in time, but it is about time in the sense that it is reasoning now by a self about what that self is going to do now or in the future. So, once we introduce the notion of time we see that the self is required both as a locus of responsibility for past actions, and as a subject of planning about present and future actions. When I plan now for the future, the subject of the planning is the same self that is going to perform the act in the future. The structuring of time that is an essential part of practical reason presupposes a self.

VIII   Summary of the Argument for the Existence of an Irreducible, Non-Humean Self

Step 1. The existence of voluntary, intentional actions requires a conscious agent who acts. Otherwise the action would just be an event that occurs. Neither a Humean bundle nor a Strawsonian "person"[8] having both mental and physical properties, nor even a Frankfurt-style[9] person who has second-order desires about its first-order desires is by itself sufficient to account for agency.

---

8. Peter Strawson, *Individuals: An Essay in Descriptive Metaphysics*, London: Methuen, 1959, pp. 87–116.
9. Harry G. Frankfurt, "Freedom of the Will and the Concept of a Person," *Journal of Philosophy*, January 1971, pp. 5–20.

Step 2. But it is logically possible to be an agent and not yet a self. In order to be a self the entity that acts as an agent must also be capable of conscious reasoning about its actions. It must be an entity capable of perception, memory, belief, desire, thought, inference, and cognition generally. Agency is not enough for rational action. The agent must be a self.

Step 3. The crucial step: There is a special logical feature of rational action explanations. Construed as causal explanations, they do not work. The causes are typically not sufficient to explain the action. Yet they are perfectly adequate as they stand. Their intelligibilty requires that we think of them not as citing causes that determine an event, but as citing the reasons that a conscious rational agent acted on. That agent is a self. Agency plus the apparatus of rationality equals selfhood.

Step 4. Once we have a self as the agent of action, then a lot of other puzzling notions can be accounted for, specifically responsibility with its attendant notions of blame, guilt, desert, reward, punishment, praise, and condemnation.

Step 5. The existence of the self accounts for the relation of agency to time. One and the same self must be responsible for the actions that it performed in the past, and it must be capable of planning about the future. All reasoning is in time, and practical reasoning is, in the sense I have tried to explain, about time.

IX Experience and the Self

What is the relationship between the self that I have described, a purely formally characterizable entity defined by a specific list of features, and our actual conscious experiences? Are we in any sense challenging Hume's conclusion that there is no experience of the self? What, in short, can we say about this "self"? So far, nothing. It is a formal requirement on rational action that there must be a self who acts, in a way that it is not a formal requirement on perception that there be an agent or a self who perceives. Consequently the Humean account of me as a sequence of impressions and ideas, even updated to include a physical body with all of its dispositions, does not capture the essential requirement for rational agency, namely selfhood.

The key to answering this question lies in examining the structure of our own consciousness, since the first condition on the self is that it should be capable of consciousness. On the account I am presenting, the self is not an experience, nor is it an object that is experienced. When, for example, I look at a table, I have a visual experience and there is a table that is the object of the experience. In contrast, there is no self-experience and no object experienced as the self. Rather, "self" is simply the name for that entity which experiences its own activities as more than an inert bundle. It is characteristic of my conscious experience that I engage in deliberation and action, I have perceptions, I use my memories in deliberation, I make decisions, I carry out my decisions (or fail to carry them out), and I feel satisfied or unsatisfied, guilty or innocent, depending on the net results of all of these activities. The line I am following here is in a sense a fine line between Hume's skepticism and the naive pretheoretical view that each of us is aware of himself or herself as a self. The point I am making is that though the self is not the name of an experience nor is it the name of an object of an experience, nonetheless there is a sequence of formal features

of our experiences that are constitutive of ourselves as
selves.

How can we be sure that the apparent requirement of
the postulation of a self is not just a grammatical illusion
foisted on us by the subject-predicate structure of the
sentences? Are we not reifying something in order to have
an object for the "I" to refer to when we say "I decided to
vote for Clinton"? No. For the grammatical requirement is
the same even in cases where I am not doing anything.
Consider "I see the rose." As far as the phenomenology is
concerned, you can describe the phenomenological facts
by saying "This sequence of experiences now includes one
of a rose." But you do not capture the active feature of
the decision by saying this sequence of experiences now
includes a decision, for the decision was something I
made, an action on my part, and the experience of the rose
was received passively.

But are we not postulating a homunculus who lives in
the gap and makes our decisions for us? And does this not
lead to an infinite regress? No, because we live in the gaps
and make the decisions.

The postulation of a self does not require that we have
any experiences of the self. An analogy will make this
point clearer. Whenever we see anything we have a visual
experience, and in order to explain the visual experience
we have to postulate a point of view from which the
experience takes place, even though the point of view is
not an experience nor is it itself experienced. Thus for
example to explain my having this visual experience of the
Pacific Ocean I have to postulate that the experience is
from a certain point of view in space, even though when I
see the Pacific I do not see the point of view from which I
see it, nor is the point of view part of the experience of

seeing. Analogously the experience of free actions requires a self even though the self is neither an experience nor an object experienced.

So Lichtenberg was wrong. We should not say "It thinks" in preference to "I think." If thinking is an active voluntary process, there must be a self who thinks.

X Conclusion

What then is the self? On his own terms, Hume was surely right. If by "self" we mean some set of experiences, such as pains, or something that is the object of our experiences, such as the table in front of me, then there is no such thing. In order to account for rational agency, we must postulate a self that combines the capacities of rationality and agency. The features of the self can be stated as follows:

There is an x such that

1. x is conscious.

2. x persists through time.

3. x operates with reasons, under the constraints of rationality.

4. x, operating with reasons, is capable of deciding, initiating, and carrying out actions, under the presupposition of freedom.

5. x is responsible for at least some of its behavior.

Implicit in this argument is a result I now want to make explicit, because it will be of some importance in later chapters. The subject matter of rationality is not formal argument structures, much less is it marginal utility and indifference curves. The central topic of discussion in a theory of rationality is the activity of human beings (and presumably some other animals, as Köhler's apes have convinced us), selves, engaged in the process of reasoning. Just as the central subject matter of the philosophy of language is neither sentences nor propositions, but speech acts, so *the subject matter of the philosophy of rationality is the activity of reasoning, a goal-directed activity of conscious selves.*

4

The Logical Structure
of Reasons

What is a reason for an action? This question is supposed to be frightfully difficult, so difficult that Phillipa Foot once wrote, "I am sure that I do not understand the idea of a reason for acting, and I wonder whether anyone else does either."[1] But why should it be so hard? After all, don't we deal with reasons for action every day? How can there be a mystery? In a Wittgensteinian style one might say: nothing is hidden.

Well, nothing is hidden and no doubt the answer is in plain sight. All the same we have to look to find it, and it will turn out that the answer is more complex than we might have expected. We can infer from previous chapters that certain formal features would be possessed by any entity that was a reason for an action. For example, its existence and operation would have to be consistent with the gap. That is, it would have to be the sort of thing that could rationally motivate an action in such a way that an agent-self could *act on* it, though it does not cause the action by sufficient conditions. Furthermore, it seems it would have to have a content that was logically related in

---

1. Quoted in G. Cullity and B. Gaut (eds.), *Ethics and Practical Reason,* Oxford: Oxford University Press, 1997, p. 53.

certain specific ways to the contents of a prior intention and an intention-in-action (both of which have the
upward direction of fit) for which it was the reason. But
how exactly? All this is very vague, and I think we cannot
say anything very substantive until we work up to our
problem more slowly. So let us start by asking, how can
anything be a reason for anything and what is a reason
for anything, anyhow? A good first step is to look at the
ordinary use of sentences containing the word "reason"
and related terms such as "explanation," "why," and
"because." The project is initially to ask: under what conditions does a statement S state a reason R for a phenomenon P? With the answer to that in hand we can then go to
the next step, which is to ask, under what conditions does
S state R for a person to have an intentional state, such
as belief or a desire? And, because prior intentions and
intentions-in-action are intentional states, if we can answer
the question about intentional states in general, it looks as
if the answer should lead us to an answer about the special cases of intending to do something. And that answer,
if we can get it, is already an answer to the question,
"Under what conditions does S state a reason R for an
agent X to perform act A?"; because a reason for intending
to do something or for trying to do something is, other
things being equal, a reason for doing it.

A reason is always a reason for an agent, so it seems we
are trying to complete the following biconditional.

A statement S states a reason R for an agent X to perform
act A if and only if. . . .

But even this formulation seems to leave too much slack,
first because it does not distinguish between good and

bad reasons, between those reasons that are rationally acceptable and those that are not; and second, because our account of reasons must distinguish, as this formulation does not, between those reasons that are available to the agent and those that are not. One may have a good reason for doing something without knowing it. For example, for a long time people had a good reason not to smoke cigarettes—smoking causes cancer—without knowing that they had such a reason. Third, the use of the apparent referring expression, "act A" is at best misleading, because at the time of planning a future act, no such act yet exists, and indeed it may never exist. So a reason for a future action is a reason to perform an act of a certain *type* A. Let's try another formulation of the biconditional:

A rational agent X correctly takes a statement S as stating a valid reason R for X to perform an act of type A iff....

Later on in this chapter we will see that even this way of formulating the question is inadequate. As usual in philosophy, the big problem is to get the right formulation of the question. However, at this point, we are still thrashing around.

Notice that such reason statements are relational in three ways. First, the reason specified is a reason for something else. Nothing is a reason just by itself. Second, reasons for action are doubly relational in that they are reasons for *an agent-self* to perform an action; and third, if they are to function in deliberation, the reasons must be *known* to the agent-self. To summarize, to function in deliberation a reason must be for a type of action, it must be for the agent, and it must be known to the agent. Such statements are typically intensional-with-an-s because they do not permit the inference that the thing the reason is a reason for actually exists. One can, for example, have a reason for performing an action that one never performs. (More about intensionality later.)

I What Is a Reason?

The notion of a reason is embedded in at least three other notions, and the four can only be understood together as a family. The other notions are "why," "because," and "explanation." Stating a reason is typically giving an explanation or part of an explanation. Explanations are given in answer to the question "Why?" and a form that is appropriate for the giving of a reason is "Because...." To the question, "Why is it the case that p?" the answer, "Because it is the case that q" gives the reason why p, if q really explains, or partly explains, p. That is the reason why all reasons are reasons why. Both "reason" and "explanation" are success notions in the sense that there can be good and bad reasons/explanations but if a putative reason/explanation is really bad enough, it fails to be a reason or an explanation at all.

"Because" is a non-truth-functional sentential connective. It connects *entire* sentences. "Why" also takes whole sentences. The requirement of entire clauses is disguised from us by the fact that sometimes, in the surface grammar of the sentence, the "why" question contains a simple expression or phrase, and the "because" answer contains a prepositional phrase. Question: "Why now?" or "Why the beard?" Answer: "Because of Sally" or "Because of laziness." But in all such cases we must hear the shorter expression as short for a whole sentence. For example:

"Why are you leaving now?" Answer, "Because Sally needs me now." "Why are you growing a beard?" Answer, "Because I am too lazy to shave."

The syntax of both "Why?" questions and "Because" answers, when fully spelled out, always requires an entire clause and not just a noun phrase. This syntactical observation suggests two semantic consequences. First, the specification of both explanans and explanandum must have an entire propositional content, and second, there must be something outside the statement corresponding to that content. Reason-statements are statements, and hence linguistic entities, speech acts with certain sorts of propositional contents; but reasons themselves and the things they are reasons for are not typically linguistic entities. With some important exceptions I will mention in a minute, the statement of a reason can give a good or adequate explanation only if both the reason statement and the clause specifying the thing to be explained are in fact true. But then, what makes the statement and the clause true will be something independent of language. So, if I am asked, "Why does California have more earthquakes than any other state?" My answer, "California is the state with the most earthquake faults," can be an explanation only if California does in fact have more eathquakes than any other state and is in fact the state with the most earthquake faults, and these faults are causally related to earthquakes. There is a general term to describe those features of the world that make statements or clauses true, or in virtue of which they are true, and that term is "fact." An explanation is a statement or a set of statements. But a reason is not a statement or a set of statements, and the thing that the reason is a reason for is not a statement or a set of statements; rather, in the cases we have considered, both explanandum and explanans are facts. A fact is a reason only relative to the fact it is a reason for, and it is a reason for that fact only if it stands in an explaining relation to that fact.[2]

It is tempting then to think that *all* reasons are facts. But what about cases where I am mistaken about the facts, but can still offer an explanation? Question: "Why are you carrying an umbrella?" Answer: "Because it is raining." Both question and answer meet the requirement of propositional content, but suppose I am mistaken and it is not raining. All the same there is a true explanation implicit in my response. In making my statement I expressed the *belief* that it is raining and that belief can be a reason for my action even if the belief is false. In such cases we can say either *the fact* that I believed it is the reason or *my belief* is the reason for my action. Furthermore, I can have a reason for doing an action that I never in fact do, but if I offer the reason as an explanation, then it can be an explanation of my intention to perform an action, even if the intention is never carried out. What such examples suggest is that both reasons and the things they are reasons for can be either facts in the world or intentional states such as beliefs, desires, and intentions. So, for example, the explanation of *why I said* that California has

---

2. Speech act fans (bless them all) will no doubt have wondered why I do not just give an analysis of the speech act of explaining. After all, explaining something is a speech act. The reason is that such an analysis would not give us answers to the questions that we want answered in this discussion. "Explaining" does not name a separate illocutionary point. Explanations are typically sets of assertive speech acts but in order that they be real explanations they must be true, and the facts that make them true must stand in explaining relations to the thing they are supposed to explain. So, no speech act analysis by itself will answer the questions that we need to answer here.

the most earthquake faults may be that I *believed* that it had the most earthquake faults. And my belief may be a reason for my action, regardless of whether the belief is true. The formal contstraint on being a reason is that an entity must have a propositional structure and must correspond to a reason statement.[3]

The hypothesis that these examples suggest is this: *All reasons are propositionally structured entities: they may be facts in the world such as the fact that it is raining, or they may be propositional intentional states such as my desire that I stay dry. They can also be propositionally structured entities that are neither facts nor intentional states, entities such as obligations, commitments, requirements, and needs.* This feature of the ontology of reasons explains the syntactical fact that reason statements require a "that" clause, or some other equivalent form, which will express a whole proposition. We do not have a single word in English to name entities of all these sorts. "Fact" and "factive" are too suggestive of truth to cover both beliefs, which may function as reasons for someone even when they are false, and facts in the world. "Proposition" and "propositionally structured entities" are too closely suggestive of linguistic and intentional entities. I propose to use the old grammatical term "factitive" to cover entities that have a propositional structure, whether they are intentional states, facts in the world, or entities that are neither, such as obligations. I stipulate that by "factitive entity" I mean any entity that has a propositional structure, a structure specified by a "that" clause. All reasons are factitive entities, or factitives for short. Thus the fact that it is raining, my belief that it is

---

3. For an interesting defense of the thesis that all reasons are facts, see Joseph Raz, *Practical Reason and Norms*, London: Hutchinson, 1975, ch. 1.

raining, my desire that it rain, and my need that it rain can all be reasons. But rain by itself cannot be a reason. The point I am making here is not the trivial point that all statements have to express propositions, but rather that the specification of a reason is essentially propositional; and the reason itself, the very entity itself, has a factitive or propositional structure. Such factitive entities include not only facts in the world such as the fact that it is raining, but also beliefs, desires, needs, obligations, commitments, and a host of other factitive entities.

Thus, for example, suppose I am asked "Why are you carrying an umbrella?" I can give the following sorts of answers.

1. It is raining.
2. I believe it is raining.
3. I do not want to get wet.
4. I am under an obligation to do so.
5. I need to stay dry.

All of these statements specify factitive entities in the sense I have introduced. The first, if true, states the fact that it is raining. But the belief, desire, obligation, and need are also factitive. Some reasons represent other factitive entities. Thus a belief represents a fact in the world, but the belief may be a reason for something even if it is not true, that is, even if the corresponding fact in the world does not exist.

Why do reasons have to have a factitive structure? I don't know. My guess is that you have to be able to reason with reasons and you can only reason with something that has a propositional structure.

Our next question is: what makes a factitive entity a reason for something else? Given what we just said, that amounts to asking: under what conditions does such an entity stand in the explaining relation to something else? On the one hand, there is a class of factitive entities, reasons, and on the other hand, there is a class of factitive entities that need explaining, and that class can include facts about just about everything from wars to earthquakes, as well as such factitive entities as desires, beliefs, etc. We can explain members of the second class by stating certain members of the first class. So what features of the first class enable them to explain the members of the second class? The varieties of explaining relations correspond to the indefinite varieties of explanations one can give for phenomena—causal, logical, justificatory, aesthetic, legal, moral, economic, etc. What, if anything, do all these have in common, other than the trivial feature that they provide explanations? I do not know, and perhaps they have nothing in common. It would seem that explanations form a family, in Wittgenstein's sense, united by family resemblance. There is a huge number of different types of explaining relations, but there is a common formal element that runs through many of them, and that is the element of modality: the modal family includes why something *had* to be or had to happen, or *should* have or *must* have, or *ought to have* have happened, etc. The explaining relation includes making something happen, causing, necessitating, making more probable, justifying, bringing about, doing something for the purpose of or for the sake of ..., and others. I think the most primitive notion here is that of making something happen and our paradigmatic forms of explanations are causal explanations. The most common way to make something happen is to cause it to happen, and the most common way to explain something is to specify its causes.

Because the explanatory force of reason statements depends on how the explaining phenomena are described, reason statements are nonextensional. The point is not just that the connective "because" is nonextensional, but that substitutability fails within the reason statements. Reason statements, in short, are intensional-with-an-s not only with respect to existential generalization but also with respect to substitutability.

Consider:

California has more earthquakes than any other state because California is the state with most earthquake faults.

This together with the identity statement:

The state with the most earthquake faults is the state with the most movie stars

does not permit the inference:

California has more earthquakes than any other state because California is the state with the most movie stars.

The failure of substitutability in such reason statements is a consequence of the fact that the explanatory force of the statement depends on how the phenomena in question are described, it depends on the aspectual shape or mode of presentation. If the specification of the explanatory aspect—in this case, the causally effective aspect—is not preserved under substitution of coreferring expressions, then truth is not preserved.

Years ago there were debates about whether reasons were causes. I always thought the debates were confused because they failed to take into account the obvious grammatical differences between reason statements and causal statements. Causes are typically events, reasons are never events. You can give a reason by stating a cause, but it does not follow that the reason and the cause are the same thing. To make this clear, let us go through an example.

(1)   Why did the elevated Oakland freeway collapse?

This question asks for an explanation, and therefore a reason. It is typically answered by specifying a cause, for example:

(2)   The Loma Prieta earthquake caused damage to the foundations.

(2) gives an adequate reason and therefore an explanation. It does so by specifying a cause of the collapse. The earthquake, the event of damaging the foundations, and the event of the collapse of the freeway are three events related causally. Earthqake caused damage, damage caused collapse. (2) specifies that sequence and thus is an explanation of the third event. The statement of the reason in stating the facts gives an explanation. The *cause* of the collapse is an *event*, the earthquake. The *reason* for the collapse is the *fact* that there was an earthquake that damaged the foundations. The statement of the fact specifies the cause, but the cause is not the same entity as the reason.

So far we have made a little progress, but not much: reasons are entities that have a factitive structure. Explaining is a speech act that consists in the giving of reasons. The statement of a reason will explain only if the reason itself stands in one or more of the explaining relations to the thing it is a reason for. But even this little progress has turned up an interesting result. Though the statement of a reason will often specify a cause, it does not follow in such cases that the cause is identical with the reason, because reasons are always factitive entities and causes are typically events, not facts.

II Some Special Features of Explanations of Intentional Phenomena

When we introduce explanations of intentional phenomena, such as actions, beliefs, desires, and hopes, as well as wars, economic policies, love affairs, and novels, we introduce a new component, rationality, and with the demand for rational explanations there typically comes a demand for justification. Intentional phenomena are subject to constraints of rationality, and a demand for an explanation of an intentional phenomenon—a belief, a desire, an action, etc.—is typically a demand to show how it is rational and how justified. That is, when we ask for an explanation by asking, "Why did you do it?" "Why do you believe that?" "Why do you hope for that?" "Why do you want that?"—as well as "Why are you in love with her?" "Why did you go to war?" "Why did you lower the interest rate?" "Why did you write that novel?"—we are introducing questions that are not only of the family "What made it happen?" but also of the family "What justification is there for its happening?" and "On what reasons did you act?" Rationality in intentional phenomena is not the same as justification, because an intentional state may be unjustified without thereby being irrational. I might buy shares on the stock market "on a hunch" where my hunch in no way justifies my choice, but my action is not thereby necessarily irrational. Both rationality and justification are normative notions, but rationality is much more general than justification. In general, justified intentional states are rational, but not all rational intentional states are justified.

Why does the introduction of explanatory reasons for intentional phenomena automatically introduce the normative categories of rationality and justification? Because it is constitutive of intentional phenomena to be subject to such norms. *Being subject to rational criteria of assessment is internal to and constitutive of intentional phenomena,* in a way that winning and losing are constitutive of football games. You don't first have beliefs, hopes, desires, and intentions, and then external to them introduce rational forms of assessment; rather to have the beliefs, etc., is already to have phenomena that are subject to these norms. Furthermore, different forms of intentionality have their own forms of normativity. Thus, for example, beliefs are supposed to be true, and for that reason they are subject to special constraints of rationality and justification, involving, for example, evidence, other reasons for truth, and consistency. Rationality requires that one cannot knowingly hold inconsistent beliefs. Rationality has no such requirement for desires: One can rationally want that p and want that not p.

Like any other real empirical phenomenon in the real world, intentional phenomena may be given straight causal explanations that have nothing to do with rationality or justification. For example, "Jones believes he is Napoleon because of a brain concussion." Such an explanation is a causal explanation, but it does not give any reason that would justify Jones's belief or show it to be rational. It gives a causal reason why he has the belief, but does not give *his* reason for holding the belief. The peculiarity of intentional phenomena is that they are, in virtue of their very nature, also subject to constraints of rationality, and as part of those constraints they are subject to the demand for justification.

All good reasons explain, and all explaining is the giving of reasons. But this point has to be understood precisely. One may have justifying reasons for believing something or for having done something even though the statement of the justification does not give the reason why one believes it or why one did it. *The reasons that justify my action, and thus explain why it was the right action to perform, may not be the same as the reasons that explain why I in fact did it.* Thus if asked to justify voting for Smith, I might say I was justified in voting for him because he was the most intelligent candidate. But so far I have not answered the question of why I voted for him. I might *justify* my vote by saying he is the most intelligent candidate even though the reason I *acted on* is that he is an old drinking buddy of mine, and that has nothing to do with intelligence. In such a case the justification that I can give for my action is still not an answer to the question, "Why did you do it?" To take a case of more gravity, much of the public discussion of whether Truman was justified in dropping the atomic bomb is not about the reasons he *acted on*, but about whether the act was justified, whether it was a *good thing* on balance. All reason statements are explanations, but the point I am making now is that the explanation of why *something should have been done or is a good thing to have been done* is not always the same as *why it was in fact done*. In this book we are primarily concerned with explanations that explain why something happened, with explanations that state the reasons that the agent acted on or will act on. We are interested in justifications only insofar as they also explain why the agent acted or will act. Therefore I will distinguish between justifications and what I will call "justificatory explanations." Justification does not always explain why something in fact happened, but an explanation of its happening, whether justificatory or not, has to explain why it happened. A subclass of genuine explanations, therefore, are justificatory explanations.

So far we have found four kinds of explanation of intentional states.

1. Straight causal explanations. Example: Jones believes he is Napoleon because of a brain concussion.

2. Reason explanations of why something happened. Example: Jones voted for Smith because Smith is an old drinking buddy of his.

3. Justificatory explanations. Example: Jones was justified in voting for Smith because Smith was the most intelligent candidate, and that is the reason he voted for him.

4. Justifications that are not explanations of why the act occurred. Example: Jones was justified in voting for Smith because Smith was the most intelligent candidate, even though that is not the reason why he in fact voted for him.

With all this in mind I want now to make a crucial point: *the introduction of normative constraints on reason explanations of why some intentional phenomenon occurred does not remove the causal constraints.* Because of the gap, the causes of actions and of many other intentional phenomena do not normally give sufficient conditions, so in a more precise formulation we should say: *where intentional phenomena are concerned, the normative constraints on the explanation of why an action occurred, why an agent accepted a belief, why an agent formed a desire, why an agent fell in love, etc. do not remove the causal constraint that an explanation of why the agent did it must state the reasons that were effective with the agent.* You can have causal explanations of intentional phenomena that are nonrational, but you cannot have rational explanations of why some intentional phenomenon occurred that do not contain the notion of causal effectiveness. In the case of actions the agent makes a reason effective by acting on it. In the case of belief the agent accepts the belief because of a reason he also accepts. In the case of motivated desires, the agent forms the desire on the basis of a reason. Thus, for example, if asked, "Why did you vote for the Democratic candidate?" someone might say, "It's just an irrational obsession I have. I cannot help myself, I was brought up always to vote for Democrats." Such an explanation gives a causal, but not a rational, much less a justificatory, explanation. But if someone says, "I voted for the Democratic candidate because the Democrats will be more supportive of the labor unions, and I am committed to supporting the labor unions," that explanation, in order to provide a rational explanation for his action, must also be a causal explanation. The agent *acts* on the belief and the commitment. One can give justifications of intentional phenomena that are not causal, but to the extent that the justification does not state a reason that was causally effective, it does not give an explanation of why the intentional phenomena occurred. This is as much true of beliefs, desires, and emotions as it is of actions.

To summarize: so far I have made three substantive claims. First, that all reasons are factitive entities that stand in one or more explaining relations to the things they are reasons for. Second, that intentional phenomena are, in addition, subject to certain normative constraints. Third, if we are explaining why someone did something or has some intentional phenomena, these normative constraints do not remove the causal constraint. Reasons and rationality, in order to explain, must function causally (modulo the gap, of course). The peculiarity of intentional phenomena is that they admit both of nonnormative causal explanations and normative explanations. *But the normative explanations, in order to explain the occurrence of the intentional phenomenon, must also be causal.* Nonintentional phenomena, such as earthquakes, admit only of nonnormative explanations. For this reason, justifications of an intentional phenomenon are not always explanations of why it occurred. So, to repeat, we have at least four kinds of cases. First, nonintentional causal explanations: for example, he believes he is Napoleon because of a brain concussion. Second, rational explanations of why it happened that are not intended to justify. Third, justifications of why it happened that also explain why it happened. And fourth, simple justifications that do not explain why it happened.

III Reasons for Action and Total Reasons

So far, everything in this chapter has been a matter of preliminary ground clearing. Now we have to go to work on the constructive part. The heart of the argument of this chapter is in this section, and for the sake of total clarity I am going to lay out the argument as a series of numbered steps. I begin with some of the points we made in the previous two sections.

1. Reasons are both propositional and relational. In order to be a reason an entity must have a propostional structure and it must be related to something else that also has a propositional structure and for which it is a reason. Thus all reasons are reasons only relative to the things they are reasons for. This trivial and grammatical point has the consequence that where intentionality is concerned, a reason is always a reason for an intentional state. It is a reason for believing a proposition or a reason for having a desire, or a reason for forming a prior intention, or a reason for an intention-in-action, that is, a reason for actually performing the action. In the special case of reasons for action, a reason is also a reason for a certain person to perform an act, and if the reason is to function in deliberation, it must be known to the agent.

2. Reasons are factitive entities. The reasons for my action can be facts in the world, such as the fact that it is raining, or they can be intentional states with a factitive structure, such as beliefs and desires, or they can be factitive entities in the world, such as duties, obligations, and commitments, all of which have an upward direction of fit.

3. We need to distinguish external and internal reasons. An external reason, in my sense of the expression, is a factitive entity in the world that can be a reason for an agent, even if he does not know of that entity, or knows of it but refuses to acknowledge it as a reason. Thus, the fact that it is raining, or the fact that one has an obligation, is an external reason. In order for such an external reason to function in actual deliberation, it must be represented by

some internal intentional state of the agent. The agent *believes* that it is raining, or the agent *recognizes* his obligation. So in an ideally rational situation, there is a match between the internal and the external reasons, because insofar as there are external reasons that play a role in deliberation, they will be represented as internal reasons in the mind of the agent. The agent's deliberation can operate only on internal reasons, but the internal reasons often are valid reasons only because they represent external reasons. Thus, for example, if I decide to carry an umbrella because I believe that it is raining, my belief is an internal reason, but it is a valid reason only if it corresponds to an external reason, only if it is, in fact, raining.

4. A reason for an action is a reason only if it is, or is part of, a total reason. I have said that reasons for action are at least three ways relative, but there is a fourth way that requires emphasis as well: a statement is a statement of a *reason for an action* only insofar as that statement is systematically related to certain other statements. You can see this by considering examples. My reason for carrying an umbrella is that I believe it is going to rain. But my reason is only a reason because it is part of a total reason that includes such things as my desire to stay dry, and my belief that if I have an umbrella I can stay dry.

A total reason is a set of factitive entities. These may be beliefs, desires, or facts in the world such as the fact that it is raining or the fact that I have an obligation to go to Kansas City. Thus in response to the question, "Why are you carrying an umbrella?" I can say such things as "It is going to rain," "I believe it is going to rain," or "I don't want to get wet."

5. A total reason, in principle, might be entirely external. For example, someone might have a reason to eat citrus

fruit without having any of the relevant intentional states. Thus, suppose it is a fact that citrus fruit contains vitamin C; vitamin C prevents scurvy; scurvy is a terrible disease. All of these might be the elements of a total reason to eat citrus even for someone who knew nothing about any of them or was indifferent about disease.

In what sense can an entirely external total reason be said to be a reason for an agent, if it could not possibly motivate the agent? The answer is that the motivational force of an external reason is defined counterfactually: if the agent did have the appropriate knowledge, that is, if he knew about his health needs, and knew about how to satisfy them, then he would, if rational, recognize these as reasons for an action. So though there is ideally a match between the external and the internal reasons, we still need a distinction between the two. A perfectly rational agent might act rationally on a rationally justified belief that turned out to be false, and a fact in the world might be a compelling reason for an agent to act even in cases where the agent had no knowledge of the fact in question, or had knowledge of it but refused to recognize it as a reason.

6. In order to function in rational deliberation, and in the rational processes leading to action, every element of an external total reason must be matched by an internal element. That is, the facts that constitute the external reason must be believed, known, recognized, or otherwise acknowledged by the agent in question. Thus a health need, or an obligation, or the fact that it is raining can function in deliberation that motivates an action only if the agent in question believes or otherwise recognizes the fact in question. The fact that it is going to rain can be a reason for me to carry an umbrella, regardless of whether

I know that fact. But the fact that it is going to rain can only play a role in my deliberations if I am aware of the fact. Furthermore, the belief that it is going to rain will play the same role in my deliberation whether or not the belief is true. This makes it look as if what really matters is not the fact itself but the belief. But that is wrong. The belief is answerable to the facts. Indeed in some cases rationality can require one belief rather than another. Thus if I look out the window and see that it is raining, it would be irrational of me, other things equal, to refuse to believe that it is raining.

It might look as if an infinite regress threatened: rationality requires the belief, but the acquisition of belief itself requires rationality. Why does this not lead to an infinite regress?

7. In order to show why such cases do not lead to an infinite regress, I need to introduce the notion of *recognitional rationality*. Rationality may require that an agent under certain epistemic conditions simply recognize a fact in the world such as the fact that he has undertaken an obligation or that he has a certain need, or that he is in a certain kind of danger, etc., even though there is no rational process, no activity of deliberation, leading to the rational result. The acquisition of a rational intentional state does not always require a rational process of deliberation, or indeed any process at all.

We can see that these acquisitions are rational by contrasting them with their irrational denials. Indeed, a common form of irrationality is called "denial," where the agent persistently denies something in the face of overwhelming evidence. For example, I once had a friend who became an alcoholic. For a long time he persistently refused to acknowledge that he was an alcoholic. He just thought he liked to drink a little bit more than other people did. Other examples are cases where people simply refuse to recognize the obligations they have undertaken, or refuse to believe that they have been betrayed, or that they are in danger. The point of such examples is that the irrational attitudes are departures from a simple rational recognition of the facts. But rational recognition of the facts does not necessarily require deliberation. I may simply look and see that a truck is bearing down on me, or look out the window and see that it is raining. I recognize in both cases that these facts provide me with reasons for action. So rationality in these cases requires that I believe that it is raining or that the truck is bearing down on me, but I do not have to engage in a process of rational deliberation in order to reach these rational conclusions. Many internal reasons are based on the rational recognition of an external reason. The rational recognition of an external reason in many cases does not require any additional deliberation. Recognitional rationality is not necessarily a matter of going through steps.

8. The set of factitive elements that constitute a total reason must contain at least one element that has the world-to-mind direction of fit. Let us call these elements that have the world-to-mind direction of fit and that are at least potentially able to function in total reasons *motivators: Every total reason must contain at least one motivator.* Why? Because rationality in deliberation about actions is a matter of finding ways to satisfy motivators. The simplest argument for the claim that a total reason must contain at least one motivator is that a total reason must be capable of rationally motivating an agent. A total reason has to provide a rational ground for a prior intention to perform the action or for an intentional performance of the action.

In order to do that, there must be some entity in the total reason that has the world-to-mind direction of fit, and that provides the ground for the world-to-mind direction of fit of the prior intention and intention-in-action.

Where the motivator is an epistemically objective fact in the world, such as that the agent has certain needs or certain obligations, the external motivator can function in deliberation only if it is recognized as such by the agent. And, to repeat the point I made in the previous section, recognitional rationality may require that the agent recognize the motivator as a motivator. The man who refuses to acknowledge that there is a truck bearing down on him, putting him in great physical danger, is to that extent simply irrational, even though he has not gone through a process of deliberation. But the point for the present discussion is that for external motivators to function in deliberation they must be recognized as such by the agent.

Motivators can be either external or internal. Desires, for example, are internal motivators, and needs and obligations are external motivators. But, to repeat, the external motivators can function in deliberation only insofar as they are represented as internal motivators. A total internal reason for action must contain at least one recognized motivator.

9. The requirement that reasoning has a motivator is as much true of theoretical as of practical reason. Thus suppose I believe propositions of the form that p and that if p then q. What has all that got to do with my accepting, recognizing, or believing q? If beliefs are just neutral objects, sets of causal relations according to one fashionable (but mistaken) theory, then why should I, this self, care about q? The answer is that a belief is a commitment to truth. And when I have a belief I am committed to all of

its logical consequences. And a commitment is a desire-independent external motivator, which has the world-to-mind direction of fit. This is the real reason why there is no principled distinction in this regard between practical and theoretical reason. Theoretical reason is that branch of practical reason that concerns reasons for accepting, recognizing, believing, and asserting propositions.

10. The list of motivators seems at first sight dauntingly heterogeneous. It includes such internal motivators as desire, hope, fear, shame, pride, disgust, honor, ambition, love, and hate, not to mention hunger, thirst, and lust. It includes such external motivators as needs, obligations, commitments, duties, responsibilities, and requirements. Notice that both of these sets of motivators are factitive in the sense I explained earlier.

11. External motivators are factitive entities in the world. Under the descriptions that identify them as external motivators, descriptions given in such terms as "need," "obligation," "commitment," "requirement," "duty," etc., they are always observer-relative. It is only relative to human intentionality that some state of affairs in the world, for example, can be identified as a health need. Observer relativity implies ontological subjectivity, but it does not necessarily imply epistemic subjectivity. What that means is that the ontology of observer-relative phenomena always contains some reference to the intentionality of the observers in question. Hence the ontology is subjective. But it is quite possible for statements about ontologically subjective entities to have epistemic objectivity. It can be an objective fact that I have a certain health need, though its identification as a "need" is observer-relative.

This is an important point so let us go through it with an example. Suppose I have a certain level of vitamin C in my body. That is simply a brute, observer-independent fact about me. But suppose that level is such that it is insufficient to prevent disease, thus

(a)   I need more vitamin C.

Now, what fact corresponds to the claim that I *need* more vitamin C? What facts are constitutive of that fact? The brute facts in the world are such things as that I have a certain level of vitamin C in my body, that my body has certain causal processes, and that the level of vitamin C is insufficient to maintain these processes. Together those facts constitute the need, but under the description "need," those facts have the upward direction-of-fit. This is shown by the fact that a need can be fulfilled or satisfied, but not true or false. A need is fulfilled or satisfied if and only if the world comes to match the propositional content of the need. The brute fact in the world, that I have a certain level of vitamin C, has no direction of fit. But that fact is sufficient to constitute an observer-relative motivator: I need more vitamin C. And under the description "need" the fact is a motivator capable of functioning as a reason for action.

Statement (a) states a fact that is a reason for action. That reason is an external motivator, my need. Needs are observer-relative. It is only relative to my health and survival that I have such a need as this. Even though the need is observer-relative and thus ontologically subjective, it is an epistemically objective fact about me that I have such a need: that is, it is not just a matter of *opinion* that I have this need, it is a plain objective medical fact.

12. Desire-independent motivators, under their descriptions as motivators, always have the upward, world-to-motivator direction of fit. For this reason their recognition under these descriptions, that is, their recognition as motivators, is already a recognition of them as reasons for action. The agent does not first have to recognize an obligation and then figure out that he has a reason for action, because to recognize something as an obligation is already to recognize it as a motivator in the sense explained.

13. Rationality in decision making involves at least the following three elements. First, the recognition of the various motivators, both external and internal, and an appraisal of their relative weights. Suppose I promised to come to your party next Wednesday night. I clearly have an obligation to come to your party, and this obligation is a desire-independent reason, and has nothing to do with my desire to come to your party. But suppose also that it is very much opposed to my interests to come to your party, that if I do I will lose a business deal that will cost me my entire fortune. That interest is a contrary external motivator whose force also has to be reckoned with. Often moral philosophers, Kant for example, say that in such a case of selfish interests versus duty, duty should always triumph. But that seems to me simply ridiculous. There are many cases where I have a minor obligation, such as my obligation to go to your party, and I also have very deep interests that are in conflict with that obligation. There is no reason why the desire-independent motivator should always triumph.

Second, there must be a correct recognition and appraisal of the nonmotivational facts that bear on the case. Thus, for example, I have to be able to know how I am going to be able to carry out all of my various obligations. Is it even physically possible for me to fulfill all the obligations that I have undertaken? Roughly speaking we can divide these nonmotivational facts into two kinds. Those that have to do with "by-means-of" and the "by" or "by-way-of" relations, in the sense explained in chapter 2. In plain English these are facts about how to satisfy the motivators and what constitutes satisfying the motivators. Let us call them respectively *effectors* and *constitutors*. And once again we have to distinguish between internal and external effectors and constitutors. A simple example will make these distinctions clear. Suppose I owe you some money (external motivator). Suppose I know this (internal motivator). Suppose I can discharge this debt by driving over to your house and giving you the cash (external effector and constitutor). Suppose I know all of this (internal effector and constitutor). Knowing all of this I might decide to drive to your house and give you the money (practical reason).

Internal effectors and constitutors are always beliefs. They are beliefs about how to do things causally (effectors), or how doing one thing constitutes doing something else (constitutors). As beliefs, internal effectors and constitutors are responsible to how things are in the real world. They have the downward direction of fit. Thus they are valid reasons for action only to the extent that they correspond to real facts in the world. The fact that I can fire the gun by pulling the trigger is an external effector. Hence, if I have a reason to fire the gun, then I have a reason to pull the trigger. The external effector will be effective in my reasoning only if there is a corresponding internal effector, my belief that by pulling the trigger I can fire the gun.

It is this combination of features, the existence of the motivators and the recognition of the facts that bear on the case, that gives people the illusion that somehow all reasoning is means-ends, or belief-desire reasoning. The motivators provide the (desired) ends, and the non-motivational facts provide the (believed) means. But this way of looking at things blurs the distinction between internal and external motivators, and correspondingly it blurs the distinction between desire-dependent reasons for action and desire-independent reasons. The great gulf between humans and chimpanzees, as far as practical reason is concerned, is that we have the capacity to create, to recognize, and to act on desire-independent reasons for action. In the history of Western philosophy the great puzzle of rationality has always been: how is it possible that an agent can be rationally motivated by a desire-independent reason? For if every action is in some sense the expression of a desire to perform that action, then where does the desire come from if the reason the agent is acting on is neither itself a desire, nor itself grounded in other desires? How can desire-independent reasons ever rationally provide the ground of a desire? The standard answer to these questions given by the Classical Model is that the agent must have some overriding or higher-order desire to act on these desire-independent reasons. So the agent must have some general desire to speak the truth or to keep his promises or to carry out his obligations. But this must be the wrong way to look at these matters, because it implies that in cases where the agent does not have these higher-order desires, he has no reason at all to speak the truth, to carry out his obligations, or to keep his promises. What we need to show is how the mere fact that an agent recognizes something as a statement, a promise, or another form of obligation is already grounds for a motivation. How is that possible? The short answer is that all of these have the upward direction of fit, and to recognize certain sorts of factitive entities as having an upward direction of fit, and as having the agent as the subject of the propositional content, is already to recognize a reason for acting on that propositional content. I will discuss this point further in chapter 6.

The third element in rational decision making, once you have assembled the total reason, is to appraise the set of motivators and nonmotivational facts in such a way as to arrive at a decision. Decision theory seems to me to give a remarkably superficial account of this because it assumes that I have a well-ordered preference schedule in advance, and that it is just a matter of making probability estimates as to how to get on the highest rung of my preference ladder. But the real difficulty is in setting the preference schedule. Most of the difficulty of rational deliberation is to decide what you really want, and what you really want to do. You cannot assume that the set of wants is well-ordered prior to deliberation. Furthermore, it is not the case that all the motivators are on the same level.[4]

On the Classical Model we assume that the set of ends is given prior to deliberation. These ends are all, broadly speaking, things that the agent desires. Deliberation then is a matter of selecting means to these ends, ways of satisfying the desires. In most accounts the set of desires is assumed to be consistent. On the rival account I am pro-

---

4. There is an anecdote told about a famous decision theorist. He was offered an attractive job at another university, which tempted him, though he was deeply committed to the university where he was then employed. He went to discuss with a friend whether or not he should accept. His friend pointed out to him that as he was a famous decision theorist, he ought to be able to apply his decision theory to making this decision. What the friend did not know is that decision theory, for the most part, only applies after the hard parts of the decision have already been made.

posing, all of this is hopelessly mistaken. The really hard part of practical reason is to figure out what the ends are in the first place. Some of these are desires, but some are rationally compelling desire-independent reasons for action. *For these, the reason is the ground of the desire; the desire is not the ground of the reason.* That is, once you see that you have a reason for doing something you do not otherwise want to do, you can see that you ought to do it and a fortiori, that you ought to want to do it. And sometimes, but by no means always, that recognition will lead you to want to do it.

Furthermore, even after you have figured out your motivators, your reasons for action both desire-dependent and desire-independent, the set is seldom consistent. You can't do all the things you want to do, or all the things you ought to do. So you have to have some way of appraising the relative strength of the motivators. But even if you can solve that problem to your rational satisfaction, you still can't make a clear ends-means distinction, because some of the means involve ends of their own and some means interfere with other ends. To take the simplest sort of example, if one of your ends is to save money, you will find that the means to many of your other ends involve spending money.

I want to make all of this clearer in the pages that follow, but right now I turn to presenting some examples.

IV   Decision Making in the Real World

In a typical case, such as me now trying to allocate my time in writing this book, I have a series of conflicting motivators that bear on the case. I have an obligation to finish this book. But I have other writing obligations that have to be fulfilled before this one. I regard this work as more important, and I have promised to have the manuscript ready at an absurdly early date. My obligation to write this book conflicts with my obligation to produce two other articles that are due this month. On the other hand I have only a very unclear conception of what has to be done with this manuscript, and some of the other writing obligations look like they will be easier to finish. I expect to be paid more for this book than for the articles. I also have teaching and family commitments that absolutely have to be fulfilled. For example, I have to give lectures in my university courses and I have to show up at home by dinnertime. Doing philosophy is satisfying, but so are a whole lot of other things, and I can't do all of them.

This is what practical reason is like in real life. Notice: I cannot make a clear distinction between duty and desire, nor between ends and means. For the most part I would not have these duties if I had not wanted to have them and if I had not wanted to do the things they obligate me to do. My desires produced these duties. Is writing this book an end or a means? The answer is that it is both, and both in several different ways. But what is the maxim of my action, and shouldn't I check to see if it can be willed as a universal law? Again, I can form a lot of different maxims, some universalizable, some not, and it does not seem to matter much. The idea that in order to be a rational agent in such a case I would first have to have a well-ordered preference schedule and then make probability estimates as to which courses of action will maximize my expected utility seems absurdly implausible.

But in all this apparent intentional chaos, there is in fact an order, and the aim of practical reason is to sharpen and extend that order.

Here is the first serious puzzle: how can facts in the world, such as the fact that I have a certain vitamin level or that I uttered certain words, constitute a rationally compelling motivator? Well, some of those facts under some descriptions are already motivators. Thus that utterance was a promise and thus the undertaking of an obligation. That vitamin level is a deficiency and thus a need. Recognitional rationality can require that I recognize my deficiencies and needs under these descriptions and thus recognize them as motivators. But how? Don't I need some other antecedent desire to keep my obligations or to satisfy my health needs? I said earlier that principles of recognitional rationality can require that certain external facts be recognized as external motivators, and thus be represented as internal motivators. But more has to be said about the principles of recognitional rationality. I said there would not be an infinite regress, but why not? Wouldn't I need a motivator for the motivator? And wouldn't that lead to another kind of infinite regress?

The trivial truth that I can engage in reasoning only with what is internal to my mind is not inconsistent with the claim that the recognition of objective facts in the world can both be rationally required and can provide external rational grounds for internal motivators.

V Constructing a Total Reason: A Test Case for the Classical Model

Assuming, then, that a total reason must contain these three sorts of elements, how exactly do we construct, appraise, and act on a total reason? I want to consider a case from real life, because it illustrates the difference between the view I am advancing and the Classical Model. I believe that the example I am about to give is an example of irrationality, but the Classical Model cannot describe its irrationality.

When I was lecturing in Denmark I had a student who smoked a great many cigarettes. I pointed out to her that smoking was very bad for her health. Yes, she agreed, it was. Well, I said, "why then do you continue to smoke?" She said she didn't care about her health, that she was perfectly happy to die much younger than she would otherwise, but right now she wanted to smoke. She was right now perfectly willing to do something that she knew would have the consequence that she would be dead at sixty years of age. I pointed out to her that when she was sixty she would not be willing to die at the age of sixty and would regret smoking now. She agreed that yes, when she was sixty, she wouldn't be willing to die at the age of sixty, and would regret having smoked at twenty, but right now at the age of twenty, when she had to make the decision, she was perfectly happy to die at the age of sixty, and right now was when she had to make the decision to smoke or not to smoke.

The interest of the case is that she agreed to all of the facts I pointed out. She agreed that smoking is likely to kill her by the age of sixty, that as she got closer to that age she would regret having smoked, that she would be unwilling then to die from smoking, but all the same right here and now, having to make the decision whether to smoke or not to smoke right here and now, the rational thing for her to do was to smoke, because she wanted to smoke right here and now. That is, she was not admitting to any form of irrationality. On the contrary, she insisted that her behavior was completely rational, that the rational thing for her to do right now was to smoke.

According to the Classical Model, her action was indeed completely rational. Her beliefs and desires were such that she achieved maximum satisfaction of her desires, given her beliefs, by smoking. It is true that she might have some subsequent desires that would not be satisfied, but those subsequent desires could not play any role in the rational decision making in which she was engaged right now, because those subsequent desires didn't even exist right now. Furthermore, she had no present second-order desires about those future desires; they were a matter of total indifference to her. She did not think, "I will desire such and such in the future, so I desire to desire it now." The expected future desires played no role for her at all.

On Williams's version of the Classical Model, we would have to say that hers was a case of perfect rationality, because she acted only on internal reasons, and the internal reasons did not include any concern about her future forty years hence. Anything I might say to urge her to stop smoking would have to appeal to an external reason, something outside her present motivational set, and for that reason, according to Williams's model, it could have no claim on her rationality. There was, in Williams's terms, a "sound deliberative route" from her *existing* motivational set to the activity of continued smoking, and there was no sound deliberative route from her existing motivational set to the policy of not smoking. On the Classical Model, hers was a case of perfect rationality.

I think this case reveals the limitations of the Classical Model quite clearly, because this is a case where somebody has to make a present decision, and a rational decision requires acting on a desire-independent reason. Why exactly was her behavior irrational? I do not think this is a difficult case. The irrationality derives from the fact that the same self that makes the decision now is the self that will die by the age of sixty. It is not enough to say that right now she had no desires about her future desires, and indeed she had no desires about her future. The problem is that, rationally speaking, she *ought* to have had desires about her future, because her present behavior is such that she is both satisfying and destroying one and the same self. Notice that I am not claiming that "deferred gratification" is always the rational choice. It seems to me clear that there are some sorts of satisfactions right now that it is worth risking your life to achieve. In such a case one can construct a total reason where one has to balance out the present satisfaction against the risk of the cessation of one's future hopes. But this case is not like that. In this case there was no weighing of the desirability of smoking now and the undesirability of dying later. The point is that on the Classical Model the undesirability of dying later doesn't count at all, because it is not represented as part of the motivational set.

V   What Is a Reason for an Action?

Our original question, what is a reason for an action, has now been transformed: as we have seen, a reason for an action is any factitive entity that is an element of a set constituting a total reason. So the target of the analysis is the concept of a total reason. What then is a total reason?

A total reason for an action has to have the following components. First, it must have one or more rational
motivators. What makes a motivator rational? Formally
speaking one can say that a rational motivator must be
either a rational desire, or some rational external motivator, such as an obligation, commitment, duty, requirement, or need. For example, my desire to eat lunch and
my need for vitamins are rational motivators. But my
sudden urge to bite a piece out of this table is not a rational motivator. In order to function in a rational decision
the motivators must be recognized as such by the agent.

Second, except in some very simple cases where I can
satisfy the motivator by performing a basic action such as
raising my arm, a total reason must contain a set of effectors and constitutors. These factitive entities have to stand
in a relation to the motivators such that they either efficiently bring about the satisfaction of the motivator (these
are the effectors), or they constitute the satisfaction of
the motivator (these are the constitutors). Rational deliberation, then, consists in appraising the motivators for
their validity and for conflicts between motivators, and
appraising the effectors and constitutors in such a way as
to bring about the maximum satisfaction of the motivators
with the least expenditure of other motivators in satisfying the effectors and constitutors. To put that point in
plain English, to think rationally about what to do, you
have to figure out what you really ought to do, and then
you have to figure out how you can best do it without
frustrating a whole lot of other things you want, or ought,
to do.

We can now, in light of the discussion, go back to
our original question in section I, and reformulate it as
follows:

Rational agent X correctly takes a set of statements S, consisting of individual statements $s1, s2, s3 \ldots$, as stating a valid total reason for himself or herself to perform an act of type A iff:

1. Each of the elements of S, $s1$, $s2$, etc., are true and are taken by X to be true.

2. S contains the statement of at least one rational motivator and that rational motivator is recognized by X as a rational motivator. Rational motivators, as we saw earlier, can be either external or internal; they can, for example, be desires or obligations, but if the obligation is to function internally, it must be recognized as such by the agent.

3. X takes S as not stating causally sufficient conditions for the performance of action A. This is where the gap comes in. In order for X to engage in rational decision making, he has to assume that he has a genuine choice.

4. X takes some of the statements in S as stating effectors or constitutors (or both) for the motivators.

5. Rational appraisal of the relations between the competing motivators, and the various requirements of the effectors and the constitutors, are sufficient to justify the choice of A as a rational decision, all things considered, given S.

So far this characterization is purely formal. We have not yet said what makes a motivator rational, or how it can be the case that recognitional rationality can require that an agent must recognize an external fact as a motivator, or what the procedures are by which we are supposed to appraise the various motivators, constitutors, and effectors so as to arrive at a rational decision. I will take up some of these questions in subsequent chapters. However,

I issue one caveat right now: a theory of rationality will not by itself give you an algorithm for rational decision making. A theory of rationality will no more give you an algorithm for rational decision making than a theory of truth will give you an algorithm for finding out which propositions are true. A theory of truth tells you what it means to say that a proposition is true, and a theory of rationality will tell you what it means to say that an action was rational.

Some Special
Features of Practical
Reason: Strong
Altruism as a Logical
Requirement

I Reasons for Actions

I have been urging that in the investigation of rationality
we should concentrate our attention on reasoning as an
activity that actual selves engage in rather than focusing
on rationality as an abstract set of logical properties. If we
do, then it seems we find in any activity of reasoning a
collection of intentional phenomena and a self that tries to
organize them so as to produce another intentional state
as the end product. In theoretical reason the end product
is a belief or acceptance of a proposition; in practical reason it is a prior intention or intention-in-action. A consequence of the analysis of the intentionality of action that I
gave in chapter 2 is that actions have intentional contents.
So it is not at all mysterious that actions can be the result of a process of reasoning. Just as theoretical reason
ends in a belief or an acceptance of a proposition, so practical reason ends in a prior intention to act or an actual
action (which has the intentional content of an intention-
in-action). Often, but not always, these are preceded by the
formation of a secondary desire. For example: I look outside and come to the conclusion that it is going to rain.

Given my primary desire to stay dry and my other beliefs, I form the secondary desire to carry my umbrella, the prior intention to carry my umbrella, and I leave the house carrying an umbrella. Each of the last three steps, including the action itself, has intentional content motivated by the prior steps. I have heard people sneer at Aristotle's apparently quaint claim that an action can be the conclusion of a "practical syllogism." Aristotle was right, the sneerers are wrong.

I have been emphasizing the sense in which theoretical reason is a special case of practical reason: deciding what beliefs to accept and reject is a special case of deciding what to do. Though both theoretical and practical reason lead to a gap where the agent just has to act, reasons for acting are in many respects different from reasons for believing. Reasons for believing allow for conclusive proof, in a way that reasons for acting do not. This is a consequence of the difference in direction of fit. In this section I want to explore some of the special features of reasons for action and their consequences for practical reason. What is special about reasons for action? What are the differences between reasons for doing something and reasons for believing or accepting something? In both cases we have a set of intentional contents with the upward and downward directions of fit. Downward direction of fitters are supposed to be true, so they are responsible to states of affairs in the world. What sort of upward direction of fitters do we have and what are they responsible to? In the case of theoretical reason, the answer is relatively easy. To have a belief is to be committed to its truth, so if I am engaged in theoretical reason on the basis of my beliefs, I am committed to truth. Commitment has the world-to-mind or upward direction of fit and commitment to truth provides a reason for acceptance of true propositions. To say that something is true implies that you ought to believe it. To spell this out in more detail: suppose I want to know whether to believe that p. Suppose I have conclusive proof that p is true. Since belief involves a commitment to truth and commitment has the upward direction of fit, I ought to believe (accept, recognize or acknowledge) that p.

Both practical and theoretical reason are subject to rational constraints, but reasons for action have some additional special features. First, reasons for action have a kind of first-person status that reasons for believing do not have. Reasons for believing are typically in the form of evidence or proof of the truth of the proposition believed, and truth is impersonal. Truth is a reason for anybody to believe. But where action is concerned, even if the reason is a reason for anybody, reasons for action still must appeal to something inner or first-personal in a way that reasons for believing do not. Once you have established *truth* there isn't any further question about whether you should believe it, because to have the belief that p is true is already to have the belief that p. But because of the difference in direction of fit between belief and intention, there is nothing analogous to truth where reasons for acting are concerned. In theoretical reason, the right reasons get you to a belief that is true. In practical reason the right reasons get you to an intention that is ... what? There is no x such that intention is to x as truth is to belief. Everyone has a reason for seeking self-preservation, flourishing, autonomy, and a whole lot of other desirable goals. But none of these stands to action as truth stands to belief, because in every case the goal has to be represented by the agents' intentional contents as a separate goal. In the case of belief, the goal of truth is built into the belief. No such goal is built into reasons for acting, prior intentions, or intentions-in-action.

Second, reasons for acting have a special relation to time that is unlike that of reasons for believing. Reasons for acting are always forward-looking. And this is true even in cases where we are giving reasons why an agent acted as he or she did in the past. A present reason for acting is always a reason for a self to perform an action either *now* or *later*. A past reason for action was a reason in the past for a self to perform that action then or later.

Related to these two is a third point. Reasons for action must be able to motivate an action. If the reason is given why a past action was performed, then the reason must have functioned causally in the performance of the action, because it must have been the reason that the agent *acted on*. If the reason is for a future action, then it must be a reason that the agent *can act on*. But to say that is to say that the reason is either actually or potentially effective, because the notion of acting on a reason, as we saw, is the notion of making the reason effective in the performance of the action. In the last chapter I called attention to the motivational feature of reasons in order to argue that every total reason must contain at least one motivator.

What sorts of factitives can be motivators? The answer to that question given by the Classical Model is brutally simple: all motivators are desires, where "desire" is broadly construed to include such things as the goals, ends, and objectives of the agent. Reason is and ought to be the slave of the passions. Recent authors are somewhat vague about what the list of motivational entities would include, and they talk generally about "pro-attitudes" (a term invented, I believe, by Patrick Nowell-Smith)[1] and the "subjective motivational set" (Williams),[2] but the general idea is clear enough. Without some kind of desire-like internal psychological state, the process of reasoning could never produce an action. Köhler's chimpanzees are the model. Without desire they would never get off the ground.

Why are the classical theorists so confident about this model? Well, its simplicity is appealing and makes its features nicely formalizable in decision theory. But there are also powerful philosophical reasons in support of it. First, in real life, a lot of cases are like that. The simplest cases are where the reason simply is a desire of a certain sort. "Why are you drinking water?" Because I am thirsty. Another sort of case is where there is some fact that the agent believes will lead to the satisfaction of his desire. "Why are you drinking water?" Because it will cure my headache. Full story: I want to cure my headache, I believe that drinking water will cure my headache, therefore I want to drink water. In such a case the desire to drink water is itself a motivated desire, motivated by another desire together with a belief about how to satisfy that desire.

Another argument for the Classical Model is that in the structure of actual deliberation the conclusion must be some desire-like intentional state such as a secondary desire, a prior intention, or an intention-in-action. And where could that state rationally come from if not from an earlier desire? Without a desire or pro-attitude as a starting

---

1. Patrick Nowell-Smith, *Ethics*, London: Penguin Books, 1954, p. 112.
2. "External and Internal Reasons," reprinted in *Moral Luck*, Cambridge: Cambridge University Press, 1981, pp. 101–113.

point, it seems there is no way that deliberation could rationally end in a desire or desire-like intentional state.

The obvious objection to the claim of the Classical Model that only desires can motivate is that there are many motivationally effective reasons for action, such as obligations, that are not desires. "Why are you drinking water?" Because I am under an obligation to do so. I promised my spouse.

To all of these examples the classical theorist gives the same answer. Your obligation, for· example, is only a reason for action because you *desire* to fulfill your obligations. One of the central points in dispute between me and the Classical Model is exactly on this issue. On my view the obligation is—or at least can be—the reason for an effective desire (i.e., a desire the agent acts on), rather than a prior desire functioning as a reason for the effectiveness of the obligation. I will come back to this point in the next chapter.

A fourth feature of reasons for acting is that if the reason is taken as a reason for the performance of a free action, it cannot be taken by the agent as causally sufficient. If he thinks of himself as truly compelled, then he cannot think of himself as freely acting on a reason. In the case of human actions, because of the gap, the reason can be a good or adequate reason without providing causally sufficient conditions for the act. And, more important from the agent's point of view, the reason must not be seen as causally sufficient. As I remarked in earlier chapters, the applicability of the concept of rationality in decision making presupposes free choice. Indeed, for rational agents free choice is both necessary and sufficient for the applicability of rationality. Free choice implies that the act is rationally assessable, and rational assessability implies

free choice. It might seem that there are plenty of counterexamples to this claim. "What about the drug addict
who cannot help himself but nonetheless is capable of
rationality in selecting the rational means, rather than
irrational means, to satisfy his craving?" But even this case
supports the general point, because we are tacitly supposing that the drug addict has a choice of the means to
satisfy his overwhelming desire. That is, to the extent that
we regard the agent as acting rationally we are supposing
that to that extent he is making free choices, even though
the overall project of satisfying his addiction is not a
matter of free choice for him and thus falls outside the
scope of rationality. The gap is a feature of both reasoning
about what to believe, and reasoning about what to do.
But it plays a special role in reasoning about what to do,
as I have tried to describe.

So, to sum up: in addition to the two general constraints
of *rationality*, (together with justification), and *the gap*,
which apply to reasons for believing as well as reasons
for doing, there are at least three additional special features of reasons for action. They are, in a special sense
first-personal, they are essentially *future-directed*, and they
are essentially *motivational* in the sense that they must be
capable of motivating an action. Just to have some grand
words, let us call these five the conditions of Rationality,
Freedom, Subjectivity, Temporality, and Causation.

Why should all of these hang together in the way that
they do? Why are there these connections? At one level, I
do not think that is a difficult question. Rationality is a
biological phenomenon. Rationality in action is that feature which enables organisms, with brains big and complex enough to have conscious selves, to coordinate their
intentional contents, so as to produce better actions than

would be produced by random behavior, instinct, tropism, or acting on impulse. To get the biological advantages of rational behavior, the animal has to have its own conscious motives (Subjectivity), some of these have to be forward-looking (Temporality), they have to be able to motivate real behavior in the form of bodily movements (Causation), and they have to do it under the presupposition of freedom operating in the gap (Freedom). "Practical reason" is the name of that capacity for coordination. Indeed, these features are not logically independent: the first two features, Subjectivity and Temporality, follow from the third feature, motivational Causation. A motive has to be someone's motive (Subjectivity) to act now or in the future (Temporality).

The connection between rationality and the gap of freedom is this: *rationality applies only where there is free choice, because rationality must be able to make a difference.* If my actions are really completely *caused* by my beliefs and desires, so that I really can't help myself, then I have no choice and rationality can make no difference at all to my behavior. If I am in the grip of causally sufficient conditions, there is no room for deliberation to operate and my action falls outside the scope of rational assessment. Furthermore a demand for justification makes sense only in cases where alternative possibilities were open to the agent.

II   Constructing a Rational Animal

To illustrate the special role and character of practical reason, I would like to present the following thought experiment. Imagine that you are designing and building a robot that will be a "rational animal." The point of the thought experiment is to illustrate the logical relations between certain crucial features of human existence. Whatever else we are, we are the products, at least metaphorically speaking, of a certain sort of engineering. I do not believe it was the divine engineering of the creationist story, but rather as far as we know it was the unintentional, metaphorical, "as-if" engineering of evolutionary processes. But one way or another, we are the result of a certain set of processes that have been guided by certain sorts of design needs. Given that we are the products of engineering, even if only "as-if" engineering, the point of asking the question how rational beings might be designed is to get us to see how much you need to put into your design in order to see how much you can get out as a result of what you put in. What do you require as an actual design feature, and what do you get for free? (Many of the questions in the history of philosophy are contained in this question, by the way.) Because rationality is not a separate faculty or module, but rather a feature internal to other cognitive and volitional capacities, I believe that we will find that we have to put in most, though not all, of human mental faculties in order to have a "machine" capable of rationality.

The first feature you have to put into your robot is consciousness. You have to build a robot brain that has the power of human brains to cause and sustain inner, qualitative, unified, subjective states of awareness and sentience. Without consciousness you cannot get into the game of rationality at all. But passive perceptual consciousness is not enough. You need the active consciousness of agency. That is, you need to build a being that is consciously able to initiate actions. But in order to do that, the robot must have desires as well as intentions. This is

because it must be able to want to do the things it tries
to do. So at a bare minimum we have to have a machine
capable of perception, action, and desire. Furthermore, if
these actions are to be rational actions, the robot has to
be able to engage in deliberation. This requirement is a
more weighty matter than it might at first seem. I do not
see how a robot could engage in deliberation without a
very large chunk of the human and animal apparatus of
intentionality. First, there must be the capacity to store
information in the form of memories, and this memory
capacity will be a source of beliefs. Second, it must have
the ability to coordinate both the downward direction-of-
fitters (beliefs, perceptions, etc.) and upward direction-
of-fitters (desires, inclinations, etc.) in a conscious stream
of thought. That is, it is not enough to have perceptions,
memories, desires, and intentions; the robot also must
be able to put all this apparatus to work in a conscious
sequence of deliberative thoughts. It has be able to think
that because so and so is the case, and it wants such and
such, it should do this act and not that act, even if it can
think these thoughts only wordlessly. In order that it
should have all this intentionalistic apparatus it must have
what (in chapter 2) I call the Background, the set of pre
intentionalistic capacities that enable it to interpret and
apply its own intentional states. Finally, the robot must be
such that the stream of thought is capable of ending in
decisions and subsequent actions.

So the additions we had to make to the robot after giving
it consciousness were quite substantial: The robot has to
have conscious perceptual phenomena, conscious conative
phenomena (desires), and conscious volitional phenomena
(both prior intentions and intentions-in-actions), and it
has to have the capacity for conscious deliberation result-

ing in decisions and actions, with all the apparatus that such a deliberative process involves. The way that I have described the case, we have already built the experiences of the gap into the robot. And because it has all of these features, as I noted in chapter 3, it already has a self in my sense. Selfhood in my sense comes for free once you have a conscious intentional being capable of engaging in free actions on the basis of reasons. Now a crucial question is raised immediately. Once the robot has all of that, does it already have the mechanism necessary for rational decision making of the fully human variety? Well, not quite. So far we have not built a humanoid robot, but, one might say, an artifical chimpanzee. To get to human decision-making powers we need to put in certain other features.

Once you have both conscious and unconscious mental states and processes together with both downward (perceptions, memories, beliefs, etc.) and upward direction-of-fitters (desires, inclinations, intentions, etc.) and you have the capacity to coordinate all this in the stream of conscious thought ending in decision making, the next central element to build into the robot is, without doubt, language. It is important to say exactly what features of language would be required by a rational agent. An animal does not require any language in order to have simple intentional states like hunger and thirst, and it does not even have to have language in order to make simple decisions, nor indeed does it need a language to engage in simple instrumental reasoning of the sort that Köhler's chimpanzees engaged in. But for full-blown rationality, certain very specific features of language are essential. Not all the features of natural human languages are essential to rationality. For example, rational thought processes do not require color words, the passive voice, or definite articles. But fully human rationality does need certain essential linguistic devices. First, our robot must have the basic speech act forms that relate language to reality with both the word-to-world direction of fit, and the world-to-word direction of fit. It must, at the bare minimum, have the capacity to represent how things are in the world (assertives), as well as the capacity to represent how it tries to get others to act in the world (directives), and how it commits itself to act in the world (commissives). Furthermore, it must have the capacity to communicate all of this to other possessors of language. Language is both to think with and to talk with, but when we are concerned with talking, we have to have a language that is public, that enables the robot to communicate with others. Because we are building this robot in our own image, so to speak, we will build it with the capacity to communicate with us. Furthermore, it seems to me the robot has to have some set of devices for representing temporal relationships. If it is going to be able to plan for the future, which is characteristic of practical reason, it has to be able to represent the future and its relation to the present and the past. What else would it need? Well, it seems to me it would have to have some way of articulating logical relations. It need not have precisely our inventory of logical vocabulary, but it must have some way of marking negation, conjunction, implication, and disjunction. Furthermore, it seems to me it would also need some set, however minimal, of metalinguistic terms for appraising success and failure in achieving direction of fit, and logical coherence. So it needs something in the range that includes "true" and "false," "valid" and "invalid," "accurate" and "inaccurate," "relevant" and "irrelevant." Now that we have given it this much of a language we might as well give it a name. Call it "the Beast."

In the course of constructing all of this representational apparatus, both mental and linguistic representations, we will have had to have given the Beast the apparatus necessary to apply these representations to concrete situations and to interpret the representations that it receives from other sources. These abilities, the abilities to apply and interpret representations, constitute what I have been calling the Background.

Now here is the point of the thought experiment: once the Beast has this much, it already has the apparatus essential for the distinctively human features of rational thought processes and rational behavior. It has a form of rationality that goes far beyond the rational chimpanzees we discussed in chapter 1. Specifically, once the Beast has the ability to perform speech acts, it has the potential for desire-independent reasons for action, indeed it inevitably has the requirement of desire-independent reasons for action, because just about every speech act involves a *commitment* of some kind or other. The famous examples are speech acts like promising, where the speaker is committed to carrying out a future course of action, but asserting commits the speaker to the truth of the proposition asserted, and orders commit the speaker to the belief that the person to whom he or she gives the order is able to do it, to the desire that he or she should do it, and to permitting the hearer to do it. In short, what people have thought of as the distinctive element of promising, namely commitment or obligation, actually pervades just about all speech acts. The only exceptions I can think of would be simple expressives like "Ouch!" "Damn!" or "Hurrah!" and even they commit the speaker to having certain attitudes.

The bizarre feature of our intellectual tradition, according to which no set of true statements describing how things are in the world can ever logically imply a statement about how they ought to be, is that the very terminology in which the thesis is stated refutes the thesis. Thus, for example, to say that something is true is already to say that you ought to believe it, that other things being equal, you ought not to deny it. The notion of a valid inference is such that, if p can be validly inferred from q, then anyone who asserts p ought not to deny q, that anyone who is committed to p ought to recognize his commitment to q.

The point of the thought experiment can also be put as follows: once you have the apparatus of consciousness, intentionality, and a language rich enough to perform the various types of speech acts and express various logical and temporal relations, then you already have the apparatus necessary for rationality. Rationality is not an extra module or faculty. It is already built into the apparatus that we have described. Furthermore, something much richer than instrumental or ends-means rationality is already built into the apparatus we have described, because we have the potential, indeed the requirement, of desire-independent, or external, reasons for action.

We have included in the Beast the experiences of the gap. But have we given it genuine free will, or only the illusion of free will? There are at least two different possibilites. First we might deceive the poor Beast by making its underlying mechanisms totally deterministic. So it has the illusion of free will, because it experiences the gap, but in fact its behavior is entirely preprogrammed with fully deterministic mechanisms. Another quite distinct possibility is that its conscious experience of decision making in the gap is matched by an indeterministic element in the hardware implementation that is carried forward through time by the conscious level of decision making. I explore both of these possibilities, as far as actual human beings are concerned, in chapter 9.

III   Egoism and Altruism in the Beast

Well, what about the favorite topics of moral philosophers, egoism and altruism? How do they stand with our robot? We have not yet explicitly built either egoism or altruism into the Beast. In our intellectual culture we take egoism and self-interest as unproblematic, and regard altruism and generosity as requiring a special explanation. In one way that is right, in another it is wrong. It is right to suppose that the Beast will prefer the satisfaction of its desires to their frustration, and will prefer the alleviation of its pains to their intensification. Other things being equal, that is part of what is involved in having a desire or a pain. And the concern with its own desires, etc. looks like egoism. But in another sense it is wrong to think of egoism as unproblematic, because satisfaction of the desires does not so far tell us the *content* of the desires and so far we have said nothing about the content of the desires in the Beast. It might well be that the Beast finds altruistic desires as natural as egoistic desires. As far as what we have said goes, the Beast might prefer the prosperity of others to its own prosperity.

So let us add another component to our Beast. Let us suppose that we program it to seek what I will vaguely call "self-interest." Let us build into our Beast a preference for survival over extinction, and a preference for its self-interest over what is not in its interest, that is, we suppose that the Beast does not wish to become injured, damaged, diseased, deprived, or dead. Once the Beast has a self and self-interest, if it also has a conception of time, as we have stipulated, then it will be able to plan for its subsequent survival and flourishing. That is, if the self has interests, and if the self persists through time, and if the self is the agent that exercises rationality, then it will be rational for the self to make plans now to secure its interest in the future, even though it has no present desire to do the things now that are necessary to secure its interests in the future. So we have now two forms of desire-independent or external reasons for action. Roughly speaking, there are commitments, typically made to others, but they can be made to oneself, as well; and there are prudential reasons.

Rational self-interest in our enlightened robot does not come for free, but it does not require much of a techno-logical investment beyond the bare minimum necessary for consciousness, intentionality, and language. If the Beast has needs and interests and the capacity to recog-nize these needs and interests, and has a self and an awareness of its self extending into the future, it is not much of an addition to give it a motivation for acting now so as to look out for its interests in the future.

Now we come to a crucial question: does the Beast have any rational basis for caring about the interests of others? What is the relation between the self-interest that we have built in and the altruism that we have neglected? The standard approach to this question by moral philosophers is to try to build altruism out of egoism. There are, if I understand them, at least three ways of doing this. First, we imagine that we simply do it as an engineering task. We put altruism into our Beast, just as we have already put egoism into the Beast. This is one way of interpreting the sociobiologists. The idea is that we are genetically inclined to at least certain forms of altruism, and we are supposed to be able to account for the genetic basis of altruism through such things as group selection or kin selection. Altruism is just a natural inclination, and insofar as it can be effective at all, it can be just as effective as any other internal reason. Our Beast simply has an inclination to look out for the interests of others. Second, and more interesting, an effort has been made by Thomas Nagel[3] to show the formal similarity between prudential reasons and altruistic reasons. To consider the interests of others is just as rationally based as considering one's own future interests. Third and finally, an effort has been made in the Kantian tradition, most notably by Christine Korsgaard,[4] to derive altruism from autonomy. If, because of my autonomy or freedom, I have to will my own actions; and if the will is subject to constraints of generality such that I am rationally required that each thing I will, I should be able to will as a universal law; then I will be rationally required to treat other people as my equals in the moral realm, because the universal laws that I will apply equally to me and to them.

There is something right about all three of these approaches, but also something unsatisfactory. If I just feel an inclination to altruism, then that is much too fragile to form the basis for practical reason where altruism is concerned. The inclination to altruism has no special

---

3. *The Possibility of Altruism*, Princeton: Princeton University Press, 1970.
4. *The Sources of Normativity*, Cambridge: Cambridge University Press, 1996.

binding force. Often one does not feel such inclinations, and many people feel counterinclinations, such as an inclination to sadism, cruelty, or indifference. And on this account, altruism would just be one inclination among others. What is special about the inclination to help others? So let's turn to Nagel's analogy between prudence and altruism. The point that is true seems to me to be this: once I have consciousness and the self and am able to use language, I am already committed to the existence of other consciousnesses and selves on a par with my own. How exactly? That there is such a thing as my conscious self makes sense to me only if it is different from other things in the universe. If there is a me, then there must be a not-me. And if the not-me entities in the universe include entities with which I communicate in the performance of speech acts, then some of the not-me's in the universe must be presupposed by me to be conscious agents with a selfhood just like my own. So I am one self among others. But the question still remains, why should I care about the others? There is indeed a formal similarity between caring about my future self and caring about another self: in both cases I have to consider the interests of entities that are not present to my consciousness here and now when I am making the decisions. But there is a drastic asymmetry: in prudential reasoning, the self I care about is me. That is, the self that makes the decisions and carries out the actions is identical with the beneficiary of the decisions and actions. For altruistic reasoning, that identity is lost. I am not attempting here to do full justice to Nagel's subtle argument. I am simply raising a difficulty that I find with it, before going on to discuss another argument for the same conclusion, and then to present my own.

Let us then turn to examine Korsgaard's Kantian account of how autonomy generates universality and universality generates altruism. Her solution is presented as an interpretation of Kant's views and here is how it goes: Kant argues that (1) we have to act under the presupposition of our own free will. He then continues that (2) free will, if it is to be a will at all, must be determined in accordance with a law. Since, therefore, (3) free will has to be determined under its *own* law (by 1), it turns out that (4) the Categorical Imperative is a law of free will.[5] The dubious step here is the second step. Why should the exercise of my free will in decision making require any sort of law at all? Why can't I freely decide what to do, just like that? Certainly no argument so far has been presented why there must be a law in order for me to make free rational decisions.

To answer this objection Korsgaard draws an analogy with causation. She says causation has two components, the notion of making something happen, and the notion of a law. We require the second component, a law, because we could not properly *identify* a case of something making something else happen if we could not assume it under a causal law. That is, she thinks regularity is necessary for the identification of causation. Then she claims the causation of the will is exactly analogous to causation in general. For if I am to act of my own free will, then I am the cause of my actions. But if that is the case, I must be able to distinguish between *myself* causing the action, and some *desire* or *impulse* that is in me that causes my body to move. I have to see myself as something distinct from my first-order impulses and desires. But if that is the case, in order that the actions should genuinely be my actions, that is, that they should come from myself rather than just be expressions of my first-order desires, I have to act

5. Korsgaard, *Sources of Normativity*, pp. 221–222.

under some universal principles. So the law that I create for myself is exactly analogous to the laws of causation. We could not *identify* acts as the acts of a self unless they were done under some universal principle. In order that the actions can be truly said to be actions of myself, it turns out that I must be a law-giving agent. Indeed it is only because we impose universal volitional principles on our decisions that we can be said to have a self at all. The self is constituted by these universalized decisions. For Korsgaard the key sentence, I believe, is the following: "For if *all* of my decisions were particular and anomalous, there would be no identifiable difference between *my acting* and *an assortment of first-order impulses being causally effective in or through my body*. And then there would *be* no self—no mind—no me—who is the one who does the act" (p. 228).

I believe this argument does not work. The basic notion of causation is, indeed, the notion of making something happen. And it is true that in order to *identify* such cases, we have to presuppose regularity. But that requirement is an *epistemic* requirement, not an *ontological* requirement on the very existence of causation. There is no self-contradiction in imagining causes that occur without instantiating any universal regularities. We might not be able to establish with certainty that such and such an event was really the cause of such and such other event unless the experiment were repeatable, unless we could test the individual case by seeing if it instantiated a regularity. But that is a matter of finding out for sure; it is not a matter of the very existence of the relation whereby one thing made another thing happen. Real-life examples make clear the distinction between causation and regularity. When, for example, we investigate the causes of the

First World War, we are trying to explain why it happened. We are not seeking universal regularities. We have to make a Background presupposition of at least some degree of regularity in order to conduct the investigation at all, and without the possibility of causally sufficient conditions and repeatable experiments we may never be completely sure of our answer. But the requirement of regularity is an epistemic requirement for the *identification* of causes; it is not an ontological requirement on the very existence of the relation by which one event makes another happen.

Indeed, the requirement of regularity is an epistemic requirement on just about any notion that has application to the real world. In order to identify something as a chair or a table or a mountain or a tree, we have to presuppose some kind of regularity in its characteristics or uses. Regularity is essential for the identification of an object as a chair, but we should not on that ground say that the notion of chair really contains two components, an object that functions for people to sit in, and a regular principle. Rather we should say a chair is an object that people use to sit in, and like other notions referring to objects, causes, etc., the concept of a chair requires a Background presupposition of regularity.

If we extend the relation of regularity to causation in the case of human beings, we can say that from the third-person point of view it is indeed an epistemic requirement on my *recognizing* somebody's decisions as truly his considered decisions, as opposed to his capricious and whimsical behavior, that they have some sort of order and regularity. But it does not follow, that in order to *be* his decisions, they have to proceed from a universal law that he makes for himself. That is to say, the passage that

I quoted makes a false dichotomy between acting on impulse, which is supposed to be not free, and acting on a universal law, which is free. But acting on impulse can be as much free as acting on a universal law. Korsgaard says that there would be no *identifiable* difference between an unfree act and a capricious act, if all of a person's acts were capricious. But if this point is true, it is still only a third-person epistemic point. From the outside, someone looking at me might not be able to tell which of my actions were truly free if I always acted on impulse. But from the inside, from the first-person point of view, acting on impulse can be as much a free act as acting on sober reflection. Some very cautious persons restrain themselves from ever acting on impulse, whereas free spirits often allow their impulses to move them. The experience of the gap can be the same in both cases. And the one is as much or as little constitutive of the self as the other, because in both cases a self is required to make the decision what to do.

Korsgaard's argument presupposes (1) that in order for the self to make decisions at all, it must make them in accord with a universal principle; and that presupposition itself presupposes (2) that acting on principle is somehow constitutive of the self. I am rejecting both of these claims. Kant was wrong: free action does not require acting according to a self-created law. And the self that engages in free action does not require universal principles in order to be a self. On the contrary, both consistent and capricious behavior in the gap, as I argued in chapter 3, require a *preexisting* self. In short there is no logical requirement whatever that in order for my acts to be free acts, and freely chosen by myself, that they have to exemplify universal principles. My acts can be absolutely capricious and still be free acts.

This is not the place to try to give a full diagnosis of Korsgaard's powerful philosophical argument, but—all too briefly—I think the source of her mistake is that she wants a gap filler. She wants the self to be the cause of free actions. If you accept that requirement, then on certain natural assumptions, the rest follows. The steps are these: (1) Free actions are caused by the self. (2) But the self in causing must instantiate a law, and the only laws that it could instantiate are self-created. (3) In creating a law the self creates itself as a self.

I am rejecting all of these. If by "cause" we imply "causally sufficient conditions," then free actions are not caused by anything. That is what makes them free. To put this point more precisely: What makes an action free at the psychological level is that it does not have antecedently sufficient psychological causal conditions (see chapter 3 for the argument). The self *performs* the act, but it does not *cause* the act. Nothing fills the gap.

IV   The Universality of Language and Strong Altruism

Well, let's take stock of where we are. We were trying to answer this question: given that the Beast has been programmed to look out for its own self-interests, is there any logical requirement on it to pay any attention to the interests and needs of other people at all? The words "altruist" and "egoist" get bandied about without much clear definition, so let's try to define them for this discussion. In one sense an egoist is someone who cares only about his own interests and an altruist is someone who cares about the interests of others. But that definition obscures a crucial distinction. An altruist might be someone who is naturally inclined to care about the interests of others, but for such an altruist acting altruistically is just acting on one inclination among others. He likes to help others the way he likes to drink beer, for example. Let us call this the weak sense of "altruism." But there is another stronger sense of "altruism" that we are trying to get at. An altruist in this sense is someone who recognizes the interest of others as a valid reason for acting even in cases where he has no such inclination. The question is: are there rationally binding *desire-independent* altruistic reasons for action? An altruist in the strong sense is someone who recognizes that there are rationally binding desire-independent reasons for him to act in the interests of others. Both Nagel and Kant-Korsgaard gave arguments to support the rational requirement of altruism in this strong sense. The sociobiologists only answer the question for the weak sense. I have rejected both the Nagel and the Kant-Korsgaard arguments. But I think their conclusion is right, and I think Kant-Korsgaard is right to see that the issue is one of generality. Granted that the Beast and ourselves have reasons to behave egoistically, is there a generality requirement that would extend those reasons to other people in a way that binds our behavior? I think there is.

The generality required to support strong altruism is already built into the structure of language. How exactly? Let us go through the steps to see how language introduces rationally required forms of generality. Both my dog and I can see that a man is at the door, that is, we can both have a visual experience that I describe in words as "seeing that a man is at the door." But there is a big difference in that if I *say* I see a man at the door in language I am committed to a kind of semantic categorical imperative that has no analogue in the dog. When I say, "That is a man," I am committed to the claim that any entity exactly like that in the relevant respects is also correctly describable as "a man." To put it in Kantian jargon: assertions are bound by the semantic categorical imperative: so assert that the maxim of your assertion can be willed by you as a universal law binding on all speakers. And the maxim is provided by the truth conditions of the proposition asserted. In this case: an object that has those features satisfies the truth conditions for "man."

When you make an assertion of the form *a* is *F*, rationality requires that you be able to will that everyone in a similar situation should assert that *a* is *F*. That is, because the predicate is general, its application requires that any user recognize its generality. Any user of language, in the Kantian formulation, has to be able to will a universal law of its application to relevantly similar cases.[6]

Furthermore, this imperative, unlike some of Kant's, actually meets Kant's condition that the insincere or dishonest person is involved in some kind of self-contradiction when he attempts to will his maxim as a universal law. Thus, suppose I am lying when I say, "That is a man," then I cannot will a universal law that everybody in a similar situation should say, "That is a man," for if they did, the word "man" would cease to have the meaning it does. That is, I cannot consistently conjoin my will

---

6. Of course, neither in my case nor in Kant's does the ability to will a universal law require that the agent think that it would be a good thing if everybody behaved the way he did. That is not the point at all. It would be at the very least boring and tiresome if everybody in my situation were to say "that is a man." The point of the categorical imperative is logical; there is no logical absurdity in my willing the maxim of the action as a universal law binding on all speakers.

that my utterance be a lie together with my will that the semantic content apply universally according to the semantic categorical imperative.

To put this point without the Kantian apparatus, we can say that any assertion by a speaker S of the form a is F commits S to a universal generalization: for any x, if x is relevantly type-identical to a, then x is correctly described as "F." We are here not talking about entailment relations between propositions, but rather about what a speaker is committed to when he performs a speech act.

Furthermore, the generality requirement applies to other people. For if I am committed to recognizing similar instances as also cases of men, my commitment in a public language requires that I think other people ought also to recognize this and similar cases as cases of men. That is, the generality is built into the structure of language itself, and indeed when it comes to the application of language, it looks as if we get ought's from is's wherever we turn. From the fact that an object is truly described as "a man," it follows that you ought to accept relevantly similar objects also as men, and that other people ought both to accept this as a man and other relevantly similar objects as men. It is impossible to use language without these commitments. I have put this in a grand-sounding termi-nology, but it is a trivial consequence of the nature of language and speech acts.

The way we get generality into reasons for action in the form of strong altruism is by simply noticing that the generality requirement that works for such predicates as "man," "dog," "tree," and "mountain" also works for "has a reason for action" and other such motivators. I will show this with an example. Suppose I have a pain, and I seek to alleviate my pain. There is a difference between me seeking to alleviate my pain, and my dog's alleviating his pain by licking his wound. What is the difference? Well, at least this much: I can bring my pain under certain universal generalizations, simply by characterizing it with a word such as "pain." That is, the same feature we found in the discussion of the word "man" will also apply to the word "pain." If I assert "This is a pain" I am committed to the claim, "For all x, if x is relevantly like this, x is a pain."

The generality of language, given certain commonsense assumptions about my own self-interests, will generate strong altruism. I will first put the point in intuitive form and then recast it in a semantic form. Intuitively it seems reasonable to suppose that if I am in pain I have a reason for wanting to alleviate my pain. My feeling this degree of pain involves feeling a need for its alleviation. My need for pain alleviation is for me a reason to alleviate my pain and I even believe that others, where they have the ability and the opportunity, have a reason to help alleviate my pain. But I cannot believe that they have a reason for helping me, without committing myself to believing that in the same situation where the pronouns are reversed, I am bound to recognize that I have a reason for helping them. It is rational of me to want them to help me, for the reason that I am now in need of help. But then in consistency when they are in need of help I am committed to recognizing the existence of their need as a reason for my helping them.

The way the generality of language works to produce strong altruism is as follows:

1. I am in pain, so I say "I am in pain." Because I said "I am in pain" I am committed by the generality requirement to recognize that in a similar situation you would be in pain. Because "pain" is a general term in the language, the truth conditions apply indifferently to you and me. I am

committed to applying the open sentence, "X is in pain" to any object that satisfies exactly these conditions.

2. My pain creates a need. Because I am in pain I need help. I am aware of both my pain and my need. So I say, "I need help because I am in pain." Now notice that this is not to be interpreted as a plea for help. It is not an indirect speech act; rather it is a statement made by me about me. The same generality requirement applies again. I am now committed to recognizing that in a similar situation with a reversal of the pronouns if you are in pain, you would need help. I am committed to applying the open sentence "X needs help because X is in pain" in any type-identical situation.

3. I am in pain and need help, and I believe that my need for help is reason for you to help me. So suppose I say, "Because I am in pain and need help, you have a reason to help me." The same generality requirement is in force. I am committed to the universal, for any situation that is relevantly type-identical to this one:

For all x and for all y, if x is in pain and x needs help because x is in pain, y has a reason to help x.

But that commits me to recognize that when you are in pain I have a reason to help you. Notice that we are talking here about the speakers' commitments in the performance of speech acts. We are not at this point concerned with truth or with entailment relations between propositions; rather we are worried about what the speaker is committed to when he or she makes an assertion of this form.

The point for the present discussion is that once we have programmed the Beast in the way that I described, that is, in addition to basic mental capacities we give it the gap, self-interest, and language, then we have already given it a sufficient logical ground for strong altruism. Notice further that we require no heavy-duty metaphysics. No noumenal world or Kantian Categorical Imperative is necessary. All this argument requires is that we, other people, and the Beast can speak English or some other language, and that we make reasonable self-interested claims. We claim, for example, that our needs are sometimes a reason for someone else to help us.

But why couldn't we block the argument by saying, for example, that my case is special. I deserve special treatment, not accorded to others. One can always make such a claim but to do so goes beyond the semantics of the indexicals. There is nothing in the semantics of "I," "you," "he," etc. that blocks the commonality of truth conditions for "pain," "need," "reason," etc. I am not here trying to eliminate the possibility of special pleading or bad faith. The history of the world is full of people, tribes, classes, nations, etc. who cheat by claiming a right to special privilege, and nothing I say will stop such people from cheating. My point is rather that the universality constraint that gets us from egoism to strong altruism is already built into the universality of language. All we have to assume is that the Beast has certain reasonable self-interested attitudes about its relations with other conscious beings and that it is prepared to state them in language. Once the Beast or anyone is prepared to say "You have a reason to help me because I am in pain and need help," then it is committed, in type-identical situations, to applying universal quantifiers to the open sentence "y has a reason to help x because x is in pain and needs help," because the use of the general terms commits the speaker to the application of those terms to situations that share the general features that the initial situation had. Language is by its very nature general.

To the extent that one resists this conclusion, I think the resistance comes from another pervasive mistake in our culture: the idea that language cannot be all that important, because it is mere words. How can the mere utterance of words commit me to anything? I encountered this same resistance a generation ago when I showed how to derive "ought" from "is."[7] Many commentators felt the mere fact that I uttered words can't commit me to anything. There must be some extra moral principle involved or some endorsement of the institutions of language. Or something!

I will have more to say about these issues in the next chapter, but for the moment, we can say the problem is not to see how the utterance of words can commit me, but rather to see how anything *other than* the utterance of words could commit me. The paradigm forms of commitment to courses of action are in the performance of speech acts.

V   Conclusion

I have had three main aims in this chapter. I have tried to describe some special features of reasons for action; I have tried to describe what features are necessary for a self-agent to be capable of rationality; and I have tried to derive the principles of strong altruism from the universality of language, together with commonsense assumptions about self-interest.

---

7. Searle, John R., "How to Derive 'Ought' from 'Is,'" *Philosophical Review*, 73, January 1964, pp. 43–58.

What implications do these arguments and those of the preceding chapters have for the Classical Model of rationality? The Classical Model, we might say, is designed for extremely clever chimpanzees. It does not deal with certain special features of human rationality, especially those special features that are made possible and indeed are required by the institution of language. So far I have discussed three ways in which the Classical Model simply fails to account for certain pervasive features of rational decision making.

1. The Classical Model cannot account for long-term prudential reasoning, where the prudential considerations are not represented in the current motivational set of the self in question. The example of the smoker in Denmark was designed to illustrate this point.

2. The Classical Model cannot account for recognitional rationality where the conscious self recognizes a desire-independent motivator as providing a reason for action. The chimpanzee can presumably recognize immediate sources of danger or desirable objects such as food, but the chimpanzee cannot recognize in that way such factitive entities as obligations, commitments, and long-term needs.

3. The Classical Model cannot account for the implications of the universality of language. Given this universality together with certain natural assumptions about the sorts of reasons one accepts for oneself, strong altruism follows.

In the next chapter we will turn to:

4. The intentional creation of desire-independent reasons by the conscious intentional actions of the self.

6

How We Create Desire-independent Reasons for Action

I The Basic Structure of Commitment

The single most remarkable capacity of human rationality, and the single way in which it differs most from ape rationality, is the capacity to create and to act on desire-independent reasons for action. The creation of such reasons is always a matter of an agent *committing* himself in various ways. The Classical Model cannot account either for the existence or for the rational binding force of such reasons, and indeed, most of the authors in the tradition of the Classical Model deny that any such things exist. We have seen that long-term prudence is already a difficulty for the Classical Model, because on that model an agent can only act rationally on a desire that she has then and there. We saw in the case of the cigarette smoker in Denmark that it can be a requirement of rationality that an agent who lacks a desire then and there to act on her long-term prudential considerations nonetheless has a reason to do so. The Classical Model cannot account for this fact. On the Classical Model, the soldier who throws himself on a live hand-grenade in order to save the lives of his fellow soldiers is in exactly the same situation, rationally speaking, as the child who selects chocolate over vanilla when picking a flavor of ice cream. The soldier prefers death, the child prefers chocolate. In each case, rationality is just a matter of increasing the probability of getting to a higher rung on the preference ladder.

However, I would not like such heroic cases to make it seem as if the creation of and acting on desire-independent reasons for action was somehow odd or unusual. It seems to me that we create desire-independent reasons pretty much whenever we open our mouths to talk. In this chapter we are going to examine a large class of cases where we create such reasons. It is important to state at the beginning exactly what is at issue. In some very broad sense of "want" and "desire," every intentional action is an expression or manifestation of a want or desire to perform that action. Of course, when I go to the dentist to have my tooth drilled, I do not have an urge, yen, passion, hankering after, Sehnsucht, lust, or inclination to have it drilled; but all the same, then and there, that is what I want to do. I want to have my tooth drilled. Such a desire is a motivated or secondary desire. It is motivated by my desire to have my tooth fixed. Now because every intentional action is the expression of a desire, the question arises: where do these desires come from? On the Classical Model there can be only two possibilities: either the action is one I desire to perform for its own sake or it is one I perform for the sake of some other desire I have. Either I am drinking this beer because I want to drink beer or I am drinking it to satisfy some other desire; for example, I believe it will be good for my health and I desire to improve my health. There are no other possibilities. On this account rationality is entirely a matter of satisfying desires.

It sounds a bit crass to say that every rational action is carried out to satisfy a desire, and it is therefore interesting to see the theorists in the classical tradition having so much heavy going when it comes to describing motivation. How exactly do they describe rational motivation? Bernard Williams, who thinks that there can be no external reasons and that every rational act must appeal to something in the agent's motivational set S, has this to say about the contents of S:

I have discussed S primarily in terms of desires, and this term can be used, formally, for all elements in S. But this terminology may make one forget that S can contain such things as dispositions of evaluation, patterns of emotional reaction, personal loyalties, and various projects, as they may be abstractly called, embodying *commitments of the agent*. (My italics)[1]

A similar bifurcation is found in Davidson's characterization of "pro-attitudes." Here is what he says. "Whenever someone does something for a reason, therefore, he can be characterized as (*a*) having some sort of pro attitude toward actions of a certain kind, and (*b*) believing (or knowing, perceiving, noticing, remembering) that his action is of that kind."[2] And of his set of pro-attitudes he lists the following. It was something the agent "wanted, desired, prized, held dear, thought *dutiful*, beneficial, *obligatory*, or agreeable" (ibid., my italics). The problem with this list, as with Williams's, is that it blurs the distinction between desire-dependent and desire-independent reasons for action. It blurs the distinction between things

---

1. Bernard Williams, "Internal and External Reasons," in *Moral Luck*, Cambridge: Cambridge University Press, 1981, p. 105.
2. Dondald Davidson, "Actions, Reasons, and Causes," reprinted in A. White (ed.), *The Philosophy of Action*, Oxford: Oxford University Press, 1968, p. 79.

you *want* to do and things you *have* to do whether you want to or not. It is one thing to want or desire something, quite something else to regard it as "obligatory" or as a "commitment" that you have to do regardless of your desires. Why don't Williams and Davidson tell us what a commitment or an obligation is? Is it just another desire, "formally" speaking?

I think the reason that both authors appear to be struggling here is that they want to assimilate desire-independent reasons for action, which obviously exist, to desires. And the way they do this is to suggest that if we construe the set that includes desires broadly enough, then a person's commitments, obligations etc. are really members of the same set as desires. I think that blurs the crucial distinction I am trying to make between desires and desire-independent reasons for action. Why is there such a distinction? Surely, people can *want* to fulfill their obligations and keep their promises. Yes, but that is not like wanting chocolate ice cream. I want chocolate and I want to keep my promise. What's the difference? *In the case of the promise the desire is derived from the recognition of the desire-independent reason, that is, the obligation. The reason is prior to the desire and the ground of the desire. In the case of chocolate the desire is the reason.*

The points at issue in this chapter are the existence of, the nature of, the creation of, and the functioning of desire-independent reasons for action. I need to give an account of desire-independent reasons for action that meets the following conditions of adequacy:

1. The account has to be completely naturalistic. That is, it has to show how the creation and functioning of such reasons is possible for biological beasts like ourselves. We

are different from chimpanzees, but our capacities are a natural extension of other primate capacities. There must not be any appeal to anything transcendental, non-biological, noumenal, or supernatural. We are just talking about certain capacities of sweaty biological beasts like ourselves.

2. I need to specify the apparatus that enables us to create desire-independent reasons for action.

3. I need to explain how, within that apparatus, people do it, how they create such reasons. I need to state exactly the logical structure of the intentionality that underlies the creation of desire-independent reasons for action.

4. I need to explain how rationality alone makes those reasons binding on the agent. For what rational reason must the agent take into account his commitments and obligations? Why can't he just ignore them?

5. I need to explain how rational recognition of such reasons is sufficient for motivation: how such entities can rationally ground secondary desires if they are themselves desire-independent.

6. I need to explain how the apparatus and the intentionality used to answer conditions (1)–(5) is sufficient for both creation and operation of such reasons. There is no need for any help from general principles, moral rules, etc. That is, the answer to (1)–(5) must explain how desire-independent reasons for action are created and how they function without the assistance of substantive moral principles. The desire-independent reasons have to be, so to speak, self-sufficient.

Anyone familiar with the history of Western philosophy will think I have set myself a daunting task. I have seen reviewers who describe this sort of enterprise as pulling a rabbit out of a hat. But I think that, in fact, if we can forget about the Classical Model and the whole tradition it embodies, the answer to our problems, though complex in detail, is rather simple in its basic structure.

It is important, however, that we give the explanation at the right level, because there are different levels at which these questions can be answered. There is the "phenomenological" level at which we describe how things seem to the agent when he is engaged in rational socially committed behavior, and there is the social or "societal" level at which we discuss the social institutions used in the creation of such desire-independent reasons for action, when we explain how such institutions are structured and what functions they play in the larger society.

I will say something about these levels later, but I want to begin by discussing the simplest and most basic level of intentionality. This is, so to speak, the atomic level that is prior to the molecular levels of phenomenology and sociology. In later sections I will put in more details about commitment, sincerity and insincerity, and the specific role of human institutions. But at the beginning, it is important to get clear about the simplest and most primitive forms of human commitments. What are the conditions of satisfaction of the intentional phenomena involved in the creation of commitments? Let us suppose that we have a speaker and a hearer who are both able to speak and understand a common language. We suppose that they are masters of the institutions of making statements, requests, promises, etc. In the simplest types of speech acts, where the speaker makes an assertion, a request, or a promise, for example, he imposes conditions of satisfaction on conditions of satisfaction. How exactly? Let us go through the example of making an assertion with some care, and see what we find. Suppose a speaker utters a sentence, for example, "It is raining," and suppose he intends to make the assertion that it is raining. His intention-in-action is, in part, to produce the utterance, "It is raining." That utterance is one of the conditions of satisfaction of his intention. But if he is not just uttering the sentence, but actually *saying that* it is raining, if he actually *means* that it is raining, then he must intend that the utterance satisfy truth conditions, the conditions of satisfaction with downward direction of fit that it is raining. That is, his meaning intention is to impose conditions of satisfaction (i.e., truth conditions) on conditions of satisfaction (the utterance). His utterance now has a status function, it represents, truly or falsely, the state of the weather. And he is not neutral vis-à-vis truth or falsity, because his claim is a claim to truth. *That imposition of that sort of status function, of conditions of satisfaction on conditions of satisfaction, is already a commitment.* Why? Because the assertion was a free, intentional action of the speaker. He undertook to claim that it is raining and thus he is now committed to the truth of the asserted proposition. When he intentionally imposes conditions of satisfaction on conditions of satisfaction, in the manner of an assertion, he takes responsibility for those conditions being satisfied. *And that commitment is already a desire-independent reason for action.* For example, the speaker has now created a reason for accepting the logical consequences of his assertion, for not denying what he has said, for being able to provide evidence or justification for what he has said, and for speaking sincerely when he says it. All of these are the result of the constitutive rules for making assertions, and the speaker invokes those rules when he imposes conditions of satisfaction on conditions of satisfaction. The creation of the commitments creates desire-independent reasons for action, and the commitment is already built into the structure of the speech act. In making an assertion the speaker presents a proposition with the downward direction of fit. But in so doing, he creates a commitment, which has the upward direction of fit. His assertion that it is raining will be true or false depending on whether it really is raining. But the commitment he makes will be satisfied only if the world really is the way he says it is, only if it is raining.

So far we have considered only assertions, but in fact all of the standard forms of speech acts with whole propositional contents involve the creation of desire-independent reasons for action, because the intentional imposition of conditions of satisfaction commits or obligates the speaker in various ways. Even requests and orders, though their propositional content refers to conditions imposed on the hearer rather than on the speaker, still commit the speaker in various ways. If I order you to leave the room I am committed to allowing you to leave the room and to wanting you to leave the room, for example.

What then is a commitment? The way to answer this question is to look at the logical structure of commitments. Commitments are factitive entities that meet our condition for reasons for action. A commitment has a propositional content and an upward direction of fit. Thus, if I have a commitment to go to San Jose next week, the propositional content is "that I go to San Jose next week," and the direction of fit is upward. The commitment is satisfied only if the world changes to match the content of the commitment, only if I actually go to San Jose. Without attempting to give "necessary and sufficient conditions" one can say this: a commitment is the adoption of a course of action or policy (or other intentional content; one can, for example, be committed to beliefs and desires) where the nature of the adoption gives one a reason for pursuing the course. Thus, for example, I am committed to the practice of philosophy. And this commitment gives me a reason to pursue it even on hard days when things are not going well. Similarly one may be committed to the Catholic faith or to the Democratic Party. When Sally says that Jimmy is unwilling to "commit" she means he is unwilling to adopt a policy that will give him a reason for continuing in certain behavior and attitudes. Such reasons are desire-independent, though this is disguised from us by the fact that the sorts of commitments I have described are commitments to do things one may want to do anyhow. In this chapter we will be primarily concerned with a special form of commitment, where one creates a commitment to another person through the imposition of conditions of satisfaction on conditions of satisfaction.

Once we see the logical structure of commitments, it is easier to see how we can create a commitment in the performance of a speech act. Not all commitments are created by way of performing a speech act. For example, one may commit oneself to a policy just by adopting a firm intention to continue with that policy, but right now I am considering the class of commitments that are created publicly, normally directed to other people. We can create such a commitment for ourselves by imposing conditions of satisfaction on some other entity. It is harder to see how this works for assertives than it is for commissives, because in the case of an assertion we are imposing conditions of satisfaction with the downward direction of fit on the utterance, that is, we are making a truth claim. But in making the truth claim we are also imposing commitments on *ourselves*. In making an assertion we take *responsibility* for truth, sincerity, and evidence. And such responsibilities, like commitments in general, have the upward direction of fit. These responsibilities are met only if the world is such that the utterance is true, the speaker is sincere, and the speaker has evidence for the assertion.

But why are such commitments, obligations, and responsibilities binding on the agent? Why can't he, rationally speaking, just ignore them? Why are they not social constructs like any others? Because the speaker stands in a special relation to his own assertions, in that he has created them as his own commitments. He has freely and intentionally bound himself by undertaking his commitments. He can be indifferent to the truth of someone else's assertion, because he has not committed himself. He cannot be indifferent to the truth of his own assertions, precisely because they are his commitments.

But how can any such an abstract, desire-independent commitment ever give rise to a secondary desire? How can it ever motivate? Well, ask yourself how evidence, proof, and even truth itself motivate someone to believe something that he does not want to believe? For example, many people did not want to believe Gödel's Theorem because it destroyed their research project. But once they recognized the validity of the proof, rationally speaking, they had no choice. To recognize the validity of the proof is already to recognize a reason for accepting it, and to recognize a reason for accepting it is already to recognize a reason for wanting to accept it. The lesson of this case, and of others that we will consider, is that desire-independent reasons motivate like any other reasons. Once you recognize something as a valid reason for acting, that is, once you recognize a factitive entity, with you as subject and an upward direction of fit, you have already recognized it as a ground for wanting to do the thing you are committed to doing. My desire to speak the truth or keep my promise is derived from the fact that I recognize that I am making a statement or have made a promise, that statements and promises create commitments and obligations, and that I am required to fulfill my commitments and obligations, in the same way that my desire to have my tooth drilled is derived from my recognition that it needs to be fixed, and from my desire to take care of my health needs.

People tend to assume that the way desire-dependent reasons motivate secondary desires is unproblematic. But the way desire-dependent reasons motivate is no more and no less puzzling than the way desire-independent reasons motivate. I recognize that my desire to have my tooth fixed is a reason for having it drilled, and therefore a reason for wanting to have it drilled. I also recognize that the fact that I owe you money is a reason to pay it back, and therefore a reason for wanting to pay it back. In each case the recognition of a valid factitive entity with me as subject and the upward direction of fit is a reason for peforming an action and therefore a reason for wanting to perform the action.

The difficulty in seeing that there is nothing especially problematic about how desire-independent reasons can motivate derives in part from a tendency in our tradition to think that motivation must be a matter of causally sufficient conditions. It is a weakness of our tradition that we suppose that any account of motivation must show how the action is necessitated, how the agent *must* perform the action if he really has the right reasons. That mistake derives from failing to recognize the gap. I might recognize my need to have my tooth drilled, just as I might recognize my obligation, and still not act on either reason. So in an account of the motivating force of desire-independent reasons for action, we are not trying to show that they cause actions by sufficient conditions. They do not. Neither do any other rational reasons for action.

An essential step in understanding motivation is to get clear about the relations between the third-person point of view and the first-person point of view. From the third-person point of view, every society has a set of institutional structures, and the members of that society are, in various ways, in the eyes of their fellow members, bound by the deontic structures within those institutional structures. They are bound as husbands, wives, citizens, taxpayers, etc. But to say that, is, so far, to say nothing about the first-person point of view. Why should I, as a conscious self, care in the least about what other people think I am bound or obligated to do? The answer is that from the first-person point of view, I, acting within those institutional structures, can voluntarily and intentionally create desire-independent reasons for myself. Institutional structures make it possible for me to do this, but—and this is the crucial point—obligations, commitments, and other motivators that I so create do not derive from the institution, but from my intentionally and voluntarily undertaking those obligations, commitments, and duties. Because of this fact, the recognition of these motivators can be rationally required of me as a conscious agent. This is obvious in the case of promises, and equally true, if less obvious, in the case of statements. Since I uttered the phrase "I promise," it is not open to me to say, "Yes I said that but I do not see why that constitutes making a promise"; and once I have made the promise, it is not open to me to say, "Yes, I made the promise, but I do not see why that places me under an obligation." Similarly, if I said, "It is raining," it is not open to me to say, "Yes, I said that but I do not see why that constitutes making a statement," and once I have made a statement it is not open to me to say, "Yes, I made a statement, but I do not see why that is any commitment to its truth."

I have so far presented, rather swiftly, an overview of the main arguments that I will be presenting in this chapter. So far I have discussed them only at the most fundamental, atomic level. We will get to higher levels later, and I will restate in more detail the argument concerning the way desire-independent reasons can motivate actions. Let us see how the account of assertions presented so far meets our conditions of adequacy.

1. The account is completely naturalistic. Our abilities are an extension of more primitive animal and especially primate abilities. Apes have the capacity for intentionality, but they do not have the capacity for the second level of intentionality where they can impose conditions of satisfaction on conditions of satisfaction. They do not have the capacity to undertake a commitment to the truth of a proposition that it is raining by imposing conditions of satisfaction on conditions of satisfaction. Furthermore, they do not have the socially created institutions whereby we can do these things in ways that are recognizable to other members of our species, and consequently enable us to communicate these commitments to other members of our species.

2. The apparatus we use for the creation of desire-independent reasons for action is the set of constitutive

rules of speech acts and their realization in the semantic structure of actual human languages. Any language rich enough to allow the speaker to make an assertion, an order, or a promise will do the job. In real life the speaker and hearer will typically be involved in other institutional structures, such as money, property, nation-states, and marriages. The structures, both linguistic and non-linguistic, are complex. But they are not mysterious, and I have described them in detail elsewhere.[3]

3. You create desire-independent reasons for action by imposing conditions of satisfaction on conditions of satisfaction. All such impositions are commitments, and all such commitments create desire-independent reasons for action. Where the condition of satisfaction makes reference to the speaker, as in the case of a vow or a promise, and the propositional content specifies some voluntary action by the speaker, there is an explicit creation of a desire-independent reason for action in the imposition of those conditions of satisfaction. In the case of the assertion, the commitment to action is only implicit, but it is a commitment nonetheless. Imposing conditions of satisfaction on the utterance imposes commitments on the speaker.

4. The commitments you undertake are binding on you, because they are *your* commitments. That is, because you freely and intentionally made the assertion and thus committed yourself to its truth, it is not rationally open to you

---

3. John R. Searle, *Speech Acts: An Essay in the Philosophy of Language*, Cambridge: Cambridge University Press, 1969; *Expression and Meaning*, Cambridge: Cambridge University Press, 1979; *Intentionality*, Cambridge: Cambridge University Press, 1983; and *The Construction of Social Reality*, New York: Basic Books, 1995.

to say that you are indifferent to its truth, or sincerity, or consistency, or evidence, or entailment. Recognitional rationality is enough. You simply have to recognize your own self-created commitments and their logical consequences.

5. The reason such reasons can motivate is that you created them as motivators. That is, you created a factitive entity with a propositional content that has the upward direction of fit, which is binding on you. By the exercise of your will in imposing conditions of satisfaction on conditions of satisfaction, you bound your will in the future vis-à-vis those conditions. This will become more obvious when we consider promises, but almost all speech acts have an element of promising. For a long time philosophers tried to treat promises as a kind of assertion. It would be more accurate to think of assertions as a kind of promise that something is the case.

6. Notice that I have stated the answer to conditions (1)–(5) without reference to any substantive external principles. Such principles as "you ought to tell the truth," "you ought not to lie," or "you ought to be consistent in your assertions" are *internal* to the notion of assertion. You do not need any external moral principle in order to have the relevant commitments. The commitment to truth is built into the structure of the intentionality of the assertion.

II Motivation and Direction of Fit

So far I have presented a bare bones account of how someone can create commitments and be motivated by them. In this section I want to add some more details to the account. Frankly, the account so far does not seem to me very contentious, or even exciting. But I have to say that it faces enormous resistance. Why? A large part of the resistance comes from our peculiar philosophical tradition according to which any such account is impossible. According to this tradition, there must be a strict distinction between fact and value, between "is" and "ought." The tradition has produced endless numbers of books about the place of values in a world of facts and the sources of normativity in such a world. The same tradition contains an unhealthy obsession with something called "ethics" and "morality," and the authors are seldom really interested in reasons for action, and are too eager to get to their favorite subject of ethics. They regard facts as unproblematic, values as requiring explanation. But if you think about matters from the point of view of sweaty biological beasts like ourselves, normativity is pretty much everywhere. The world does indeed consist of facts that are largely independent of us, but once you start representing those facts, with either direction of fit, you already have norms, and those norms are binding on the agent. All intentionality has a normative structure. If an animal has a belief, the belief is subject to the norms of truth, rationality, and consistency. If an animal has intentions, those intentions can succeed or fail. If an animal has perceptions, those perceptions either succeed or fail in giving it accurate information about the world. And the animal cannot be indifferent to truth, success, and accuracy, because the intentional states in question are the states of that very animal. If *you* have a belief, I may be indifferent to the truth or falsity of your belief, but if *I* have a belief I cannot be similarly indifferent, because it is my belief and the normative requirement of truth is built into the belief. From the point of view of the animal, there is no escape from normativity. The bare representation of an *is* gives the animal an *ought*.

What is special about human animals is not normativity, but rather the human ability to create, through the use of language, a *public* set of commitments. Humans typically do this by performing public speech acts where the speaker intentionally imposes conditions of satisfaction on conditions of satisfaction. These speech acts are made possible by the existence of institutional structures that the speaker uses to perform meaningful speech acts and to communicate them to other speakers/hearers. Using this apparatus the speaker can undertake commitments when he imposes conditions of satisfaction on conditions of satisfaction. Indeed there is no way to avoid undertaking commitments. The speech act of asserting is a commitment to truth, the speech act of promising is a commitment to a future action. Both arise from the fact that the speaker imposes conditions of satisfaction on conditions of satisfaction. Speech acts commit the speaker to the second set of conditions of satisfaction. In the case of an assertion, he is committed to the truth of the assertion, in the case of a promise, he is committed to carrying out the act that he has promised to perform.

Once a motivation is created, its recognition provides an internal reason for action. It is important to get clear about this point. The acceptance of any external motivator, however crazy, can provide an agent with an internal reason for an action. If I irrationally become convinced that there is a tiger hiding behind my desk, then I have accepted the existence of a danger, and I consequently have a reason for acting, however irrational my reason may be. The point, however, about the desire-independent reasons for action is that their acceptance is rationally required as a matter of recognitional rationality, once the agent has intentionally and freely created the reason in question.

Consider the case I discussed earlier where I make a statement that it is raining. Whenever I make a statement I have a reason to speak truthfully. Why? Because a statement simply *is* a commitment to the truth of the expressed proposition. There is no gap at all between making a statement and committing oneself to its truth. That is, there are not two independent features of the speech act, first the making of a statement and second committing myself to its truth; there is only making the statement, which is *eo ipso* a commitment to truth. Suppose you ask me, "What's the weather like outside?" And I say "It's raining." I have *thereby* committed myself to the truth of the proposition that it is raining. My commitment to truth is most obvious in cases where I am lying. If I don't in fact believe that it is raining, but I lie and say, "It's raining," my utterance is intelligible to me as a lie precisely because I understand that the utterance commits me to the truth of a proposition I do not believe to be true. And the lie can succeed as a lie precisely because you take me to be making a statement and therefore committing myself to the truth of the expressed proposition. A similar point can be made about mistakes. Suppose I am not lying but am genuinely mistaken. I sincerely said it is raining, but all the same it is not raining. In such a case there still is something wrong with my speech act, namely, it is false. But why is that wrong? After all, for every true proposition there is a false one. It is wrong because the aim of a statement is to be true, and this one fails, because it is false. When I make a statement I commit myself to its truth, and here my mistake makes me fail in the commitment.

There is no way that the Classical Model can account for these simple facts. The Classical Model is forced to say that there are two separate phenomena, the institution of statement making and then, external to that, the principle that one should try to speak the truth. What reason have I to try to tell the truth when making a statement? The classical theorist is forced to say that I have *no reason at all just in virtue of making a statement*. The only reason I could have would be that I felt there would be bad consequences if I lied, or that I hold a moral principle, which is logically independent of making a statement, to the effect that falsehood is wrong, or that I just felt an inclination to tell the truth, or had some other reason external to making the statement. On the Classical Model all such reasons are independent of the nature of statement making as such. I am claiming, on the contrary, that there is no way to explain what a statement is without explaining that the commitment to truth is *internal* to statement making.

But why is the commitment to truth internal to statement making? Why couldn't we have a different sort of institution of statement making, where we make statements, but are not committed to their truth? What is the big deal about commitment? Well, in a sense you can perform speech acts without their normal commitments. That is what happens in works of fiction. In works of fiction nobody holds the author responsible for the truth of the utterances that she makes in the text. We understand those cases as derivative from, and parasitic on, the more fundamental forms, where the commitments are to the truth conditions of the actual utterance. So, to repeat the question, why? And the answer follows from the nature of meaning itself. The reason why I am committed to the truth of the claim that it is raining when I say that it is raining is that, in making the utterance that it is raining, I have intentionally imposed certain conditions of satisfaction on that utterance. Assuming I am not just practicing my pronunciation, or rehearsing for a play, or reciting a poem, when I seriously assert that it is raining, I am committed to the truth of the proposition, because I have intentionally imposed the commitment to that truth on the utterance when I intentionally imposed the conditions of satisfaction that it be raining on the conditions of satisfaction of my intention-in-action that that intention-in-action should produce the sounds, "It is raining." And, to repeat, what makes it possible for me to do that in a publicly accessible manner is the fact that I am a participant in the human institution of language and speech acts.

Now I want to apply some of these lessons to practical reason as it is more traditionally construed. In many cases of practical reason, one creates a reason now for performing an act in the future. I believe the only way to understand how voluntary rational action can create reasons for future actions is to look at the matter from close up. So, let us consider the sorts of cases that happen in everyday life. Suppose I go into a bar and order a beer. Suppose I drink the beer and the time comes to pay for the beer. Now the question is, granted the sheer fact that I intended my behavior to place me under an obligation to pay for the beer, must I also have a reason independent of this fact, such as a desire to pay for the beer, or some other appropriate element of my motivational set, in order to have a reason to pay for the beer? That is, in order to know if I have a reason to pay for the beer, do I first have to scrutinize my motivational set to see if there is any desire to pay for the beer, or to see if I hold any general principles about paying for beer that I have drunk? It seems to me the answer is, I do not. In such a case, by ordering the beer and drinking it when brought, I have already intentionally created a commitment or obligation to pay for it, and such commitments and obligations are species of reasons.

It is an absurdity of the Classical Model that it cannot account for such an obvious case. As in the case of truth telling, the defender of the Classical Model is forced to say that I have a reason to pay for the beer only if I can locate the relevant desire in my "motivational set." In opposition to this I want to claim that in this situation I have simply created a reason for myself to pay for the beer by ordering the beer and drinking it.

What exactly are the formal features of the situation that have enabled me to create such a reason? What exactly are the truth conditions of the claim: Agent A has a desire-independent reason to perform act X in the future? What fact about him makes it the case that he has such a reason? Well, one sort of fact that would be sufficient is: Agent A has *created* a desire-independent reason for himself to perform act X in the future. So our question now boils down to: how does one go about such a creation? I have already answered that question as a logical question about conditions of satisfaction, but let us now consider it "phenomenologically." How did it seem to Agent A when he ordered the beer? Well, if I am the agent, the way that it seems to me is this: I am now performing an act such that I am in that very act trying to get the man to bring me a beer on the understanding that I am under an obligation to pay for it if he brings it. But if that is the intention, then, by this very performance, if the man brings the beer, I have made it the case that I now have an obligation, and therefore a reason, which will be a reason for me to act in the future, and that reason that I now create will be independent of my other future desires. In such a case, a sufficient condition for an act to create a reason for me is that I intend that it create a reason for me.

The formal mechanism by which I created the obligation is exactly parallel to the formal mechanism by which I created a commitment in the case of statement making. In this case, however, I imposed conditions of satisfaction on my utterance, which had an upward direction of fit. I undertook an obligation to do something. It is hard to see this, because I did not do this explicitly in the utterance. I just said, "Bring me a beer," and that utterance has the conditions of satisfaction with the upward direction of fit, that the hearer should bring me a beer. But the total understanding of the situation, which we will have occasion to explore in detail when we consider promising, is that I have also imposed conditions of satisfaction on myself, on my future behavior. And I have imposed these in the form of a conditional obligation. Obligations have the upward, or world-to-obligation, direction of fit. The obligation is satisfied or fulfilled only if the world changes, typically in the form of the behavior of the person who has the obligation, to match the content of the obligation. Obligations, therefore, are a species of external motivators. Typically their existence is epistemically objective, though because they are always created by human beings, and exist only relative to the attitudes of human beings, they are ontologically subjective. And as we have had occasion to see over and over, ontological subjectivity does not imply epistemic subjectivity. It can be a plain matter of fact that I am under an obligation, even though the creation and the existence of the obligation are observer-relative.

The presupposition of the freedom of the agent is crucial to the case as I have described it. From the first-person point of view, by freely undertaking to create a reason for myself, I have already manifested a desire that such and such be a reason for me. I have already bound my will in the future through the free exercise of my will in the present. In the end all these questions must have trivial answers. Why is it a reason? Because I created it as a reason. Why is it a reason *for me*? Because I have freely created it as a reason for me.

In the discussion of the gap in chapters 1 and 3, we found that all effective reasons are agent created. But the peculiarity of the creation of desire-independent reasons for future actions is that I now, through the exercise of an effective reason, have created a potentially effective reason for me to act in the future. The philosophical tradition has the problem exactly back to front. The problem is not, "How could there be desire-independent reasons for me?"; the problem is rather, "How could anything be a reason of any kind for me that I did not create as a reason for me, including desire-independent reasons?" In the performance of a voluntary action, there is a gap between the causes and the actual carrying out of the action, and that gap is crossed when I simply perform the action; and in this case, the performance of the action is itself the creation of a reason for a subsequent action.

As far as motivation is concerned, in the cases I have described *the reason can be the ground of the desire and not conversely.* In ordinary English the correct description of this case is, "I want to pay for it because I have an obligation to pay for it." And the connection between reason, rationality, and desire is as follows: the recognition of something as a binding obligation is already the recognition of something whose ontology is that of an external motivator, that is, an entity that has the upward direction-of-fit. To recognize the validity of such an entity is already to recognize a reason for acting. And the recognition of something as a reason for acting is already the recognition of that thing as a reason for desiring to perform the action.

III   Kant's Solution to the Problem of Motivation

Kant, in *Groundwork of the Metaphysic of Morals*,[4] faced a problem that is formally similar to the one I am discussing. My problem is, how can desire-independent reasons actually motivate actions, if every action is the expression of a desire to perform that action? Kant phrases his problem in the form, "How can pure reason be practical?" And he explains that by saying that it is the question of why we can take an *interest* in the Categorical Imperative. An interest is that in virtue of which reason becomes practical, that is, it becomes a cause determining the will to action. It seems to me that Kant's answer to this question is inadequate. Here is what he says: "If we are to will actions for which reason by itself prescribes an 'ought' to a rational, yet sensuously effected, being, it is admittedly necessary that reason should have a power of *infusing a feeling of pleasure* or satisfaction in the fulfilment of duty, and consequently that it should possess a kind of causality by which it can determine sensibility in accordance with rational principles" (p. 128). So, on Kant's view, pure rea-

---

4. Immanuel Kant, *Groundwork of the Metaphysic of Morals*, New York: Harper Torchbooks, 1964.

son has to cause a feeling of pleasure, and it is only because of that feeling of pleasure that we are actually able to act in accordance with the dictates of pure reason. Kant admits that it is totally unintelligible to us how pure reason could ever cause such a feeling of pleasure, because we can only discover cause and effect relations among objects of experience, and pure reason is not an object of experience.

I think this is a bad argument. Kant's claim is that we could not act on a desire-independent reason for action unless, somehow or other, we would get a "feeling of pleasure" from doing so. I think Kant fails to understand direction of fit. That is, I think we can perform many actions in which there is no "feeling of pleasure," only the recognition that we have a valid reason for doing them. I no more have to have a "feeling of pleasure" when I get my tooth drilled than I have to have a feeling of pleasure when I keep my promises. I might get some satisfaction out of the tooth drilling and from the fulfillment of my promise, but it is not logically necessary that I get any such feeling in order for me to have my tooth drilled or to keep my promise. *On the view that I am presenting, the recognition of the validity of the reason is enough to motivate the action.* You do not need to have any extra pleasure, desire, or satisfaction. The motivation for performing the action is precisely the motivation for wanting to perform the action.

This is an absolutely crucial point, both for Kant's argument, as well as for the argument of this book, and indeed for the debate about the Classical Model in general. Kant, though he attacks the Classical Model in various ways, accepts one of its worst features. Kant assumes that I could not intentionally and voluntarily perform an action here and now, unless I got a "feeling of pleasure" here and now, in the performance of that action. If every action is really done to satisfy a desire, and if every action is itself the expression of a desire to perform that action, then there must be some desire satisfaction in the performance of any action. But this is a nest of confusions, and I intend now to sort them out. First let us consider the cases where an action is done to satisfy a desire. I get my tooth drilled to satisfy my desire to have it fixed. And I get it drilled because I want then and there to get it drilled. But it does not follow that there need be any "feeling of pleasure" in any sense at all in my intentional action. The primary desire to get my tooth fixed can motivate a secondary desire to have it drilled, which in turn can motivate the action. But the pleasure or satisfaction that I get from having a repaired tooth does not carry over to the activity of getting it drilled, nor need it. This is a case where I have a desire-dependent reason for desiring something, but the way that the desire-dependent reason grounds the secondary desire is exactly the same way that a desire-independent reason grounds a secondary desire. My desire to keep my promise derives from the desire-independent fact that I have made a promise, and therefore have an obligation. But it is no more necessary that I derive a feeling of pleasure from keeping my promise in order that I intentionally perform the action of keeping my promise, than it is necessary that I derive a feeling of pleasure from having my tooth drilled in order that I satisfy my primary desire of getting my tooth fixed. Kant's mistake makes fully explicit a mistake that is only implicit in most of the authors in the Classical tradition. If every action is the expression of a desire to perform that action, and every successful action results in the satisfaction of desire, then it seems that the only thing that can motivate an action is desire satisfaction, that is, a feeling of pleasure. But this is a fallacy. From the fact that every action is indeed the expression of a desire to perform that action, it does not follow that every action is done for the *purpose* of satisfying a desire, nor does it follow that actions can be motivated only by desire satisfaction, in the sense of a feeling of pleasure.

IV   Promising as a Special Case

Discussions of these issues usually spend a lot of time on promising, but I am trying to emphasize here that the phenomenon of agent-created desire-independent reasons is pervasive. You could not begin to understand social life without it, and promising is only a special and pure kind of case. However, the history of the debates about promising is revealing, and I will be able to explain better what I am arguing for if I explain the obligation to keep a promise and expose some of the standard mistakes. The question is: what reason do we have for keeping a promise? And to that the obvious answer is: promises are by definition creations of obligations; and obligations are by definition reasons for action. There is a follow-up question: what is the *source* of the obligation to keep a promise?

There is no way that the Classical Model can account for the fact that the obligation to keep a promise is internal to the act of promising, just as the commitment to truth telling is internal to the act of statement making. That is, promising is by definition undertaking an obligation to do something. The tradition is forced to deny this fact, but in order to deny it, the defenders of the Classical Model are typically forced to say some strange, and I believe mistaken, things. In this section I offer a brief list of the most common mistakes I have encountered.

There are three common but I believe mistaken claims that can be disposed of quickly. The first is to suppose there is some special *moral* obligation to keep a promise. On the contrary, if you think about it you will see that there is no special connection between promising and morality, strictly construed. If I promise to come to your party, for example, that is a social obligation. Whether it is a moral obligation as well would depend on the nature of the case, but for most parties I go to it would not be a moral obligation. Often we make promises where some grave moral issue is concerned but there is nothing about promising as such that entails that any promise at all involves moral issues. There is nothing in the practice of promising as such that guarantees that every obligation to keep a promise will be grave enough to be considered a moral obligation. One may make promises over matters that are morally trivial.

A second, related mistake is to suppose that if you promise to do something evil there is no obligation at all to keep the promise. But this is obviously wrong. The correct way to describe such cases is to say that you do indeed have an obligation to keep the promise but it is overridden by the evil nature of the promised act. This point can be proved by the method of agreement and difference: there is a difference between the person who has promised to do the act and the person who has not. The person who has made the promise has a reason that the person who has not made the promise does not have.[5]

---

5. In law, a contract to do something illegal is considered null and void and cannot be enforced in court. That is not because there was no contract, but because the law voids it.

A third, and I believe the worst of the three mistakes, is to suppose that the obligation to keep a promise is only a prima facie obligation, as opposed to a flat outright obligation. This view was formulated (by Sir David Ross)[6] to try to get around the fact that obligations typically conflict and you often can't fulfill them all. When obligation A overrides obligation B, says Ross, B is only a prima facie obligation, not an honest-to-john outright obligation. I have argued in detail elsewhere[7] that this view is confused, and I won't repeat the arguments here except to say that when B is overridden by some more important obligation, this does not show that B was not an all-out, unconditional, etc. obligation. You can't override it if there there is nothing really there to override in the first place. "Prima facie" is an epistemic sentence modifier, not a predicate of obligation types, and could not possibly be an appropriate term for describing the phenomenon of conflicting obligations, where one is overridden by another. The theory of "prima facie obligations" is worse than bad philosophy, it is bad grammar.

I believe the following are the most common serious mistakes about the obligation to keep a promise, and they all derive in their different ways from an acceptance of the Classical Model:

Mistake number 1: The obligation to keep a promise is prudential. The reason for keeping a promise is that if I don't I will not be trusted in the future when I make promises.

---

6. W. D. Ross, *The Right and the Good*, Oxford: Oxford University Press, 1930, p. 28.
7. John R. Searle, "Prima Facie Obligations," in Zak van Straaten (ed.), *Philosophical Subjects: Essays Presented to P. F. Strawson*, Oxford: Oxford University Press, 1980, pp. 238–260.

Famously, Hume held this view. But it is subject to a decisive, and equally famous, objection: on this account, in cases where no living person knows of my promise, I would be under no obligation at all to keep it. On this view the deathbed promise, made by the son in private to his dying father, would involve no obligation at all because the son need not tell anyone about the promise.

Furthermore, why would I not be trusted in the future? Only because I undertook an obligation and failed to carry it out. The failure to fulfill obligations as a ground for mistrust is quite unlike the mere fact of disappointing expectations. For example, Kant famously took his walks so regularly that his neighbors could set their clocks by him. But if he failed to take his walk at the regular time, he may have disappointed, but he would not have inspired mistrust in the way that a person who reneges on his obligations would. In the promising case the mistrust arises not just from the failure of an expectation, but from the fact that the promissor gave his word.

Mistake number 2: The obligation to keep a promise derives from the acceptance of a moral principle to the effect that one ought to keep one's promises. Without such an acceptance the agent has no reasons, except perhaps prudential reasons to keep a promise.

The mistake here is the same as the mistake we found in the case of the commitment to truth when making a statement. The Classical Model tries to make the obligation in promising external to the act of promising, but then it becomes impossible to explain what a promise is, just as it becomes impossible to explain what a statement is if one tries to make the relation between stating and committing oneself to the statement's truth purely external. That is, the decisive answer to this objection is to point out that the relations between promising and obligations are internal. By definition a promise is an act of undertaking an obligation. It is impossible to explain what a promise is except in terms of undertaking an obligation.

Just as we saw in the case of statement making, that the commitment to truth is most obviously revealed in the case of the person who deliberately lies, so in the case of promising we can show that the obligation is internal to the act of promising most obviously in the case of the person who makes an insincere promise. Suppose I make an insincere promise, a promise I have no intention to keep. In such a case my act of deception is fully intelligible to me, and may later be seen by the promisee as a dishonest act, precisely because it is understood that when I made the promise I was binding myself, undertaking an obligation, to do the thing I promised to do. When I make a promise I am not hazarding a guess or making a prediction about what is going to happen in the future; rather I am binding my will as to what I am going to do in the future. *My dishonest promise is intelligible to me as a promise in which I undertook an obligation without any intention to fulfill the obligation I have undertaken.*

Mistake number 3 (this is a more sophisticated variant of number 2): If obligations really were internal to promising then the obligation to keep a promise would have to derive from the institution of promising. The fact that someone made a promise is an institutional fact, and any obligation would have to derive from the institution. But then what is to prevent any institution from having the same status? Slavery is as much an institution as promising. So if the view that promises create desire-independent reasons were right, then the slave would have as much an obligation as does the promissor, which is absurd. That is, the desire-independent view of promising leads to absurd results and so must be false. The correct way to see matters is to see that the institution is indeed the ground of the obligation but only because independently of the institution we accept the principle that one ought to keep one's promises. Unless you approve of the institution or somehow endorse it or favorably evaluate it, there would be no obligation of promising. We are typically brought up to keep our promises and thus to adopt a favorable attitude toward the institution, so we fail to notice that our endorsement of the institution is the essential source of the obligation. As institutions, promising and slavery are on all fours; the only difference as far as our present debate is concerned is that we happen to think the one is good, the other bad. But the obligation is not internal to the act of promising, it derives externally from the attitude that we have toward the act of promising. The only way the obligation of promising could be created is that we accept the principle "Thou shalt not break thy promise."

This objection encapsulates the view of the Classical Model on this issue. The simplest answer to it is this: *The obligation to keep a promise does not derive from the institution of promising.* When I make a promise, the institution of promising is just the *vehicle*, the tool that I use to create a reason. The obligation to keep a promise derives from the fact that in promising I freely and voluntarily create a reason for myself. The free exercise of the will can bind the will, and that is a logical point that has nothing to do with "institutions" or "moral attitudes" or "evaluative

utterances." This is why the slave does not have any reason to obey the slave owner, except prudential reasons.
He has not bound his will by an exercise of his freedom.
Viewed externally, the slave may look exactly like the
contract laborer. They might even be given the same
rewards. But internally it is quite different. The contract
laborer has created a reason for himself that the slave has
not created. To think that the obligation of promising
derives from the institution of promising is as mistaken as
to think that the obligations I undertake when I speak
English must derive from the institution of English: unless
I think English is somehow a good thing, I am under no
obligations when I speak it. On the Classical Model, the
obligation to keep a promise is always something external
to the promise itself. If I have an obligation to keep a
promise it can only be because I think (a) that the institution of promising is a good thing, or (b) I hold a moral
principle to the effect that one ought to keep one's promises. There is a simple refutation of both of these views:
they have the consequence that in the absence of either of
these conditions, there would be no obligation whatever
to keep a promise. So, for someone who did not think the
institution of promising was a good thing, or for someone
who did not hold a moral principle that one ought to keep
one's promises, there is no reason whatever to keep a
promise. I believe that is absurd, and I have been pointing
out its absurdity at various points throughout this book.

Mistake number 4: There are really two senses of all these
words, "promise," "obligation," etc., a descriptive and an
evaluative sense. In the descriptive sense, when we use
these words, we are just reporting facts and not actually
endorsing any reasons for action. When we use them in

an evaluative sense, more is involved than just stating facts, for in these cases we must make some moral judgement, and such moral judgements can never follow from the facts by themselves. So, really, there is a systematic ambiguity in the whole discussion. The ambiguity is between the descriptive and the evaluative meanings of the words.

I will be brief in answering mistake number 4. There are no such two senses of these words any more than there are two senses of "dog," "cat," "house," or "tree." Of course one can always use words in a way that does not involve the normal commitments. Instead of saying "That's a house," I can say "That's what they call 'a house,'" in which case, I don't commit myself one way or another to whether it is actually a house (though I do commit myself to some people calling it that). Now, similarly, if I say "He made a promise" or "He undertook an obligation," I can put quotation marks around the words "promise" and "obligation" and thus remove the commitment carried by the literal meaning of the words. But this possibility doesn't show that there are two senses to any of these words or that there is some ambiguity in their literal use. The literal meaning of "promise" is such that someone who has made a promise has thereby undertaken an obligation to do something. It is an evasion of these matters to try to postulate extra senses of these words.

V   Generalizing the Account: The Social Role of Desire-independent Reasons

So far in this chapter I have tried to describe what I call the atomic structure of the creation of desire-independent reasons for action, and I have discussed some of the special features of assertions and promises with emphasis on criticizing the philosophical tradition in its discussion of the institution of promising. I have also briefly discussed the "phenomenological level" of desire-independent reasons for action, where one acts on the understanding that one's action will create a reason for oneself to do something in the future. I now want to try to state a more general account of the role of desire-independent reasons in social life in general, at a higher level than the level of the atomic structure. I want, among other things, to explain why the creation of desire-independent reasons by free, rational selves in possession of a language and operating within institutional structures is pervasive. This is what happens when you get married, order a beer in a bar, buy a house, enroll in a college course, or make an appointment with your dentist. In such cases you invoke an institutional structure in such a way that you create a reason for yourself to do something in the future regardless of whether in the future you have a desire to do that thing. And in such cases it is a reason for you because you have voluntarily created it as a reason for you.

A general account of the role of reasons in practical rationality involves understanding at least the following five features: *(1) freedom; (2) temporality; (3) the self, and with it the first-person point of view; (4) language and other institutional structures; and (5) rationality.* Let us consider each in order.

Freedom

I have already argued that rationality and the presupposition of freedom are coextensive. They are not the same thing, but actions are rationally assessable if and only if the actions are free. The reason for the connection is this: *rationality must be able to make a difference*. Rationality is possible only where there is a genuine choice between various rational and irrational courses of action. If the act is completely determined then rationality can make no difference. It doesn't even come into play. The person whose act is entirely caused by beliefs and desires, à la the Classical Model, is acting compulsively outside the scope of rationality altogether. But the person who freely *acts on* those same beliefs and desires, who freely makes them into *effective* reasons, acts within the realm of rationality. Freedom of action, the gap, and the applicability of rationality are coextensive.

Acting freely, I can, by imposing conditions of satisfaction on conditions of satisfaction, create a reason that will be a reason for me to do something in the future, regardless of whether I feel like doing it when the time comes. The ability to bind the will now can create a reason for the future act only because it is a manifestation of freedom.

Temporality

Theoretical reason statements are untensed in a way that practical reason statements are inherently tensed. "I am going to do act A because I want to make it the case that B" is essentially future referring, in the way that "Hypothesis H is substantiated by evidence E" is not essentially tensed at all. It is timeless, although of course in particular instances, it may make reference to particular historical situations. For nonhuman animals, there really are only immediate reasons, because without language you cannot order time.

The self and the first-person point of view

In the cases we will be considering, it is essential to see that we are examining the logical structure of the behavior of rational selves engaged in creating reasons for themselves. No external or third-person point of view can explain the processes by which a free agent can create a reason now that will be binding on him in the future, regardless of how he may feel in the future.

Language and other institutional structures

In order to create desire-independent reasons an agent has to have a language. One can imagine primitive pre-linguistic beings imposing conditions of satisfaction on conditions of satisfaction. But the systematic creation of such reasons, and their communication to other people, requires conventional symbolic devices of the sort that are characteristic of human languages. Furthermore, social relations require that we be able to represent the deontic relations involved in the creation of desire-independent reasons for action, and we also need language to order time in the required way. That is, we have to have ways of representing the fact that one's present action creates a reason for a future action, and we have to have linguistic ways of representing the temporal and deontic relations in question.

In addition to language narrowly construed, that is, in addition to such speech acts as statement making or promising, there are extralinguistic institutional structures that also function in the creation of desire-independent reasons. So, for example, only if a society has the institution of property can there be desire-independent reasons

involving property, and only if a society has the institution of marriage can there be desire-independent reasons
involving the institution of marriage. The point, however,
which must be emphasized over and over, is that the
reason does not derive from the institution, rather the
institution provides the framework, the structure, within
which one creates the reason. The reason derives from
the fact that the agent binds her will through a free and
voluntary act.

Rationality

In order that the practice of creating desire-independent
reasons can ever be socially effective, it must be effective
in virtue of the rationality of the agents involved. It is only
because I am a rational agent that I can recognize that
my previous behavior has created reasons for my present
behavior.

Combining all five elements

How let us try to put these points together into a general
account. To begin with, how can we organize time? The
obvious answer is that we do things now that will make
things happen in the future in a way they would not have
happened if we did not act now. That is why we set our
alarm clocks. We know we have a reason to get up at
6:00 A.M., but we also know that at 6:00 A.M. we will not
be able to act on that reason because we will be asleep. So
by setting the alarm clock now, we will make it possible
to act on a reason in the future. But suppose I don't have
an alarm clock and I have to try to get some other person
to wake me up. What is the difference between setting an

alarm clock for 6:00 A.M. and asking someone to wake me up at 6:00 A.M., for example? In both cases I do something now to make it the case that I will wake up at 6:00 A.M. tomorrow. The difference is that in the alarm clock case only causes are created, whereas in the latter case, new reasons for action are created. How? Well, there are different sorts of cases. If I don't trust the person in question I might say, "If you wake me up at 6:00 A.M. I will give you five dollars." In that case I have made a promise, a conditional promise to give the other person five dollars, and, if he accepts the offer, he has promised to wake me up on the condition that I pay him five dollars. This is typical of contracts. Each party makes a conditional promise, conditional on receiving a benefit from the other party.

In the more realistic case I simply extract from him a promise to wake me up. I say, "Please wake me up at 6:00 A.M.," and he says, "OK." In that context he has made an unconditional promise and created a desire-independent reason.

In a third sort of case, no promise need be made at all. Suppose I do not trust the person at all, but I know that he makes his breakfast everyday at 6:00 A.M. I simply position all the breakfast food so that he can't get at it without waking me up. I take it in my room and lock the door, for example. To get breakfast he has to bang on my door to wake me up. Now this third sort of case also creates a reason to wake me up, but this one is a prudential or desire-dependent reason. He has to reason: "I want breakfast, I can't have breakfast unless I wake him up, so I will wake him up."

All three of these methods might on occasion work equally well, but I want to call attention to what a bizarre

case the third one is. If the only way we could get cooperation from other people was by getting them in a position where they, independently of us, want to do what we
want them to do, most forms of human social life would
be impossible. *In order that we can organize time on a social
basis it is necessary that we create mechanisms to justify reasonable expectations about the future behavior of members of the
community, ourselves included.* If we only had desires, in
the manner of Köhler's apes, we would never be able to
organize time in a way that would enable us to organize
our own behavior, and to coordinate with other selves. In
order to organize and coordinate our behavior, we need to
create a class of entities that will have the same logical
structure as desires, but will be desire-independent. We
need, in short, to create a class of external motivators that
will provide a reason for an action—that is, a propositional content with an upward direction-of-fit, and the
agent as subject. The only way that such entities can be
binding on rational selves is precisely if the rational selves
freely create them as binding on themselves.

Let us turn to the role of language and other institutional structures. There are many features of institutional
facts that require analysis; I have elsewhere tried to give
an analysis of several of them and I won't repeat it here.[8]
However, there is one feature that is essential for the
present discussion. In the case of institutional facts, the
normal relationship between intentionality and ontology
is reversed. In the normal case, what *is* the case is logically
prior to what *seems to be* the case. So, we understand that
the object seems to be heavy, because we understand what
it is for an object to be heavy. But in the case of institu-

---

8. *The Construction of Social Reality*, New York: The Free Press, 1995.

tional reality, the ontology derives from the intentionality. In order for a type of thing to be money, people have to think that it is money. But if enough of them think it is money and have other appropriate attitudes, and act appropriately, and if the type of thing satisfies all the other conditions set by their attitudes, such as not being counterfeit, then it is money. If we all think that a certain sort of thing is money and we cooperate in using it, regarding it, treating it as money, then it is money. In this case, "seems" is prior to "is." I cannot exaggerate the importance of this phenomenon. The noises coming out of my mouth, seen as part of physics, are rather trivial acoustic blasts. But they have remarkable features. Namely, we think they are sentences of English and that their utterances are speech acts. If we all think of them as sentences and speech acts, and if we all cooperate in using, interpreting, regarding, responding to, and generally treating them as sentences and speech acts, then they are what we use, regard, treat, and interpret them as. (I am being very brief here. I do not wish to suggest that these phenomena are in any way simple.) In such cases we create an institutional reality by treating a brute reality as having a certain status. The entities in question—money, property, government, marriage, universities, and speech acts—all have a level of description where they are brute physical phenomena like mountains and snowdrifts. But by collective intentionality we impose statuses on them, and with those statuses we impose functions that they could not perform without that imposition.

The next step is to see that in the creation of these institutional phenomena we can also create reasons for action. I have a reason for preserving and maintaining the rather uninteresting bits of paper in my wallet, because I know that they are more than just bits of paper. They are valuable pieces of United States currency. That is, given the institutional structure, there are whole sets of reasons for actions that could not exist without the institutional structure. So, "it seems to be the case" can create a set of reasons for action, because what seems to be the case (appropriately understood) is the case, where institutional reality is concerned. If I borrow money from somebody, or order a beer in a bar, or get married, or join a club, I use institutional structures to create reasons for action and the reasons exist within institutional structures.

But so far this doesn't answer our crucial question, namely, how can we use such structures to create desire-independent reasons? I have very good reasons for wanting money, but they are all desire-dependent, because they derive from the desires I have for the things I can buy with the money. But what about the obligations I have to pay money? Or pay my debts to other people? Or fulfill my promises to deliver money on such and such occasions? If a group of people creates an institution whose sole function is that I should give them money, I have, so far, no obligation whatever to give them money, because though they might have created what they think is a reason, it is not yet a reason for me. So, how can I use institutional reality to create desire-independent reasons for me?

It is at this point that we have to introduce the features of freedom and the first-person point of view. Our question now is, how can I create a reason for myself, a reason that will be binding on me in the future, even though I may not at that time have any desire to do the thing I created a reason for doing. I think the question becomes impossible to answer if you look at the phenomena from the third-person point of view. From a third-person point of view, someone makes a bunch of noises through his mouth. He says, "I promise to wake you up at 6:00 A.M." How can his doing that ever create a reason that will bind his will? The only way to answer this question is to see, from the first-person point of view, what I think is going on, what I am trying to do, what my intention is when I make these sounds through my mouth. And once we see the matter from the first-person point of view, we can, I believe, see the solution to our puzzle. When I say "I promise to wake you at 6:00 A.M.," I see myself as freely creating a special type of desire-independent reason, an obligation, for me to wake you at 6:00 A.M. This is the whole point of promising. Indeed, that is what a promise is. It is the intentional creation of certain sort of obligation—and such obligations are by definition independent of the subsequent desires of the agent. But all I have said so far is that I made noises with certain intentions and that because I have those intentions, such and such seems to me to be the case. But how do we get from "it seems to be the case" to "it is the case," and to answer that question, we have to go back to what I just said about institutional structures. It is characteristic of these structures that *seems* is prior to *is*. If it seems to me that I am creating a promise, because that was my intention in doing what I did, and it seems to you that you have received a promise, and all of the other conditions (which I will not enumerate here but have enumerated in detail elsewhere),[9] if all the other conditions on the possibility of creating a promise are present, then I have created a

---

9. *Speech Acts: An Essay in the Philosophy of Language*, Cambridge: Cambridge University Press, 1969, chap. 3.

promise. I have intentionally created a new entity, which is binding on me in the future; it is a desire-independent reason for me, because I have freely and intentionally created it as such.

The ability to bind the will now creates a reason for the future act only because it is a manifestation of my freedom now. I said earlier that this shows why the slave doesn't have any reason to obey the slave owner, except desire-dependent reasons, even though both promissor and slave act within institutional structures. The only reasons the slave has are prudential reasons. The slave never exercised any freedom in creating a reason for himself to act. To see how within the institutional structure an agent can create external reasons for acting, it is essential to see that within the institutional structure, there is the possibility of the agent freely creating reasons for himself. There cannot be any question that it is a reason for him because he has freely and voluntarily created it as a reason for himself. Now, this is not to say, of course, that it is a reason that will override all other reasons. On the contrary, we know that in any real-life situation, there is likely to be a large number of competing reasons for any action, or against doing that action. When the time comes, the agent still may have to weigh his promise against all sorts of other competing reasons for doing or not doing something.

We have so far considered four features, time, institutional structures, the first-person point of view, and freedom. I now turn to the fifth: rationality. The ability to act rationally is a general set of capacities involving such things as the ability to recognize and operate with consistency, inference, recognition of evidence, and a large number of others. The features of rationality that are important for the present discussion involve the capacity to operate in various ways with reasons for action. I want that to sound vague at this point because clarifying it is our next essential task.

Suppose I have freely acted with the intention of creating a desire-independent reason for me, suppose I have met all the conditions (on promising, or ordering a beer, or whatever), so that I really succeeded in creating that reason. Then, when the time comes, what do I need in order to recognize that there is such a reason? Assuming that I know all the facts, recognitional rationality is sufficient for acknowledging that the prior creation of a reason is now binding. The important thing is that you don't have to have some extra moral principle about promising or beer drinking in order to understand that the reason you created in the past as a binding reason for the present moment is precisely a binding reason in the present moment. It is sheer logical inconsistency to grant all the facts, about the creation and continuation of the obligation, and then to deny that you have a reason for acting.

VI   Summary and Conclusion

In this chapter I have been concerned to show how human beings can create and be motivated to act on desire independent-reasons for action. What facts correspond to the claim that the agent has created such a reason, and what facts correspond to the claim that such a reason is a rational form of motivation to action? I have tried to discuss these questions at three levels. The first and most basic level is that of the atomic structure of the fundamental intentionality by which an agent can commit himself by imposing conditions of satisfaction on conditions of satisfaction. The second level is the level of "phenomenology" where we discuss how it seems to the agent. The way it seems to the agent is that he is undertaking commitments through the free and intentional exercise of his will, in such a way as to bind his will in the future so that in the future he has a reason for an action that is independent of whether he desires to perform the action. And the third level is that of society in general—what are the social functions of having such systems of desire-independent reasons for action?

The basic facts that correspond to the claims that humans can create and be motivated to act on desire-independent reasons are these:

1. There must exist a structure sufficient for the creation of such institutional facts. These structures are invariably linguistic but they may involve other institutions as well. Such structures enable us to buy a house, order a beer, enroll in a university, etc.

2. Within these structures, if the agent acts with the appropriate intentions, that is sufficient for the creation of desire-independent reasons. Specifically, if the agent acts with the intention that his action should create such a reason, then if the circumstances are otherwise appropriate, he has created such a reason. The crucial intention is the intention that it be a reason. The reason does not derive from the institution; the institution provides only the vehicle for the creation of such reasons.

3. The logical form of the intentionality in the creation of such reasons is invariably the imposition of conditions of satisfaction on conditions of satisfaction. The purest case, so to speak, of the creation of a desire-independent reason for an action is the promise. Promising is, however, peculiar among speech acts in that it has the maker of the

promise as the subject of the propositional content, and has a self-referential component imposed on the conditions of satisfaction. The conditions of satisfaction of the promise are not only that the speaker do something, but that he do it because he made a promise to do it. There is, therefore, a self-referential component in promising, and this self-referential component does not exist in certain other sorts of speech acts. For example, it does not exist in assertions.

4. Once the obligation is created, it is a requirement of recognitional rationality that the agent should recognize it as binding on his subsequent behavior. The obligation has the structure of reasons for action. There is a factitive entity with the upward direction of fit, and the agent as subject.

5. Once a valid desire-independent reason for action has been created, that reason can motivate a desire to perform the action, just as the recognition of any other reason can motivate a desire to perform the action. To recognize a valid reason for doing something is already to recognize a valid reason for wanting to do it.

Appendix to Chapter 6: Internal and External Reasons

I have objected to Bernard Williams's claim that there are no such things as external reasons, that all reasons for an agent have to be internal to his motivational set. No doubt there are various objections one could make to this view, but the main thrust of my objection has been that there can be facts external to the agent's motivational set, such that rationality requires that the agent recognize these facts as reasons for action, even if there is nothing in his motivational set then and there that disposes him to recognize them as reasons. The two sorts of facts I have concentrated on are facts about long-term prudence and facts about the existence of desire-independent reasons such as obligations undertaken by the agent.

One last feature of the doctrine of internalism deserves special mention. There are interpretations of internalism on which the claim that there are no external reasons comes out as tautologically true, and I would not wish to be thought to be disagreeing with those. The problem is that the true tautological versions can easily be interpreted as substantive versions, which are false. (I am not suggesting that Williams himself makes this confusion.) And in this appendix I am going, all too briefly, to state the tautological versions and contrast them with the substantive versions.

The basic argument for internalism is that unless an agent has internal reasons, he would have nothing to reason *from*. An external reason, by definition, is one that is external to the agent, and consequently one he could not use to reason from. A corollary to this argument, and in a way the most powerful way of stating the argument, is that we could not explain an agent's actions in terms of his reasons unless they were internal reasons, for only an internal reason can actually *motivate* the agent to act. So there are two closely related arguments for internalism, one about the process of reasoning, and one about motivation. Each of these admits of a tautological formulation, and of course I do not disagree with the tautological formulation.

Tautology A, reasoning: In order to reason in the mind on the basis of a reason, an agent has to have a reason in the mind to reason from.

The tautological version of a motivational thesis is as follows:

Tautology B, motivation: In order to be motivated by a reason in his mind, an agent has to have a reason in the mind that motivates him.

Both of these tautologies admit of a substantive reformulation that seems to me not tautological, but false. The substantive reformulation embodies the disagreement between the internalist and the externalist, where rationality is concerned.

Substantive thesis A: In order for any fact or factitive entity R to be a reason for agent X, R must already be a part of, or represented, in X's motivational set S.

And the nontautological version of B is:

Substantive thesis B: All rational motivations are desires broadly construed, in the way that Williams describes S.

The substantive versions of internalism are immediately subject to counterexamples. Thesis A has the immediate consequence that facts about an agent's desire-independent

reasons for actions, such as facts about his long-term prudential interests and facts about his undertakings and
obligations, cannot be reasons for action, even in cases
where the agent is aware of these facts, unless the agent
is disposed in his motivational set to act on these facts.
Thesis B has the immediate consequence that at any point
in an agent's life, and for any act type T, unless the agent
right then and there has some desire, where desire is
broadly construed, either to do an act of type T, or a desire
for something such that there is a sound deliberative route
from that desire to doing an act of type T as a means to
satisfy the desire, then the agent has no reason to perform
an act of type T. We have seen a number of cases where
that is false, where the agent has a reason to perform an
act even though these conditions are not satisfied.

So the dispute between the internalist and the externalist is about the existence of desire-independent reasons for
action. The question is: are there reasons such that rationality alone requires the agent recognize them as motivations, whether or not they appeal to something in the
agent's motivational set? According to the internalist,
all reasons for action must be based on desires, broadly
construed. According to the externalist, there are some
reasons for actions that can themselves be the ground for
desiring to do something, but are themselves neither
desires nor based on desires. For example, I can have a
desire to keep my promise because I recognize it as an
obligation, without its being the case that the only reason I
want to keep it is that I antecedently had a desire to keep
all my promises.

Williams sometimes talks as if the recognition of an
obligation already is an internal reason for action. But that
claim is ambiguous. To say that A knows he has an obligation allows for at least two distinct possibilities.

1. *A* knows that he has an obligation, which he recognizes as a valid reason for acting and therefore as a reason for wanting to act.

2. *A* knows that he has an obligation, but he doesn't care a damn about it. Nothing in his motivational set inclines him to act on it.

Now the dispute between the internalist and the externalist comes out right here: for the externalist in both cases there are reasons for action. Indeed in both cases there are desire-independent reasons for action. For the internalist, only in case (1) is there a reason for action. Furthermore, according to the externalist, case (1) is misdescribed by internalism. The internalist thinks the recognition of a binding obligation as a valid reason is already a desire for action. The externalist thinks of it as the ground of a desire, which is itself a desire-independent reason for action.

In such cases it seems to me the defender of the internalist point of view might argue that the external reason can still function only if the agent has the capacity to recognize it as a binding obligation. And this leads to a third tautological version of internalism:

Tautology C: In the exercise of his internal dispositional capacities, in order for an agent to recognize an external reason as a reason, the agent has to have the internal capacity to recognize it as a reason.

But this is easily reinterpreted in a nontautological substantive version, which is false:

Substantive C: In order that any external fact can be a reason for an agent, the agent must have an internal disposition to recognize it as a reason.

It is easy to see how you can confuse the substantive with the tautological, but they are quite distinct. The tautological just says that in order to exercise a capacity the agent has to have the capacity. The substantive version says that nothing is a valid reason unless the agent is disposed to recognize it as such, and that, I have argued, is mistaken. It is part of the concept of rationality that there can be desire-independent reasons, reasons that are binding on a rational agent, regardless of desires and dispositions in his motivational set.

Sometimes, indeed all too frequently, it happens that one goes through a process of deliberation, makes a considered decision, thereby forms a firm and unconditional intention to do something, and when the moment arrives, because of weakness of will, does not do it. Now, if the relation between deliberation and intention is both causal and rational or logical, that is, if the rational processes cause intentions, and if intentions in turn cause actions by intentional causation, then how could there ever be genuine cases of weakness of will? How could there be cases where an agent forms an all-out inclusive, unconditional intention to do something, nothing prevents him from doing it, and yet he still does not do it? Amazingly, many philosophers think that such a thing is impossible and have advanced ingenious arguments to show that it is impossible, and that the apparent cases of weakness of will are really cases of something else. Alas, it is not only possible but quite common. Here for example is an all-too-common sort of case: a student forms a firm and unconditional intention to work on his term paper Tuesday evening. Nothing prevents him from working on it, but when midnight comes, it turns out that he has spent the evening watching television and drinking beer. Such cases, as any teacher can attest, are not at all unusual. Indeed we ought to insist that it is a condition of adequacy on any account of weakness of will, what the Greeks called *akrasia*, that it allow for the fact that *akrasia* is very common in real life and involves no logical errors. In earlier chapters we discovered a gap between intentions and actions, and this gap will provide the explanation of weakness of will.

Well, how can *akrasia* be possible? Let us turn the question around and ask, why would anyone doubt or even be puzzled by its possibility since in real life it is so common? I think the basic mistake, and it is a mistake that has a long history in philosophy, is to misconstrue the relationships between the antecedents of an action and the performance of an action. There is a long tradition in philosophy according to which in the case of rational action, if the psychological antecedents of the act are all in order, that is, they are the right kind of desires, intentions, value judgments, etc., then the act must necessarily follow. According to some authors it is even an analytic truth that the act will follow. A typical statement of the idea of causal necessitation is in J. S. Mill:

... volitions do in point of fact, follow determinate moral antecedents with the same uniformity, and (when we have sufficient knowledge of the circumstances) with the same certainty as physical effects follow their physical causes. These moral antecedents are desires, aversions, habits and dispositions, combined with outward circumstances suited to call those internal incentives into action. ... A volition is a moral effect, which follows the corresponding moral causes as certainly and invariably as physical effects follow their physical causes.[1]

---

1. J. S. Mill, *The Examination of Sir William Hamilton's Philosophy*, quoted in Timothy O'Connor (ed.), *Agents, Causes and Events: Essays on Indeterminism and Free Will*, Oxford: Oxford University Press, 1995, p. 76.

I think it is clear that anyone who holds such a view is going to find weakness of will a problem, because if the causes are of the appropriate sort, then the action should follow by causal necessity. There is a tradition in twentieth-century analytic philosophy according to which pure cases of weakness of will never really occur, and according to which it is impossible that they should occur. On R. M. Hare's[2] account, if the agent acts contrary to his professed moral conviction, that shows that he really did not have the moral conviction that he claimed to have. On Donald Davidson's[3] account, if the agent acts contrary to his intentions, then he really did not have an unconditional intention to perform the action. Both Hare and Davidson hold variations of the basic idea that someone who makes a certain sort of evaluative judgment in favor of doing something must then of necessity do that thing (unless, of course, he is prevented, etc.). Consequently, on this view, if the action is not performed, then it follows that the evaluative judgment of the right sort simply was not present. On Davidson's account it turns out that the judgment was only a prima facie or conditional value judgment. On Hare's account it turns out that the evaluation in question could not have been a moral evaluation.

The general pattern in all of these cases is to suppose that if the antecedents of the action are rationally structured in a certain way, then the action will follow by causal necessity. Thus Davidson endorses the following two principles:

(P1)   If an agent wants to do x more than he wants to do y and he believes himself free to do either x or y, then he will intentionally do x if he does either x or y intentionally. (Ibid., p. 23)

---

2. R. M. Hare, *The Language of Morals*, Oxford: Oxford University Press, 1952.
3. "How Is Weakness of the Will Possible?" in *Essays on Actions and Events*, Oxford: Oxford University Press, 1980.

and

(P2)   If an agent judges that it would be better to do x than to do y then he wants to do x more than he wants to do y. (Ibid.)

Taken together these imply that an agent who judges that it would be better to do x than y will intentionally do x if he does either x or y intentionally. These two principles appear to be inconsistent with the principle that there are weak-willed acts, which Davidson states as:

(P3)   There are incontinent actions. (Ibid.)

That is, there are actions where the agent judges that it would be better to do x than y, believes himself free to do either, and yet intentionally does y rather than x.

   Davidson's solution to the apparent paradox is to say that cases where the agent apparently acts contrary to his best judgment in doing y rather than x are really cases where the agent did not make an *unconditional* judgment to the effect that the better course of action was x. Hare's view is slightly more complex, but it is the same basic idea. His idea is that if we accept an imperative, or a command, then it follows by causal necessity that our acceptance of that imperative will lead to the performance of the action, and, on his view, to accept a moral judgment is to accept an imperative. Hare writes: "I propose to say that the test, whether someone is using the judgement 'I ought to do X' as a value-judgement or not is, 'Does he or does he not recognise that if he assents to the judgement, he must also assent to the command "Let me do X"?'"[4] He also writes, "It is a tautology to say that we cannot sincerely assent to a second-person command addressed

---

4. R. M. Hare, *Language of Morals*, pp. 168–169.

to ourselves, and *at the same time* not perform it, if now is the occasion for performing it and if it is in our (physical and psychological) power to do so."[5]

In both authors we get the view that the appropriate causal antecedents of the action must cause the action, hence apparent cases of *akrasia* are really cases where there was something wrong with the causes of the action in the form of the antecedent psychological states.

All of these authors in effect deny the existence of the gap, and that is why the problem of weakness of will arises in such a stark form for them and why they are forced to deny, either implicitly or explicitly, that there really are any such things as cases of *akrasia* strictly speaking. So the deep dispute between me and the tradition is a dispute about the gap. The Classical Model denies the existence of the gap. I, on the contrary, think the gap is an obvious fact of our conscious life. I have presented arguments for the existence of the gap in earlier chapters and won't repeat them here. In this chapter I want to adopt a different approach. I regard the Hare-Davidson approach to *akrasia* as a kind of reductio ad absurdum of this feature of the Classical Model. On my view, in the case of free actions, no matter what type of antecedents the action has—moral judgments, unconditional value judgments, firm and unconditional intentions, anything you like—weakness of will is always possible. So if you get the conclusion that it is not possible, you have made a mistake and have to go back and revise the premises that led to the mistake. In this case the false premise is the denial of the gap. Davidson's account is the more recent, so I will focus most of my attention on it.

---

5. Ibid., p. 20.

What exactly is the thesis that there are weak willed actions? That is, we need to state the thesis in a way that makes it clear whether or not it really is inconsistent with (P1) and (P2). Davidson states it in this form:

(P3)   There are incontinent actions.

But what is an "incontinent" action? On a natural interpretation, it seems to me the thesis is that there are acts such that the agent judges unconditionally it would be better to do x than to do y, believes that he is able to do either, and yet he intentionally does y rather than x. That thesis is genuinely inconsistent with the conjunction of (P1) and (P2), and it is a thesis that I believe is true. Davidson denies that it is true and says that in cases that appear to be "incontinent" what is really happening is that the agent did not judge unconditionally that it would be better to do x than y, but rather only made a conditional, or prima facie, judgment to the effect that x was better than y. He judged that x was better than y "all things considered," where, according to Davidson, "all things considered" does not mean literally "*all* things considered," it just means something like "relative to a certain set of considerations that the agent happens to have in mind."

The first thing to note about Davidson's thesis is that no independent argument is given for saying that the weak-willed agent cannot make an unconditional evaluative judgment in favor of performing any action other than the one he performs. That is, no independent reason is given for motivating the thesis, no cases are examined to show that only a conditional judgment was made. Rather, the notion of prima facie and conditional evaluations is introduced as a way of overcoming the apparent inconsistency between (P1), (P2), and (P3). If in the case of weak-willed actions the agent did not make an unconditional judgment in favor of doing the action that he did not perform, but only a prima facie, "all things considered" judgment, then the inconsistency is removed. For now (P3) is read as

(P3*) Sometimes an agent makes a conditional, prima facie, judgment that it would be better to do x than y, believes he is able to do either, and then he intentionally does y.

And so construed, (P1), (P2), and (P3) are consistent.

What then is the logical status of the solution? The claim is this: all weak-willed actions are preceded by conditional value judgments (or conditional intentions, which Davidson takes to be the same thing). On its face that looks like an empirical hypothesis: there is a one hundred percent correlation between the experience of weakness of will and the making of conditional rather than unconditional value judgments. But if this is supposed to be an empirical hypothesis, it is an astonishingly ambitious claim made on the basis of little or no empirical evidence.

And even aside from the fact that no independent argument is given for claiming that the weak-willed agent did not make an unconditional judgment, there is still another, and worse, problem. The problem is this: no matter what the form of the judgment is, an agent can still suffer from weakness of will. An agent can say, "Unconditionally I think x is better than y," and nonetheless do y rather than x. The only way I can see out of this is to make the argument circular, to make the criterion for whether or not the person had an unconditional judgment to be

whether or not he did in fact perform the action intentionally. The circle is this: the thesis is that all weak-willed
actions are preceded by conditional, rather than unconditional intentions. The argument for the thesis is that the
actions were weak-willed, and therefore *must* have been
preceded by a conditional rather than an unconditional
intention, for if they had been preceded by an unconditional intention, the action would have had to have taken
place. I believe this circle is implicit in Davidson's article.
For Davidson an agent does something intentionally if
and only if he holds an all-out unconditional evaluative
judgment in favor of doing that thing. So it follows trivially from this conception that in cases where the agent
says that x is better than y but still intentionally does y
rather than x, the judgment cannot have been unconditional. But this gets us out of the frying pan and into the
fire, because it is obviously false on any ordinary sense of
making all-out unconditional evaluative judgments that it
is impossible for someone to make such a judgment and
then not do the thing that he judges it best to do. Indeed,
that is precisely the problem of weakness of will. One
often makes an all-out unconditional judgment and then
does not do the thing one judges to be the best thing to do.
Davidson simply solves the problem of weakness of will
by fiat when he declares that in all such cases the agent
fails to make an all-out unconditional judgment.

My diagnosis of what is going on is this: what looks like
an empirical claim—all cases of weakness of will are cases
of conditional value judgments—is not in fact empirical.
Rather Davidson assumes (P1)–(P3) are true and that (P1)
and (P2) are unproblematic, and thus that there must be
an interpretation of (P3) where it is consistent with (P1)

and (P2). The claim about conditional value judgments is that interpretation.

But this solution has absurd consequences, which I will now spell out. Consider the sorts of cases of weakness of will that typically arise in real life. Let us suppose that I decide, after considering all the facts known to me that bear on the issue, that it is best for me not to drink wine at dinner tonight, because let us suppose I want to do some work on weakness of will after dinner. But let us suppose that as it turns out, I do drink wine at dinner. The wine being served looked rather tempting, and so in a moment of weakness, I drank it. On the Davidsonian account, here is the sum total of my intentional states that bear on the case:

1. I made a conditional judgment: All things considered, it is best not to drink wine.

2. I made an unconditional judgment: It is best to drink wine.

And, that being the case, I drank the wine.

What is wrong with this account? It is simply false to say that I must have made any unconditional value judgment to the effect that it is best to drink the wine. I just drank the wine. That is what made my action a case of weakness of will. I drank the wine in the teeth of my *unconditional* judgment that it is better not to drink the wine. So the false claim that my intention to do the right thing could not have been unconditional, but must have been only prima facie or conditional, is matched by another false claim to the effect that when I did the wrong thing I had to have made an unconditional judgment to the effect that it was then and there the right thing to do.

Both claims are wrong. I can make an unconditional value judgment and still, in a weak-willed act, do something contrary to it, and my weak-willed act need not be accompanied by any judgment to the effect that it was the right thing to do.

The problem of weakness of will is *not* how I can reconcile two apparently inconsistent *judgments*; rather the problem is, how is it that having made only one judgment I can then act contrary to that judgment? And the answer is that I do not have to make another judgment in order to act; I can just act. That is, in this sort of case, I have an intention-in-action with no prior intention and no prior deliberation.

What the whole discussion shows is that the conjunction of (P1) and (P2) is false. It is not the case that everything that one judges to be the best to do, one really wants to do, and it is not the case that when you have made up your mind and you really want to do something, that you will therefore necessarily do it. There are a lot of things I judge it best to do, and things I really want to do, but I do not in fact do them, even though I have both the ability and the opportunity to do them.

The key sentence, I believe, in Davidson's article is the following: "If *r* is someone's reason for holding that *p*, then his holding that *r* must be, I think, a cause of his holding that *p*. But, and this is what is crucial here, his holding that *r* may cause his holding that *p* without *r* being his reason; indeed, the agent may even think that *r* is a reason to reject *p*."[6] Let's try to apply this account to the example of drinking the wine. I hold a set of reasons *r*, and those reasons cause me to hold that it is best to drink

---

6. "How Is Weakness of the Will Possible?" p. 41.

the wine, p. However, they cause me to hold that it is best to drink the wine without actually being a reason for drinking the wine. Indeed, in my case I think that they are a reason to reject the claim that it is best to drink the wine.

I do not find this even remotely plausible as an account of what happened when I, in a moment of weakness of will, drank wine in the teeth of my better judgment. I think a much more plausible account, which I will explain in more detail later, is that I held an unconditional judgment to the effect that it was best *not* to drink the wine, but when confronted with the wine I found it tempting, and I simply failed to resist the temptation.

How did we get into this mess? Davidson, in company with a whole lot of other philosophers,[7] thinks that in the case of rationally motivated actions, there is some sort of causally necessary connection between the psychological antecedents of an action and the intentional performance of the action, or at least the intentional attempt to perform the action, that the action follows from its antecedents by a kind of causal necessity. But that is a mistake. That denies the existence of the gap. Once you deny the existence of the gap, you get into all of the problems that we have been examining, and in particular you get into the problem that weakness of will, strictly speaking, becomes impossible.

In response to these claims that the proper psychological antecedents lead to the action in question by causal necessity, let us ask, are there indeed such cases? Are there cases where the psychological antecedents are causally sufficient to produce the action? It seems to me quite

---

7. For example, Peter van Inwagen, "When Is the Will Free?" in Timothy O'Connor (ed.), *Agents, Causes, and Events: Essays on Indeterminism and Free Will*, New York: Oxford University Press, 1995.

obvious that there are many such cases, but they are typically cases where there is no free will, rather than cases of the standard sort of voluntary action. Thus, for example, a drug addict might well have psychological antecedents for drug use that are causally sufficient to guarantee his drug use, simply because he is unable to help himself. In such cases, as we have seen earlier, there is no gap of the familiar sort. The action is genuinely causally determined by antecedently sufficient psychological causes. We now, by the way, have pretty good evidence that these psychological causes are grounded in the appropriate neurobiology. When people crave satisfaction of their addiction, the mesolimbic dopamine system is activated. This system runs from the amygdala and the anterior singulate to the tip of both temporal lobes. Its activation is, according to at least some current views, the neurological correlate of addictive behavior.

In normal cases we can make the obvious objection that you can make any kind of evaluative judgment you like and still not act on that judgment. The problem of *akrasia*, to repeat, is that if we leave aside the cases of addiction, compulsion, obsession, etc., then any antecedent whatever, provided that it is described in a non-question-begging way that does not trivially entail the performance of the action, is such that it is always possible for a fully conscious rational agent to have the antecedent (e.g., the relevant moral judgment, unconditional intention, anything you like) and still not act in accordance with the content of that antecedent. Furthermore, this is not a rare occurrence. It happens all the time. Ask anybody who has ever tried to lose weight, give up smoking, or keep all their New Year's resolutions.

In its crudest form, the mistake that makes it seem puzzling that there can be *akrasia* derives from a mistaken conception of causation. If, for example, we think of causation on the model of billiard balls hitting billiard balls or gear wheels activating other gear wheels, then it just seems impossible that we should have the causes without the effects. If intentions cause behavior and the intention was present and the agent did not undertake the intended action, it can only be because some other cause interfered, or it was not the type of intention we thought it was, or some such.

But intentional causation is in certain important respects unlike billiard-ball causation. Both are cases of causation, but in the case of desires and intentions, in the case of normal voluntary actions, once the causes are present they still do not compel the agent to act; the agent has to *act on* the reasons or on his intention. In the case of voluntary action there is, as we saw in chapters 1 and 3, a gap, a certain amount of slack between the process of deliberation and the formation of an intention, and there is another gap between the intention and the actual undertaking.

Where intentionality is concerned, it is best to think from the first-person point of view. Well, what is it like for me to form an intention and then not act on it? Am I always prevented from acting on it, and am I always compelled by causes, conscious or unconscious, to act contrary to my intention? Of course not. Well, does it always turn out in such cases that the intention was somehow defective, conditional, or inappropriate, that it was not an all-out, unconditional, no-holds-barred intention, but only a prima facie, conditional intention? Once again, of course not. It is possible, as we all know, for an intention to be as strong and unconditional as you like, for nothing to interfere, and still the action does not get done.

To see how *akrasia* occurs we have to remind ourselves how actions proceed in the normal, non-*akrasia* cases. When I form an intention I still have to act on the intention that I have formed. I can't just sit back and wait to see the action happen, in the way that I can in the case of the billiard balls. But from a first-person point of view, the only view that really matters here, actions are not just things that happen, they are not just events that occur; rather, from the first-person point of view, they are *done*; they are, for example, undertaken, initiated, or performed. Making up your mind is not enough; you still have to do it. It is in this gap between intention and action that we find the possibility, indeed the inevitability of at least some cases of weakness of will. Because of the inevitability of conflicting desires and other motivators, for most premeditated actions there will be the possibility that when the time comes to perform the action the agent will find himself confronted with desires not to do the thing he has made up his mind to do.

What would it be like if *akrasia* were genuinely impossible? Imagine a world in which once a person had formed an unconditional intention to perform an action (and had satisfied any other antecedent conditions you care to name, such as forming an all-out value judgment in favor of performing it, issuing a moral injunction to himself to perform it, etc.), the action then followed by causal necessity, unless some other cause overcame the causal power of the intention or the intention grew weak and lost its power to cause action. If that were how the world worked in fact, we would not have to *act on* our intentions; we could, so to speak, wait for them to act by themselves. We could sit back and see how things turned out. But we can't do that, we always have to act.

Akrasia in short is but a symptom of a certain kind of freedom, and we will understand it better if we explore that freedom further. On a certain classical conception of decision making, we, from time to time, reach a "choice point": a point at which we are presented with a range of options from which we can—or sometimes must—choose. Against that conception I want to propose that at any normal, conscious, waking moment in our lives we are presented with an indefinite, indeed strictly speaking infinite, range of choices. We are always at a choice point and the choices are infinite. At this moment, as I am writing this chapter, I can wriggle my toes, move my left hand, my right hand, or set out for Timbuktu. The experience of any normal, conscious, free action contains within it the possibility of not performing that action, but doing something else instead. Many of these options will be out of the question as fruitless, undesirable, or even ridiculous. But among the range of possibilities will be a handful we would actually like to do, for example, have another drink, go to bed, go for a walk, or simply quit work and read a novel.

There are many different forms of *akrasia*, but one way in which *akrasia* typically arises is this: as a result of deliberation we form an intention. But since at all times we have an indefinite range of choices open to us, when the moment comes to act on the intention several of the other choices may be attractive, or motivated on other grounds. For many of the actions that we do for a reason, there are reasons for not doing that action but doing something else instead. Sometimes we act on those reasons and not on our original intention. The solution to the problem of *akrasia* is as simple as that: we almost never have just one choice open to us. Regardless of a particular resolve, other options continue to be attractive.

It might seem puzzling then that we ever act on our best judgment with all these conflicting demands made on us. But it is not so puzzling if we remind ourselves why we have deliberation and prior intentions at all. A large part of the point of these is to regulate our behavior. Sane behavior is not just a bundle of spontaneous acts, each motivated by the considerations of the moment; rather we bring order into our life and enable ourselves to satisfy more of our long-range goals by the formation of prior intentions through deliberation.

It is common to draw an analogy between *akrasia* and self-deception, and there are indeed certain similarities. A characteristic form of *akrasia* is that of duty versus desire, just as a characteristic form of self-deception is evidence versus desire. For example, the lover deceives himself that his beloved is faithful to him in the teeth of blatant evidence to the contrary, because he desperately wants to believe in her faithfulness. But there are certain crucial differences between *akrasia* and self-deception, mostly having to do with direction of fit. The weak-willed person can let everything lie right on the surface. He can say to himself, "Yes I know I shouldn't be smoking another cigarette and I have made a firm resolve to stop, but all the same I do want one very much; and so, against my better judgment, I am going to have one." But the self-deceiver cannot say to himself, "Yes I know that the proposition I believe is certainly false, but I want very much to believe it; and so, against my better judgment and knowledge, I am going to go on believing it." Such a view is not self-deception, it is simply irrational and perhaps even incoherent. In order to satisfy the desire to believe what one knows to be false, the agent must suppress the knowledge. *"Akrasia"* is the name of a certain type of conflict between intentional states, where the wrong side wins. "Self-deception" is not so much the name of a type of conflict at all, but rather a form of conflict-avoidance by suppression of the unwelcome side. It is a form of concealment of a conflict, indeed what would in some cases be an inconsistency, which if it were allowed to come to the surface could not be maintained. The form of the conflict is:

I have overwhelming evidence that *p* (or even perhaps, I know that *p*) but I wish very much to believe that not *p*.

That conflict cannot be won by the desire if it emerges in that form. If desire is to win, the conflict itself requires suppression. That is why it is a case of self-deception. *Akrasia* is a form of conflict but not a form of logical inconsistency or logical incoherence. Self-deception is a way of concealing what would be a form of inconsistency or incoherence if it were allowed to surface. For these reasons self-deception logically requires the notion of the unconscious; *akrasia* does not. *Akrasia* is often supplemented by self-deception as a way of removing the conflict, for example, the smoker says to himself: "Smoking isn't really so bad for me, and besides, the claim that it causes cancer has never been proved."

To summarize these differences: *akrasia* and self-deception are not really similar in structure. *Akrasia* typically has the form:

It is best to do *A* and I have decided to do *A*, but I am voluntarily and intentionally doing *B*.

There is no logical absurdity or inconsistency here at all, though there is a conflict between inconsistent reasons for action, and the act is irrational to the extent that the agent intentionally and voluntarily acts on a reason that he believes is the wrong reason to act on.

Self-deception typically has the form:

The agent has the conscious state: I believe not p. He has the unconscious states: I have overwhelming evidence that p and want very much to believe that not p.

Self-deception, thus, involves irrationality and in some cases even logical inconsistency. It can exist only if one of the elements is suppressed from consciousness.

In weak-willed actions, the self acts on a reason that that very same self judges to be not the best reason to act on, and the self acts against the very reason that the self has judged the best reason to act on. There are many different forms this pattern can take, and many different degrees of weakness of will. It is tempting to think that in cases of weakness of will the self is overcome by some strong desire, so that the desire that the self acts on provides a genuinely sufficient causal condition for acting. No doubt there are such cases, but they are not the typical case. In the typical case the gap exists as much for the weak-willed action as it did for the strong-willed action. I had another glass of wine in the teeth of my judgment that I should not have another glass of wine. But my taking the glass of wine was no more compelled or forced or determined than was my strong-willed action when I acted according to my best judgment. The gap is—or can be—the same in both types of case. And that is why the weak-willed act is to that extent irrational. It is irrational of me when I genuinely have a choice to make the wrong choice when I know that it is the wrong choice. The metaphor of "weakness" is, I believe, exactly right in these cases, because the question at issue is about the self. The question at issue is not about the weakness of my desires or my convictions, but it is about the weakness of myself in carrying out the decisions I have made.

On the account I have presented the problem of weakness of will is not a serious problem in philosophy. It is serious only if we make the wrong set of assumptions about the causal antecedents of action. But it is illuminating in that it enables us to see the gap from a different point of view. The question remains, however: what is or could be the neurobiological reality of the gap? That is a question I postpone until the last chapter.

8   Why There Is No Deductive Logic of Practical Reason

I   The Logic of Practical Reason

Practical reason, we are usually told, is reasoning about what to do, and theoretical reason is reasoning about what to believe. But if this is so, it ought to seem puzzling to us that we do not have a generally accepted account of the deductive logical structure of practical reason in a way that we apparently do for deductive theoretical reason. After all, the processes by which we figure out how to best achieve our goals seem to be just as rational as the processes by which we figure out the implications of our beliefs, so why do we seem to have such a powerful logic for the one and not for the other? Aristotle more or less invented the theoretical syllogism and, though generally it has been less influential, he also invented the practical syllogism. Why is there no accepted theory of the practical syllogism in the way there is an accepted theory of the theoretical syllogism and a theory of deductive logic generally?

To see what the problem is, let us review how it is apparently solved for theoretical reason. We need to distinguish questions of logical relations from questions of philosophical psychology. Great advances in deductive logic were made when, in the nineteenth century, Frege separated questions of philosophical psychology (the "laws of thought") from those of logical relations. After Frege, it has seemed that if you get the logical relations right the philosophical psychology should be relatively easy. For example, once we understand the relations of logical consequence between propositions then many of the corresponding questions about belief seem fairly simple. If I know that the premises "all men are mortal" and "Socrates is a man" jointly entail the conclusion "Socrates is mortal" then I already know that someone who *believes* those premises is *committed* to that conclusion; that someone who *knows* the premises to be true is *justified* in *inferring* the truth of the conclusion, etc. There seems in short to be a fairly tight set of parallels within theoretical reason between such "logical" notions as premise, conclusion, and logical consequence on the one hand and such "psychological" notions as belief, commitment, and inference on the other. The reason for this tight set of parallels is that the psychological states have propositional contents and therefore inherit certain features of the logical relations between the propositions. Because logical consequence is truth-preserving, and belief is a commitment to truth, the features of logical consequence can be mapped onto the commitments of belief. If q is a logical consequence of p, and I believe p, then I am committed to the truth of q. The tacit principle that has worked so well in assertoric logic is that if you get the logical relations right, then most of the philosophical psychology will take care of itself.

Now, supposing we accept this distinction between the logical relations and the philosophical psychology, how is it supposed to work for practical reason? What are the logical relations in practical reason and how do they bear on the philosophical psychology? Some of the questions about logical relations would be: What is the formal logical structure of practical argument? In particular, can we get a definition of formal validity for practical reason in the way that we can for deductive "theoretical" reason? Does practical logic exhibit the same or does it require different rules of inference than assertoric logic? The questions about the philosophical psychology of deliberation would concern many of the issues that we have been discussing in this book, especially the character of the intentional states in practical reasoning, their relation to the logical structure of deliberation, their relations to action, and their relations to reasons for action generally. What sorts of intentional states figure in deliberation and what are the relations between them? What sorts of things can be reasons for action? What is the nature of motivation, and how does deliberation actually motivate action?

In light of our distinction between logical theory and philosophical psychology, the question we are asking is, "Are there formal patterns of practical validity, such that the *acceptance* of the premises of a valid practical argument commits one to the acceptance of the conclusion, in the way that is characteristic of theoretical reason?" We have seen that in theoretical reason belief in the premises of a valid argument commits you to a belief in the conclusion. Could we get similar commitments to desires and intentions as conclusions in practical reason? The aim of a formal logic of practical reason, it seems to me, would have to be to get a set of valid forms of practical inference; and a test for any such a project would be whether the agent who accepted the premises of a putatively valid practical inference would be committed to desiring or intending the conclusion, in a way that the agent who accepts the premises of a valid theoretical inference is committed to believing the conclusion.

II   Three Patterns of Practical Reason

To begin, let us consider some attempts to state a formal logical structure of practical reason. I will confine the discussion to so-called means-ends reasoning, since most authors on the subject are in the tradition of the Classical Model and think that practical reason is a matter of deliberating about means to achieve ends. Oddly enough it is not at all easy or uncontroversial to state the formal structure of means-ends reasoning, and there is no general agreement on what it is. In the philosophical literature there is a bewildering variety of formal models of such reasoning, and even fundamental disagreements over what its special elements are supposed to be—are they desires, intentions, fiats, imperatives, norms, *noemata*, actions, or what?[1] I think the reason for this variety is that the authors in question are coping with the fact that the elements in reasoning are factitives, and factitives can come in different forms. Many philosophers speak rather glibly about the belief-desire model of explanation and deliberation, but what exactly is the structure of this

---

1. For a good survey of the literature up to the mid-1970s, see Bruce Aune, *Reason and Action*, Dordrecht-Holland: D. Reidel Publishing Company, 1977, ch. 4, pp. 144–194.

model supposed to be? Anthony Kenny suggests that the structure of practical reason is quite different from theoretical reason. He gives the following example:

I'm to be in London at 4.15
If I catch the 2.30 I will be in London at 4.15
So I'll catch the 2.30.[2]

Because the premises exhibit both directions of fit, we can represent the form of the argument generally with the following symbolism, using "↑" and "↓" for the upward and downward directions of fit respectively, and using "E" and "M" for ends and means:

↑ (E).

↓ (If M then E).

Therefore, ↑ (M).

In the case where one has beliefs and desires as "premises" this pattern of inference can be represented as follows:

DES (I achieve E).

BEL (If I do M I will achieve E).

Therefore, DES (I do M).

But it seems this could not be right, because two premises of this form simply do not commit one to accepting the conclusion. You do not get a commitment to a desire, much less an intention, as the conclusion of this form of argument. To see this note that a lot of the Es one can think of are quite trivial and many Ms are ridiculous. For

---

2. Anthony Kenny, *Will, Freedom and Power*, New York: Barnes and Noble, 1976, p. 70.

instance I want this subway to be less crowded and I believe that if I kill all the other passengers it will be less crowded. This does not commit me to desiring to kill the other passengers. Of course one *might* form a homicidal desire on a crowded subway, but it seems absurd to claim that rationality *commits* me to a desire to kill just on the basis of my other beliefs and desires. The most that this pattern could account for would be *possible* motivations for forming a desire. Someone who has the appropriate beliefs and desires has a possible motive for desiring M. But there is no *commitment* to such a desire.

It is sometimes said that this pattern fails because there is no entailment relationship between the propositional contents of the premises and the conclusion. Indeed, if we just look at the propositional contents, the inference is guilty of the fallacy of affirming the consequent. Some philosophers think the standard form of practical reason is to be found in cases where the means is a necessary condition of achieving the end. Thus they endorse the following (or variations on it):

↑ (I achieve end E).

↓ (The only way to achieve E is by means M) (sometimes stated as "M is a necessary condition of E", or "to achieve E, I must do M").

Therefore, ↑ (I do M).

In this case the satisfaction of the premises guarantees the satisfaction of the conclusion, but the acceptance of the premises still does not commit one to a desire or intention in the conclusion. If you think about this pattern in terms of real life examples it seems quite out of the question as a general account of practical reason. In general there are

lots of means, many of them ridiculous, to achieve any
end; and in the rare case where there is only one means, it
may be so absurd as to be out of the question altogether.
Suppose that you have any end you care to name: you
want to go to Paris, become rich, or marry a Republican.
Well, in the Paris case, for example, there are lots of ways
to go. You could walk, swim, take a plane, ship, kayak, or
rocket; you could tunnel through the earth or go via the
moon or the North Pole. In very rare cases there may be
only one means to an end. As far as I know there is no
quick way to get rid of flu symptoms short of death.
Therefore, on the above model, if I desire to get rid of my
flu symptoms immediately, and I believe the only way to
do it is death, I am committed to desiring my death. This
model, like the first one, has very little application. Most
means-ends reasoning is not about necessary conditions,
and even when it is, desiring the end does not commit me
to desiring the means.[3]

In the first of these examples there was no entailment
relation between the propositional contents of the premises and the conclusion; but in the second there was. The
fact that entailment relations do not generate a commitment to a secondary desire reveals an important contrast
between the logic of beliefs alone and the logic of belief-
desire combinations. If I believe both p and (if p then q),
then I am committed to the belief that q. But if I want p
and believe that (if p then q), I am not committed to
wanting q. Now why is there this difference? When we
understand that, we will go a long way toward understanding why there is no plausible logic of practical reason.

---

3. Aune, *Reason and Action*, who sees that the first model is inadequate
for reasons similar to those I have suggested, nonetheless fails to see that
the same sorts of objections seem to apply to the second model.

Let's try again to construct a formal logical model of practical reason. Generally when you have a desire, intention, or goal you seek not just *any* means; nor do you search for the *only* means; you seek the *best* means (as Aristotle says you seek the "best or easiest" means). And if you are rational, when there isn't any good or at least reasonable means you give up on the goal altogether. Furthermore, you don't just have a goal, but if you are rational, you appraise and select your own goals in the light of—well, what? We will have to come back to this point later. In the meantime let us suppose you have seriously selected a goal and appraised it as reasonable. Suppose you seriously want to go to Paris, that is, you have "made up your mind," and you try to figure the best way to get there and conclude that the best way is to go by plane. Is there a plausible formal model of the logic of means-ends reasoning for such a case?

The form of the argument seems to be:

Des (I go to Paris).

Bel (the best way, all things considered, is to go by plane).

Therefore, Des (I go by plane).

If we separate the questions of logical relations from the questions of philosophical psychology—as I have been urging—we see that from a logical point of view this argument, as it stands, is enthymematic. To be formally valid it would require an extra premise of the form:

Des (If I go to Paris I go by the best way, all things considered).

If we add this premise, the argument is valid by the standards of classical logic. Let $P = $ I go to Paris, $Q = $ I go by the best way, and $R = $ I go by plane. Then its form is:

$$P$$
$$P \to Q$$
$$Q \leftrightarrow R$$

$$\therefore R$$

And though the argument is not truth-preserving because two of its premises and its conclusion don't have truth values, this doesn't really matter since the argument is satisfaction-preserving, and truth is just a special case of satisfaction. Truth is satisfaction of representations with the word-to-world direction of fit.

But once again, as in the earlier examples, it seems the logical relations don't map onto the philosophical psychology in the right way. It is by no means obvious that a rational person who has all those premises must have, or be committed to having, a desire to go by plane. Furthermore, to make it plausible, we had to introduce a fishy-sounding premise, about wanting to do things "by the best way all things considered." Indeed it looks as if any attempt to state formally the structure of a practical argument of this sort would in general require such a premise, but it is not at all clear what it means. What is meant by "the best way," and what is meant by "all things considered"? Notice furthermore that such premises have no analogue in standard cases of theoretical reason. When one reasons from one's belief that all men are mortal and that Socrates is a man to the conclusion that Socrates is mortal, one does not need any premise about what is the best thing to believe, all things considered.

I have tried to make a sympathetic attempt to find a formal logical model of the traditional conception of means-ends reasoning, the conception that goes back to Aristotle, and this is the best that I can come up with. I have also tried to give a statement of its formal structure that seems to me an improvement on other versions I have seen. But I think it is still hopelessly inadequate. After various unsuccessful tries I have reluctantly come to the conclusion that it is impossible to get a formal logic of practical reason that is adequate to the facts of the philosophical psychology. To show why this is so, I now turn to the discussion of the nature of desire. The essential feature of desire for the present discussion is that it has the upward direction of fit. Many of the features that I will specify as features of desire are also features of other factitives with the upward direction of fit such as obligations, needs, commitments, etc. However, for the sake of simplicity I will state most of the discussion in terms of desire and generalize it to other upward direction-of-fit factitives later.

III   The Structure of Desire

In order to understand the weaknesses in my revised logic for practical reasoning, and in order to understand the general obstacles to a formal logic of practical reasoning, we have to explore some general features of desire and especially explore the differences between desires and beliefs. I will use the general account of intentionality that I gave in chapter 2, as well as other features of the theory of intentionality that I presented in the book of that name.[4] Specifically, I am going to assume that contrary to the surface grammar of sentences about desire, all desires have whole propositions as intentional contents (thus "I want your car" means something like "I want that I have

---

4. John R. Searle, *Intentionality: An Essay in the Philosophy of Mind*, Cambridge: Cambridge University Press, 1983.

your car"); that desires have the world-to-mind direction of fit, whereas beliefs have the mind-to-world direction of fit; and that desires do not have the restrictions on intentional contents that intentions have. Intentions must be about future or present actions of the agent and must have causal self-referentiality built into their intentional content. Desires have no such causal condition, and they can be about anything, past, present, or future. Furthermore, I am going to assume that the usual accounts of the de re/ de dicto distinction are hopelessly muddled, as is the view that desires are intensional-with-an-s. The de re/de dicto distinction is properly construed as a distinction between kinds of *sentences* about desires, not between kinds of desires. The claim that all desires, beliefs, etc. are in general intensional is just false. *Sentences about* desires, beliefs, etc. are in general intensional. Desires and beliefs themselves are not in general intensional, though in a few oddball cases they can be.[5]

Where a state of affairs is desired in order to satisfy some other desire, it is best to remember that each desire is part of a larger desire. If I want to go to my office to get my mail, there is indeed a desire the content of which is simply: I want that (I go to my office). But it is part of a larger desire whose content is: I want that (I get my mail by way of going to my office). This feature is shared by intentions. If I intend to do *a* in order to do *b*, then I have a complex intention whose form is I intend (I do *b* by means of doing *a*). I will say more about this point later.

The first feature about desiring (wanting, wishing, etc.), in which it differs from belief is that it is possible for an agent consistently and knowingly to want that *p* and want

5. For a discussion of these points about intensionality-with-an-s and the de re/de dicto distinction, see Searle, *Intentionality*, chaps. 7 and 8.

that not p in a way that it is not possible for him consistently and knowingly to believe that p and believe that not p. And this claim is stronger than the claim that an agent can consistently have desires that are impossible of simultaneous satisfaction because of features he doesn't know about. For example, Oedipus can want to marry a woman under the description "my fiancee" and want not to marry any woman under the description "my mother" even though in fact one woman satisfies both descriptions. But I am claiming that he can consistently both want to marry Jocasta and want not to marry Jocasta, under the same description. The standard cases of this are cases where he has certain reasons for wanting to marry her and reasons for not wanting to. For example, he might want to marry her—because, say, he finds her beautiful and intelligent, and simultaneously not want to marry her—because, say, she snores and cracks her knuckles. Such cases are common, but it is also important to point out that a person might find the same features simultaneously desirable and undesirable. He might find her beauty and intelligence exasperating as well as attractive, and he might find her snoring and knuckle-cracking habits endearing as well as repulsive. (Imagine that he thinks to himself: "It is wonderful that she is so beautiful and intelligent, but at the same time it is a bit tiresome; her sitting there being beautiful and intelligent all day long. And it is exasperating to hear her snoring and cracking her knuckles, but at the same time there is something endearing about it. It is so human.") Such is the human condition.

The possibility of rationally and consistently held inconsistent desires has the unpleasant logical consequence that desire is not closed under conjunction. Thus if I desire that p and desire that not p, it does not follow that I desire that (p and not p). For example I want to be in Berkeley right now and I want to be in Paris right now but knowing that these are inconsistent desires, it is not the case that I am rationally committed to wanting: (I am simultaneously in Berkeley and Paris right now).

In order to understand the possibility of rationally and consistently held inconsistent desires and its consequences for practical reason, we need to probe a bit deeper. It is customary, and I think largely correct to distinguish, as the Classical conception does, between primary and secondary or derived desires. It is literally true to say to my travel agent, "I want to buy a plane ticket." But I have no lust, yearning, yen, or passion for plane tickets—they are just "means" to "ends." A desire that is primary relative to one desire may be secondary relative to another. My desire to go to Paris is primary relative to my desire to buy a plane ticket, secondary relative to my desire to visit the Louvre. The primary/secondary desire distinction will then always be relative to some structure whereby a desire is motivated by another desire or some other motivator. This is precisely the picture that is incorporated in the classical conception of practical reason. In such cases, as I just noted, the complete specification of the secondary desire makes reference to the primary desire. I don't just want to buy a ticket, I want to buy a ticket in order to go to Paris.

Once we understand the character of secondary desires we can see that there are at least two ways in which fully rational agents can form conflicting desires. First, as noted earlier, an agent can simply have conflicting inclinations. But second, he can form conflicting desires from consistent sets of primary desires together with beliefs about the best means of satisfying them. Consider the example of the man who reasons that he wants to go to Paris by plane. Such a man has a secondary desire to go by plane, motivated by a desire to go to Paris, together with a belief that the best way to go is by plane. But the same man might have constructed a practical inference as follows: I don't want to do anything that makes me nauseated and terrified, but going anywhere by plane makes me nauseated and terrified, therefore I don't want to go anywhere by plane, therefore I don't want to go to Paris by plane. It is easy enough to state this according to the pattern of practical reasoning I suggested above: all things considered the best way to satisfy my desire to avoid nausea and terror is *not* to go to Paris by plane. Since this can be stated as a piece of practical reasoning, it seems that *the same person, using two independent chains of practical reason, can rationally form inconsistent secondary desires from a consistent set of his actual beliefs and a consistent set of primary desires.* A consistent set of "premises" will generate inconsistent secondary desires as "conclusions." This is not a paradoxical or incidental feature of reasoning from beliefs and desires; rather, it is a consequence of certain essential differences between practical and theoretical reason.

Let's probe these differences further: in general it is impossible to have any set of desires, even a consistent set of primary desires, without having, or at least being rationally motivated to having, inconsistent desires. Or, to put this point a bit more precisely: if you take the set of a person's desires and beliefs at any given point in his life, and work out what secondary desires can be rationally motivated from his primary desires, assuming the truth of his beliefs, you will find inconsistent desires. I don't know how to demonstrate this, but any number of examples can be used to illustrate it. Consider the example of going to

Paris by plane. Even if planes do not make me nauseated and terrified, still I don't want to spend the money; I don't want to sit in airplanes; I don't want to eat airplane food; I don't want to stand in line at airports; I don't want to sit next to people who put their elbow where I am trying to put my elbow. And indeed, I don't want to do a whole host of other things that are the price, both literally and figuratively, of satisfying my desire to go to Paris by plane. The same line of reasoning that can lead me to form a desire to go to Paris by plane can also lead me to form a desire *not* to go to Paris by plane.

A possible answer to this, implicit in at least some of the literature, is to invoke the notion of preference. I prefer going to Paris by plane and being uncomfortable to not going to Paris by plane and being comfortable. But this answer, though acceptable as far as it goes, mistakenly implies that the preferences are given *prior* to practical reasoning, whereas, it seems to me, they are typically the product of practical reasoning. And since ordered preferences are typically products of practical reason, they cannot be treated as its universal presupposition. Just as it is a mistake to suppose that a rational person must have a consistent set of desires, so it is a mistake to suppose that rational persons must have a rank ordering of (combinations of) their desires prior to deliberation.

This points to the following conclusion: even if we confine our discussion of practical reasoning to means-ends cases, it turns out that practical reason essentially involves the adjudication of conflicting desires and other sorts of conflicting motivations (i.e., factitives with upward direction-of-fit) in a way that theoretical reason does not essentially involve the adjudication of conflicting beliefs. Practical reasoning is typically about adjudicating between conflicting desires, obligations, commitments, needs, requirements, and duties. That is why in our attempt to give a plausible account of the Classical conception of practical inference we needed a step about wanting to go by "the best way, all things considered." Such a step is characteristic of any rational reconstruction of a process of means-ends reason, because "best" just means the one that best reconciles all of the conflicting desires and other motivators that bear on the case. However, this also has the consequence that the formalization of the classical conception I gave is essentially a trivialization of the problem, because the hard part has not been analyzed: how do we arrive at the conclusion that such and such is "the best way to do something all things considered" and how do we reconcile the inconsistent conclusions of competing sets of such valid derivations?

If all one had to go on were the Classical conception of reasoning about means to ends, then in order to reach a conclusion of the argument that could form the basis of action one would have to go through a whole set of other such chains of inference and then find some way to settle the issue between the conflicting reasons. *The Classical conception works on the correct principle that any means to a desirable end is desirable at least to the extent that it does lead to the end. But the problem is that in real life any means may be and generally will be undesirable on all sorts of other grounds, and the model has no way of showing how these conflicts are adjudicated.*

The matter is immediately seen to be worse when we consider another feature of desires, which we already noticed in passing. A person who believes that p and that (if p then q) is committed to the truth of q; but a person who desires that p and believes that (if p then q) is not committed to desiring that q.[6] You can want that p and believe that (if p then q) without being committed to wanting that q. For example, there is nothing *logically* wrong with a couple who want to have sexual intercourse and who believe that if they do she will get pregnant but who do not want her to get pregnant.

We can summarize these points about desire and the distinction between desire and belief as follows: desires have two special features that make it impossible to have a formal logic of practical reason parallel to our supposed formal logic of theoretical reason. The first feature we might label "the necessity of inconsistency." Any rational being in real life is bound to have inconsistent desires and other sorts of motivators. The second we might label "the nondetachability of desire." Sets of beliefs and desires as "premises" do not necessarily commit the agent to having a corresponding desire as "conclusion" even in cases where the propositional contents of the premises entail the propositional content of the conclusion. These two theses together go a long way to account for the fact that there is in the philosophical literature no remotely plausible account of a deductive logical structure of practical reason.

The moral is: as near as I can tell, the search for a formal deductive logical structure of practical reason is misguided. Such models either have little or no application, or, if they are fixed up to apply to real life, it can only be by trivializing the essential feature of practical

---

6. Of course you are not committed to a belief in the sense that you must actually have *formed* the belief that q. You might believe that p and that (if p then q) without having thought any more about it. (Someone might believe that 29 is an odd number and that it is not evenly divisible by 3, 5, 7, or 9 and that any number satisfying these conditions is prime, without ever having actually drawn the conclusion, i.e., formed the belief, that 29 is prime.)

deliberation: the reconciliation of conflicting desires and conflicting reasons for action generally and the formation of rational desires on the basis of the reconciliation. We can always construct a deductive model of any piece of reasoning; but where an essential feature of the reasoning contains both p and not p—as in I want that p and I want that not p, or I am under obligation to bring it about that p and under an obligation to bring it about that not p—deductive logic is unilluminating, because it cannot cope with such inconsistencies. The models either have to pretend that the inconsistencies do not exist or they have to pretend that they have been resolved ("by the best way all things considered"). The first route is taken by the models I criticized at the beginning, the second route is taken by my revised version. The possibility, indeed the inevitability, of contradictory desires, obligations, needs, etc. renders the Classical conception unilluminating as a model of the structure of deliberation. Furthermore even if you do fudge to the extent of trivializing the problem you still do not get a commitment to a desire as the conclusion of the argument. Modus ponens simply doesn't work for desire/belief combinations to produce a commitment to desiring the conclusion.

Does modus ponens work for desire/desire combinations? This is not the standard subject matter of means-ends reasoning, but it is worth considering the question. It seems to me that if you want that p and want that if p then q, you are committed to wanting that q, but you may still rationally also want that not q. Thus I might want for me to be very rich, and as a matter of public policy I want the very rich to be very heavily taxed, and logically speaking this commits me to the desire that if I become rich I should be very heavily taxed. I am indeed committed to such a desire, but at the same time I do not want for me to be very heavily taxed. Thus I have a commitment to a desire that is inconsistent with another desire I also have.

IV   Explanation of the Differences between Desire and Belief

Now why should there be these differences? What is it about the philosophical psychology of desire that makes it logically so unlike belief? Well, any answer to that has to be tautological, and so disappointing, but here goes anyhow.

Both desires and beliefs have propositional contents, both have a direction of fit, both represent their conditions of satisfaction, and both represent their conditions of satisfaction under certain aspects. So, what is the difference that accounts for the different logical properties of desires and beliefs? The difference derives from two related features, the difference in direction of fit and the difference in commitment. The job of beliefs is to represent how things are (downward direction of fit) and the holder of a belief is committed to its truth. To the extent that the belief does this or fails to do it, it will be true or false respectively. The job of desires is not to represent how things are, but how we would like them to be. And desires can succeed in representing how we would like things to be even if things don't turn out to be the way we would like them to be. In the case of belief, the propositional content represents a certain state of affairs as actually existing. But in the case of desire, the propositional content does not function to represent an actual state of affairs, but rather a *desired* state of affairs, which may be actual, nonexistent, possible, impossible, or what have you. And the propositional content represents the state of affairs under the aspects that the agent finds desirable. There is nothing wrong with unsatisfied desires, qua desires, whereas there is something wrong with unsatisfied beliefs, qua beliefs, namely, they are false. They fail in their job of representing how things are. Desires succeed in their job of representing how we would like things to be even in cases where things are not the way we would like them to be, that is, even in cases where their conditions of success are not met. Roughly speaking, when my belief is false, it is the belief that is at fault. When my desire is unsatisfied, it is the world that is at fault.

The two logical features of desire, inconsistency and nondetachability, both derive from this underlying feature of desire: desires are inclinations toward states of affairs (possible, actual, or impossible) under aspects. There is no necessary irrationality involved in the fact that one can be inclined and disinclined to the same state of affairs under the same aspect; and the fact that one is inclined to a state of affairs under an aspect together with knowledge about the consequences of the existence of that state of affairs does not guarantee that, if rational, one will be inclined to those consequences.

But if you try to state parallel points about belief it doesn't work. Beliefs are convictions that states of affairs exist under aspects. But one cannot rationally be convinced both that a state of affairs exists and does not exist under the same aspect. And the fact that one is convinced of the existence of a state of affairs under an aspect together with knowledge about the consequences of the existence of that state of affairs does guarantee that, if one is rational, one will be convinced of (or at least committed to) those consequences. It is important to emphasize that

these features of belief follow from two of its characteristics: downward direction of fit and commitment. If
you just have downward direction of fit that is not
enough. Thus hypotheses that one may form about how
things might be also have the downward direction of fit.
But one can consistently and rationally entertain inconsistent hypotheses in a way that one cannot consistently and rationally hold inconsistent beliefs, and this is
because beliefs, unlike hypotheses, though both involve
the downward direction of fit, have the additional feature
of commitment.

These features of desire are characteristic of other sorts
of representations with the world-to-word direction of fit.
The features of inconsistency and nondetachability apply
to needs and obligations as well as desires. I can consistently have inconsistent needs and obligations and I do
not necessarily need the consequences of my needs, nor
am I obligated to achieve the consequences of my obligations. Examples of all these phenomena are not hard
to find: I might need to take some medicine to alleviate
one set of symptoms, but I need to avoid that medicine
because it aggravates another set of symptoms. I have an
obligation to meet my class at the university, but I also
have an obligation to give a lecture at another university,
because I promised to do so a year earlier. I need to take
aspirin to avoid heart ailment, but aspirin upsets my
stomach, and so I need to avoid aspirin. Jones has an
obligation to marry Smith because she made a promise,
but marrying Smith will make her parents unhappy, and
she does not have an obligation to make her parents
unhappy. It is amazing, by the way, how much the ref-
erential opacity of all of these concepts, "obligation,"
"need," etc., is neglected in the literature.

In objecting to this account, one might say, "Look, when I believe something, what I believe is that it is true. So, if I believe something and know that it can't be true unless something else is true, then my belief and knowledge must commit me to the truth of that other thing as well. But now why isn't it the same for desire? When I want something what I want is that something should happen or be the case, but if I know that it can't happen or be the case unless something else happens or is the case then surely I must be committed to wanting that something else." But the analogy breaks down. If I want to drill your tooth to fill your cavity and I know that drilling the tooth will cause pain it simply does not follow that I am in any way committed to causing pain, much less committed to wanting to cause pain. And the proof of this distinction is quite simple: if I fail to cause pain one of my beliefs is thereby false, but none of my desires is thereby unsatisfied.

When I want something, I want it only under certain aspects. "Yes, but when I believe something I believe it only under certain aspects as well. Sentences about belief are just as opaque as sentences about desire." Yes, but there is this difference: when something is desired under certain aspects it is, in general, the aspects that make it desirable. Indeed the relation between the aspects and the reasons for desiring are quite different from the case of belief, since *the specification of the reasons for desiring something is, in general, already a specification of the content of the desire;* but the specification of the evidence on the basis of which I hold a belief is not in general itself part of the specification of the belief. The reasons for believing stand in a different relation to the propositions believed than the contents of reasons for wanting do to the proposition that is the content of the desire, because in general the statements of the reasons for wanting state part of what one wants. If one wants something for a reason then that reason is part of the content of one's desire. For example, if I want it to rain in order to make my garden grow, then I both want that it should rain and that my garden should grow. If I believe it will rain and I believe that the rain will make my garden grow, then I both believe that it will rain and that my garden will grow. But there is still a crucial difference. If I want it to rain *in order to* make my garden grow, then my reason for wanting it to rain is part of the whole content of the entire complex desire. My reason for believing both that it will rain and that the rain will make my garden grow, on the other hand, has to do with a lot of evidence about meteorology, the reliability of weather predictions, and the function of moisture in producing plant growth. All of these considerations count as evidence for the truth of my belief, but they are not themselves the content of that very belief. But in the case of my desire, the role of reasons is not at all like that of evidence, for the reasons state the aspects under which the phenomenon in question is desired. The reasons, in short, are part of the content of the complex desire.

In sum: beliefs have the mind-to-world direction of fit, and the holder of the belief is committed to the fit actually existing, that is, he is committed to the truth of the belief. Desires have the world-to-mind direction of fit, and the holder of a desire need not be committed to its ever being satisfied. The job of desire is not to represent how things are, but how we would like them to be. It is the notion of "the commitment to how things are" that blocks the simple possibility of consciously held contradictory beliefs, and that requires a commitment to the consequences of one's beliefs, but there is no such block and no such requirement when it is a question of how we would like things to be. In spite of certain formal similarities, belief is really radically unlike desire in both its logical and its phenomenological features.

For these reasons, it is misleading to think of theoretical reason as reasoning about what to believe in the way that we think of practical reason as reasoning about what to do. What one should believe is dependent on what is the case. Theoretical reasoning, therefore, is only derivatively about what to believe. It is primarily about what is the case—what must be the case given certain premises. Furthermore, we can now see that it is misleading to think even that there is a "logic" of theoretical reason. There is just logic—which deals with logical relations between, for example, propositions. Logic tells us more about the rational structure of theoretical reason than it does about the rational structure of practical reason, because there is a close connection between the rational constraints on belief and the logical relations between propositions. This connection derives from the fact that, to repeat, beliefs are meant to be true. But there is no such close connection between the structure of desire and the structure of logic. Because of the upward direction of fit of desires, I both can and do have conflicting desires even after all the facts are in.

V Some Special Features of Intentions

I have been concentrating on desires, but intentions are in important respects different from desires. Like desires, intentions have the upward direction of fit, but unlike desires, the are always about the agent as subject matter and they are causally self-referential. My intention is carried out only if I act by way of carrying out the intention. For this reason intentions have a logical constraint quite unlike desire. It is logically inconsistent to have inconsistent intentions in a way that it is not logically inconsistent to have inconsistent desires. Intentions are designed to cause actions, and for that reason they cannot function if they are inconsistent. This prohibition against inconsistency is shared by other causally self-referential motivators, such as orders and promises, even though they also have the world-to-mind direction of fit. It's okay—up to a point—for a speaker to say reflectively "I both wish you would go and wish you would stay." But he is irrational if he says simultaneously "Go!" and "Stay!" and you are equally irrational if you form the simultaneous intentions to to go and to stay, or make simultaneous promises both to go and to stay. One cannot consistently have inconsistent intentions or make inconsistent promises and issue inconsistent orders, because intentions, orders, and promises are designed to cause actions, and there cannot be inconsistent actions. For the same reason intentions, orders, and promises commit the agent to the belief that the action is possible, but it is not possible to carry out both of two inconsistent actions. Desires and obligations in general have no such condition. One can hold inconsistent desires and be under inconsistent obligations.

Does this feature give us the possibility of a principle of detachment for intentions? If I intend that p and I believe that if p then q, am I committed to intending that q? I think not; however, the question is trickier than it might appear at first sight, and because it ties in with Kant's famous principle, I now turn to a discussion of Kant.

VI "He Who Wills the End Wills the Means"

No discussion of the logic of practical reason would be complete without at least some mention of Kant's famous doctrine that he who wills the end wills the means. Does this give us a deductive logical principle of practical reason? That is to say, does the statement "I will end E" logically commit me to "I will means M" at least in cases where M is a necessary condition of achieving E? Is it analogous to the way "I believe p" commits me to "I believe q," in cases where q is a logical consequence of p?

Well, it all depends on what we mean by "will." On a perfectly natural interpretation the doctrine is just false, for reasons that I have stated earlier. If willing is a matter of having a very strong desire or pro-attitude toward some future course of action that I am capable of engaging in, then it is simply not the case that when I will the end I am logically committed to willing the means. As I suggested earlier, it may be the case that the means are out of the question for one reason or another. I very much want to eliminate my flu symptoms, but the only way to eliminate the symptoms is to commit suicide, there being no known cure, but all the same, I am not committed to willing suicide.

So if we interpret "will" as desire, Kant's principle comes out false. But suppose we interpret it as intention, both prior intention and intention-in-action. Suppose I have a prior intention to do E and I believe that doing M is a necessary condition of doing E. Am I committed to the intention to do M? It seems to me we need to distinguish between having a commitment to doing something that I know will involve doing M and having a commitment to doing M intentionally. Trivially it follows from the fact that I intend to do E and I know that doing E necessarily involves doing M that I have a commitment to doing something intentionally that will involve M. But I need not thereby have any commitment at all to doing M

intentionally. Thus consider our earlier example of my intention to fix your tooth. We have as premises:

Intend (I fix your tooth).

Bel (If I fix your tooth I cause you pain).

But I am not thereby committed to the conclusion

Intend (I cause you pain).

An intention commits me to a course of action, but it does not commit me to doing all of the things that I know are involved in carrying out the original intention. So the fact that I have an intention to bring it about that p and I have a belief that if p then q does not commit me to having the intention to bring it about that q. The argument for this claim, using the above example, is that when I cause you pain, I do not do so intentionally, but only as a by-product of my intentional action. And the argument for that point, in turn, is that causing you pain is not part of the conditions of satisfaction of my intention, nor is it implied by the conditions of satisfaction of my intention, because if I fail to cause you pain, I do not fail in what I was trying to do. When I fix your tooth I may have a firm belief to the effect that fixing your tooth will cause you pain, but I am not thereby committed to the intention to cause you pain. And the conclusive proof is given if we ask what counts as succeeding or failing. If I fail to cause you pain, it is not my original intention that has failed; rather one of my beliefs has turned out to be false. So it is simply not the case in general that anybody who wills the end (in the sense of having an intention to achieve that end) thereby wills everything that occurs as a known part of carrying out that intention.

However, there is a type of case in which Kant's principle is true. Suppose I have the intention-in-action to fix
your tooth, and suppose that I also have the belief that the
necessary condition of fixing your tooth is that I *intentionally* drill your tooth. This case differs from the previous
case because drilling your tooth is not a collateral part of
fixing your tooth in the way that causing you pain is a
collateral part of fixing your tooth. Rather, it is a *means*
that must be intended in order that the original intention
can be carried out. So, there is a natural interpretation of
Kant's principle where it turns out to be correct, and that
interpretation is as follows:

If I intend an end E, and I know that in order to achieve
E I must intentionally do M, then I am committed to
intending to do M. In that sense it does seem to me that
"he who wills the end" is committed to willing the means.

VII Conclusion

The moral of this discussion can be stated quite briefly.
Deductive logic deals with logical relations between
propositions, predicates, sets, etc. In the strict sense there
is no such thing as a deductive logic of practical reason,
but then in the strict sense there is no such thing as a
deductive logic of theoretical reason. Because of the combination of commitment and direction of fit of beliefs, it is
possible to get a mapping of the logical relations occurring
in theoretical reason onto deductive logic of a sort that is
not possible for practical reason. Why the difference? In
two important respects desire is unlike belief. Desire has
the upward direction of fit, and a person with a desire is
not committed to the satisfaction of that desire in the way

that a person who holds a belief is committed to the truth of the belief. This allows for the two features of desire we noted earlier, the necessity of inconsistency and the non-detachability of desire. Intentions are a bit more like belief because they do involve a commitment to the satisfaction of the intention. Nonetheless, the person who has an intention is not committed to intending to achieve all of the consequences of the achievement of his intention. He is committed only to those means that are necessarily intended in order to achieve his ends. For these reasons there will not be a "deductive logic of practical reason" even in the limited sense in which we found that it is possible to have a deductive logic of theoretical reason.

9   Consciousness, Free Action, and the Brain

I   Consciousness and the Brain

Much of this book is about the gap and its implications for the study of rationality. The gap is a feature of human consciousness, and in that sense the book is about consciousness. The gap is that feature of the consciousness of voluntary actions, whereby the actions are experienced as not having sufficient psychological causal conditions to determine them. That is part of what is meant by saying that they are, psychologically at least, free. There is no doubt that the gap is psychologically real, but is it otherwise empirically real? Is it neurobiologically real? If human freedom really exists, it must be a feature of brain function. The aim of this chapter is to situate an account of volitional consciousness, or the consciousness of free action, within an account of consciousness generally, and in turn to situate that account within an account of brain functions.

Because we are about to launch into a discussion of a traditional philosophical problem, it is a good idea to step back and ask why we still have such a problem. I said in chapter 1 that such problems typically arise when we have a conflict between two apparently inconsistent views, neither of which we feel we can give up. In this case the belief in free will is based on our conscious experiences of the gap, but we also have a fundamental metaphysical assumption that the universe is a closed physical system entirely determined by the laws of physics. What to do? The first thing to notice is that the most fundamental laws of physics, at the quantum mechanical level, are not deterministic. The second thing to notice is that the laws of physics do not actually determine anything. The laws are a set of statements that describe the relations between various physical quantities, and sometimes these statements describe causally sufficient conditions in particular situations, and sometimes they do not. The third thing to notice is that the claim that the universe is a closed physical system, insofar as it has a clear meaning at all, is a proposition that, over the centuries, we have rendered true by stipulation. As soon as we think that something really exists in the empirical world and we think we understand it even remotely, we call it "physical." As parts of the real world, consciousness, intentionality, and rationality are "physical" phenomena, like anything else. Such reflections do not solve our problem but they should lead us to think about it in less restricted ways. Let us begin by asking how consciousness fits into the "physical" universe.

In the past ten years or so, a certain conception of consciousness and its relation to the brain has been emerging and becoming more commonly accepted in philosophy and neuroscience. It is profoundly opposed to both dualism and materialism, as they have been traditionally construed. In particular it is opposed to those conceptions of consciousness that attempt to deny the irreducible subjectivity of conscious states, or attempt to reduce consciousness to behavior, to computer programs, or to functional states of a system. This conception of consciousness is becoming more commonly accepted, but it is still controversial.

Here it is: consciousness is a real biological phenomenon. It consists of inner, qualitative, subjective, unified states of sentience, awareness, thoughts, and feelings. These states begin when we awake in the morning from a dreamless sleep, and they continue throughout the day until we become unconscious again. Dreams are a form of consciousness on this account, though they are in many respects different from normal waking consciousness. The key features of consciousness, on this conception, are that it is qualitative, subjective, and unified, in ways that I will now explain. For every conscious state, there is a certain qualitative feel to the state. There is something that it is like, or something that it feels like, to be in a state of that type. This is as much true of thoughts, such as the thought that two plus two equals four, as it is of the taste of the beer, the smell of the rose, or the sight of the blue of the sky. All conscious states, whether perceptions or thought processes, are, in the sense that I am trying to explain, qualitative. They are furthermore subjective in the sense that they exist only as experienced by a human or animal subject. And they have an additional feature that is worth emphasizing: conscious experiences, such as the taste of beer or the smell of a rose, always come as part of a unified conscious field. I do not, for example, right now feel just the pressure of the shirt on my back and the aftertaste of coffee in my mouth, and the sight of the computer screen in front of me; but I have all of those as part of a single unified conscious field.

What is the relationship between consciousness so defined, and brain processes? You will recognize that as the traditional mind-body problem. I believe that in its philosophical form (though—alas—not in its neurobiological form), the mind-body problem has a rather simple solution. Here it is: all of our conscious states are caused by lower-level neuronal processes in the brain, and they are themselves features of the brain. You can see this quite obviously in the case of pains. My present pains are caused by a series of neuron firings that begin at peripheral nerve endings, and continue up the spinal column, through the tract of Lissauer, and into the thalamus and other basal regions of the brain. Some of these spread out into the sensory cortex, especially Zone 1, and eventually this sequence causes me to feel a pain. What are these pains? The pains themselves are simply higher-level or system features of the brain. The subjective, qualitative experiences of pain in the total conscious field are caused by neurobiological processes in the brain and the rest of the central nervous system, and they are themselves, as elements of the unified field of consciousness, features of the system of neurons and other cells that constitute the human brain.

What exactly are the neuronal processes that cause these conscious experiences? At present we do not know the answer to that question. We are making some progress, but progress has been slow. Currently there are, as far as I know, at least two general approaches to the problem of consciousness, and in order to get into the main topic of this discussion, I have to say a little bit about each of these. The first approach I call "the building block approach." The idea is that our conscious field consists of a series of separate components, which are the individual conscious experiences. These elements make up the total field in the way the building blocks of a house make up the house. The assumption behind the building block research project is that if we could find exactly how even one building block works, how, for example, we visually experience the color red, that might give us a key to the whole problem of consciousness, because the mechanisms by which the conscious experiences of red are produced would presumably resemble the mechanisms by which the experiences of sounds or tastes are produced. The idea is to find the neuronal correlate of consciousness (NCC) for individual sensory experiences, and then generalize from them to an account of consciousness generally.

For reasons I have tried to explain elsewhere[1] I think the building block approach is wrong. Each building block occurs only in a subject who is already conscious. I do not believe that we can discover, for example, the mechanisms that produce consciousness by trying to discover the mechanisms that produce the experience of red, because only a subject who is *already* conscious can have the experience of red. The building block approach would predict that in an otherwise unconscious subject, if you could produce the NCC for a single building block, say, the experience of red, then that subject would suddenly have a flash of red and no other conscious state. This is a possible empirical hypothesis, but it seems to me most unlikely, given what we know about how the brain works. It seems to me much more likely that we will come to understand how the brain causes consciousness if we can find the difference between the neurophysiological

1. "Consciousness," *Annual Review of Neuroscience* 2000, vol. 23, pp. 557–578.

behavior of an unconscious brain and a conscious brain. What we would really like to know is, how does the subject become conscious in the first place? Once the subject is conscious, particular experiences can be induced that will modify the existing unified conscious field.

There is another line of research, which I call "the unified field approach." Instead of thinking of consciousness as made up of a series of little bricks, a series of building blocks, we should take seriously the unity that I spoke of earlier and think of the entire conscious field as a unity. We should think of the individual perceptual inputs not as *creating* consciousness, but as *modifying* a preexisting consciousness. On this account, instead of looking for the NCC of red, for example, we should try to find the differences between the conscious brain and the unconscious brain.

On the account that I am presenting, the three features I mentioned, qualitativeness, subjectivity, and unity, are not three distinct features, but different aspects of the same feature. Once a feature is qualitative, in the sense I have explained, it must be subjective, because the notion of qualitativeness that we are talking about is something that is experienced by a subject. And once there are experiences that are subjective and qualitative, they are necessarily unified. You can see this again with a thought experiment. If you imagine your present state of consciousness broken into seventeen pieces, you are not imagining a single conscious field with seventeen parts, you are imagining seventeen different conscious fields. Qualitativeness, subjectivity, and unity are not different features; rather they are all aspects of the one feature, and that feature is the very essence of consciousness.

II Consciousness and Voluntary Action

When we explore the character of the conscious field, we discover a remarkable fact. There is a striking and dramatic difference between the qualitative character of perceptual experiences and the qualitative character of voluntary actions. In the case of perceptual experiences, I am a passive recipient of experiences that are caused by the external environment. So if I hold up my hand in front of my face, for example, it is not up to me whether or not I see a hand. The perceptual apparatus and the external stimuli are sufficient by themselves to cause in me a visual experience of my hand in front of my face. I do not have a choice in the matter; the causes are sufficient to produce the experience.

If, on the other hand, I decide to raise my right hand over my head, it is entirely up to me. It is up to me whether I raise my right hand or my left hand, how far up I raise each one, etc. Voluntary action simply has a different conscious feel to it than perception. I am not, of course, suggesting that there is no voluntaristic element at all in perception. I think there is. For example in the Gestalt switching examples one can at will shift one's perception from the duck to the rabbit and back. At present I just want to call attention to some of the striking features of voluntary action that are in sharp contrast to the experience of perception.

The gap that we have been discussing arises only for voluntary action. First there is a gap between the reasons for a decision and the decision, second, a gap between the decision and its execution, and third, a gap between the initiation of an action and its continuation to completion. At bottom I think all three gaps are manifestations of the same phenomenon, because all three are manifestations of volitional consciousness.

As we saw in chapter 3, the logical structure of explanation of human behavior where the agent voluntarily acts on a reason requires us to postulate an irreducible self. We can now add to this purely formal notion of self the point that the self so construed requires the unified field of consciousness. We had to postulate a self to make intelligible the phenomenon of free rational actions. But the self so postulated requires a unified conscious field. The self is not identical with the field, but its operations, whereby it makes decisions on the basis of reasons and acts to carry out those decisions, requires a unified field containing both cognitive elements such as perceptions and memories as well as volitional elements such as deliberations and actions. Why? Well, if you try to imagine the mind as a Humean bundle of unconnected perceptions, there is no way that the self can operate in the bundle. In order for the self to operate in making decisions you would have to have a different self for each different element of the bundle.

III Free Will

I now want to apply the lessons we have learned so far to a discussion of the traditional problem of the freedom of the will. There are no doubt many different senses of "free will" and "determinism"; but for this discussion, the problem of the freedom of the will arises for those parts of the conscious field in which we experience the gap. These are the cases that are traditionally called "volition." There is no question that we have experiences of the sort that I have been calling experiences of the gap; that is, we experience our own normal voluntary actions in such a way that we sense alternative possibilities of action open to us, and we sense that the psychological antecedents of the action are not sufficient to fix the action. Notice that on this account the problem of free will arises only for consciousness, and it arises only for volitional or active consciousness; it does not arise for perceptual consciousness.

What then, exactly, is the problem of the freedom of the will? Free will is typically taken to be opposed to determinism. The thesis of determinism about actions is that every action is determined by antecedently sufficient causal conditions. For every action, the causal conditions of the action in that context are sufficient to produce that action. Thus, where actions are concerned, nothing could happen differently from the way that it does in fact happen. The thesis of free will, sometimes called "libertarianism," states that some actions, at least, are such that the antecedent causal conditions of the action are not causally sufficient to produce the action. Granted that the action did occur, and that it did occur for a reason, all the same, the agent could have done something else, given the same causal antecedents of the action.

The most widely held contemporary view on the topic of free will is called "compatibilism." The compatibilist view is that if we properly understand these terms, freedom of the will is completely compatible with determinism. To say that an action is determined is just to say that it has causes like any other event, and to say that it is free is just to say that it is determined by certain kinds of causes, and not others. So if someone puts a gun to my head and tells me to raise my arm, my action is not free; but if I raise my arm by way of voting, as we say, "freely," or "of my own free will," then my action is free. Though in both cases, both in the case of voting and the case with the gun at my head, my action is completely causally determined.

I think compatibilism simply misses the point about the problem of free will. As I have defined it, libertarianism is definitely inconsistent with determinism. To repeat, the determinist says, "Every action is preceded by causally sufficient conditions that determine that action." And the libertarian asserts the negation of that: "For some actions the antecedent causal conditions are not sufficient to determine the action."

I think there is no doubt a sense of "free" and "determined" in which compatibilism is right. When for example people march in the streets waving signs demanding "freedom," they are usually not much interested in the laws of physics. They typically want fewer government restrictions on their actions, or some such; and they are not concerned with the causal antecedents of their actions. But this sense of "freedom," where it means absence of external constraints, is irrelevant to the problem of the freedom of the will, as I have stated it. I cannot think of any interesting philosophical problem of free will to which compatibilism provides a substantive answer.

We come by the conviction of the freedom of the will, in my sense, because of the experiences of the gap. So the problem of the freedom of the will can be posed as follows: what reality corresponds to those experiences? Granted that we experience our actions as not having antecedently sufficient, psychological, causal conditions, why should we take this psychological fact seriously? Is it not possible that the neurobiological underpinnings of the psychology are causally sufficient to determine the action, even though the psychological level by itself is not causally sufficient? And could there not be unconscious psychological causes determining the act? Even granted the psychological reality of the gap, we still have a problem of free will left over. What exactly is it and how exactly might we go about solving it?

To make the problem completely clear, consider the following example. Suppose I am offered a choice at time t_1 between two glasses of red wine, a Burgundy and a Bordeaux, on a table in front of me. Let us suppose that I find both attractive, and that after 10 seconds, at time t_2, I decide in favor of the Burgundy and I reach out and lift it from the table and take a drink from it. Call that Act A, and we will suppose it begins at t_2 and continues for a few seconds until t_3. For the sake of simplicity we will suppose there is no psychological time gap between the decision and its execution. The instant I decided on the Burgundy at t_2, the intention-in-action began and I was reaching for the glass. (In real time, of course, there is a time gap of about 200 milliseconds between the onset of my intention-in-action and the actual onset of the muscle movements.) Let us suppose also that this was a voluntary action with a gap: I was not in the grip of an obsession or other sufficient cause that determined the action. We will simply stipulate that in this example there were no unconscious psychological causes sufficient to determine the action. My action was free in the sense that the psychological causes, conscious and unconscious, operating on me were not sufficient to determine Act A. What does that mean exactly? At least this much. A complete specification of all the psychological causes operating on me at t_1, with all their causal powers, including any psychological laws relevant to the case, would not be sufficient to entail that I would perform Act A *under any description*. They would fail to entail not only: "JRS will select the Burgundy," but also: "This arm will move in this direction and these fingers will close over this object." In this respect the psychological causes at t_1 are unlike standard physical causes. If while reaching for the Burgundy I inadvertently knock an empty glass off the table, a description of the causes operating on the glass beginning at the moment of impact will be sufficient to imply that the glass will fall to the floor.

I said earlier that all of these psychological processes are themselves caused by and realized in the brain. So at t_1, my conscious perception of the two glasses of red wine, and my conscious reflections on their relative merits, were caused by lower level neurobiological processes in the brain and realized in the structure of the brain. Now here is the problem: Assuming there were no further inputs to the brain, such as further perceptions, were the neurobiological processes occurring in me at t_1 causally sufficient to determine the total state of my brain at t_2? And was the total state of my brain at t_2 sufficient to cause the continuation of the brain processes that went on between t_2 and t_3? If so then there is a description of the act A under which it has antecedently sufficient causal conditions, because the state of my brain at t_2 was one in which the neurotransmitters were causing the onset of the muscle contractions that constituted the bodily component of act A, and the continuation of the processes from t_2 to t_3 was sufficient to cause the continuation of the muscle contractions to the completion of the action at t_3. The problem of the freedom of the will comes down to this: assuming no further relevant external stimuli enter the brain, was the brain state at t_1, neurobiologically described, causally sufficient to determine the brain state at t_2, and was the state at t_2 sufficient to carry it to t_3? *If the answer to those questions is yes, for this and all other relevantly similar cases, then we have no free will.* The psychologically real gap corresponds to no neurobiological reality and the freedom of the will is a massive illusion. *If the answer to that question is no, then given certain assumptions about the role of consciousness, we really do have free will.*

Now, why does everything come down to this? Because the brain state at t_2 was sufficient to cause the muscle movements of the action to begin, and the brain states from t_2 to t_3 are sufficient to carry the muscle movements through to the completion of the action. Once the acetylcholene hits the axon end plates of the motor neurons, then assuming the rest of the physiological apparatus is functioning normally, the muscles are going to move by straightforward causal necessity. The first two gaps occur prior to the onset of the muscle movements, and the third gap occurs between the onset of the action and its continuation to completion. The gap is a real psychological phenomenon, but if it is a real phenomenon that makes a difference to the world, it must have a neurobiological correlate. As a neurobiological question, the reality of the gap comes to this: are the states of the brain from t_1 to t_3 sufficient so that each state determines the next state by causally sufficient conditions? The problem of the freedom of the will is a straight problem in neurobiology about the relations of certain sorts of consciousness to neurobiological processes. If it is an interesting question at all, it is a scientific question about the causation of certain sorts of conscious actions. I intend now to go over this matter carefully and try to get to the bottom of it.

IV   Hypothesis 1: Psychological Libertarianism with Neurobiological Determinism

To begin, we have to remind ourselves of what we know so far. All of our states of consciousness are caused by bottom-up neurobiological processes in the brain. They themselves can cause subsequent conscious states or bodily movements because they are grounded in the neurobiology. Thus, in cases where there are no gaps, the left-right causation through time at the top level is exactly matched by a left-right causation through time at the bottom level. For example, my intention-in-action is caused by lower level processes in the brain. It in turn causes my arm to go up. The neurobiological processes that cause the intention-in-action in turn cause a series of physiological changes that cause and realize my arm movements. These relations are typical of any system that has causally real levels of description. Thus a car engine has the same set of formal relationships. No epiphenomenalism is a result of these relations. The intention-in-action is as causally real as the solidity of the piston. Furthermore, there is no causal overdetermination. We are not talking about independent causal sequences, but rather the same causal sequences described at different levels. Once again, the analogy of the car engine works perfectly. We can describe the causation at the level of molecules or we can describe it at the level of pistons and cylinders. These are not independent causal sequences, but the same causal sequence described at different levels.

In earlier writings[2] I represented these relations that make up voluntary action as a parallelogram that looks like this:

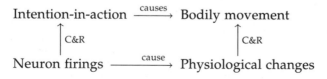

2. John R. Searle, *Intentionality: An Essay in the Philosophy of Mind*, New York: Cambridge University Press, 1983, p. 270.

At the top level, the intention-in-action causes the bodily movement, at the bottom level the neuron firings cause physiological changes, and at each point the bottom level causes and realizes (C&R) the top level. As represented the whole structure is deterministic at every stage.

What about cases with a gap, when I deliberate and then form a decision, for example? It seems to me there are at least two possibilities. The first possibility (hypothesis 1) is this: the indeterminacy at the psychological level is matched by a completely deterministic system at the neurobiological level. So, though we have a psychological gap between the reasons for action and the decision, we do not have any gap at the neurobiological level between the neurophysiological realization of the reasons for the action in the form of beliefs and desires, and the subsequent neurophysiological realization of the decision. Here is what it would look like:

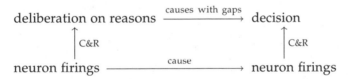

deliberation on reasons $\xrightarrow{\text{causes with gaps}}$ decision

$\uparrow$ C&R $\uparrow$ C&R

neuron firings $\xrightarrow{\text{cause}}$ neuron firings

In this case the gap produces an asymmetry between the parallelogram of voluntary action and the parallelogram of cognition. You can see this if you contrast decision and action with memory. Suppose I see a dramatic scene, say, a car accident, and I then have a memory of the car accident that I saw. I had a psychological event, the perceptual experience, and that psychological event was sufficient causal grounds for the subsequent psychological event of the recollection of the incident that I observed. But we know that all of that is made possible because we have a sequence of causally sufficient conditions in the neurobiology. The actual perception, neurobiologically speaking, is sufficient to lay down memory traces in short-term and long-term memory, whereby I remember the psychological event. That is to say, in the case of cognition, such as the relation of perception and memory, sufficient conditions at the top, or psychological, level, are matched by sufficient conditions at the bottom, or neurophysiological, level. You get a perfect parallelogram. For volition, as opposed to cognition, you do not get such a parallelogram. In the case of volition, psychological indeterminacy would coexist with neurobiological determinism.

If this is how nature works, then we would have a kind of compatibilism. Psychological libertarianism would be compatible with neurobiological determinism. The psychological processes, though they are themselves caused by lower-level neuronal processes, would nonetheless not be sufficient causal conditions for the subsequent psychological event of intentional action. At t_1, the psychological processes by which I am deciding which glass of wine to drink are entirely causally determined by lower-level neuronal processes by bottom-up causation. At t_2 I decide on the Burgundy. That decision, again, is entirely fixed by bottom-up causation, even though there is a gap at the psychological level between my reflection on the reasons and my decision. From t_2 to t_3, the muscle movement components of action A, my taking the wine in my hand and to my mouth, are caused by neurobiological processes, by bottom-up causation, even though, again, there is a gap at the psychological level between the initiation of the action and its continuation to completion. So we have gaps at the psychological level, but no gap in the form of bottom-up causation between the neurobiological level

and the psychological level, and no gaps at the neurobiological level between any state of the system and the
next state of the system. This would give us physiological
determinism with psychological libertarianism.[3]

This result, however, is intellectually very unsatisfying,
because, in a word, it is a modified form of epiphenomenalism. It says that the psychological processes of
rational decision making do not really matter. The entire
system is deterministic at the bottom level, and the idea
that the top level has an element of freedom is simply a
systematic illusion. It seems to me at t_1 that I have a choice
between the Burgundy and the Bordeaux and that the
causes operating on me are not sufficient to determine the
choice. But I am mistaken. The total state of my brain at t_1
is entirely sufficient to determine every bodily movement
as well as every thought process from t_1 to t_2 to t_3. If hypothesis 1 is true, then every muscle movement as well as
every conscious thought, including the conscious experience of the gap, the experience of "free" decision making,
is entirely fixed in advance; and the only thing we can say
about psychological indeterminism at the higher level is
that it gives us a systematic illusion of free will. The thesis
is epiphenomenalistic in this respect: there is a feature of
our conscious lives, rational decision making and trying to
carry out the decision, where we experience the gap and
we experience the processes as making a causal difference
to our behavior, but they do not in fact make any difference. The bodily movements were going to be exactly the
same regardless of how these processes occurred.

---

3. I said this is a form of compatibilism, but it differs from traditional
compatibilism, because the traditional version postulates determinism at
every level. This version postulates psychological indeterminism with
neurobiological determinism.

Maybe that is how it will turn out, but if so, the hypothesis seems to me to run against everything we know about evolution. It would have the consequence that the incredibly elaborate, complex, sensitive, and—above all—biologically expensive system of human and animal conscious rational decision making would actually make no difference whatever to the life and survival of the organisms. Epiphenomenalism is a possible thesis, but it is absolutely incredible, and if we seriously accepted it, it would make a change in our worldview, that is, in our conception of our relations to the world, more radical than any previous change, including the Copernican Revolution, Einsteinian relativity theory, and quantum mechanics.

Why would hypothesis 1 render consciousness any more epiphenomenal than any other higher-level feature of a physical system? After all, the solidity of the piston in the car engine is entirely explained by the behavior of the molecules but that does not render solidity epiphenomenal. The difference is this: the essential characteristics of solidity matter to the performance of the engine, but the essential characteristic of conscious decision making, the experience of the gap, would not matter in the least to the performance of the agent. The bodily movements would have been the same, regardless of the experiences of the gap.

V   Hypothesis 2: System Causation with Consciousness and Indeterminacy

On the alternate view (hypothesis 2), the absence of causally sufficient conditions at the psychological level is matched by a parallel lack of causally sufficient conditions at the neurobiological level. But what could that possibly mean? What is the diagram supposed to look like on any such hypothesis? At this point it seems to me we have to examine critically the assumptions built into our diagrammatic representation with its metaphors of "bottom-up," "top-down," "levels of description," etc. I think they are going to prove inadequate at this stage. The problem is this: the idea that consciousness is a higher-level or surface feature of the brain gives us a picture of consciousness as like the paint on the surface of the table. Then the question of top-down and bottom-up causation is one of reaching up or reaching down. All of that is wrong. Consciousness is no more on the surface of the brain than liquidity is on the surface of the water. Rather the idea we are trying to express is that consciousness is a *system feature*. It is a feature of the whole system and is present—literally—at all of the relevant places of the system in the same way that the water in a glass is liquid throughout. Consciousness does not exist in an individual synapse any more than liquidity exists in an individual molecule. But then the picture of different levels moving in parallel, which is represented in our diagram, is wrong. The whole system moves at once. What we have to suppose, if we believe that our conscious experience of freedom is not a complete illusion, is that the whole system moves forward toward the decision making, and toward the implementing of the decision in actual actions; that the conscious rationality at the top level is realized all the way down, and that means that the whole system moves in a way that is causal, but not based on causally sufficient conditions.

In order to ask how the gap might work in the neurobiology, we have to be clear about how it works in the conscious psychology. In the case of conscious rationality, nothing fills the gap. A person simply makes up his or her mind, and then simply acts. Those facts are intelligible to us only if we postulate a conscious rational agent, capable of reflecting on its own reasons, and then acting on the basis of those reasons. I am reluctant to use the traditional jargon, but I argued earlier that that postulation amounts to a postulation of a self. We can make sense of rational, free conscious action, only if we postulate a conscious self. But that postulation makes sense only relative to the fact of a unified conscious field of subjectivity. You cannot account for the rational self just in terms of a Humean bundle of disconnected perceptions. So the second hypothesis is not that you get a split between the indeterminacy at the level of the psychology, and the determinacy at the level of the neurobiology, but rather that the whole system moves forward at once, as a conscious, rational system, which, as far as its third-person ontology is concerned, consists entirely of neurobiological elements; and the lack of causally sufficient conditions at the psychological level goes all the way down. That will seem less puzzling to us if we reflect that our urge to stop at the level of the neurons is simply a matter of prejudice. If we keep on going down to the quantum-mechanical level, then it may seem less surprising that we have an absence of causally sufficient conditions.

Sperry somewhere uses an example of "top-down" causation that I once thought was weak but now seems to me enlightening. Think of a single molecule in a wheel that is rolling. The whole structure of the wheel and its movements as a wheel determine the movements of the molecule, even though the wheel is made of such molecules. And what is true of one molecule is true of all the molecules. The movements of each molecule are affected by the system even though the system consists entirely of the molecules. The right way to think of this is not so much "top-down" but as system causation. The system, as a system, has causal effects on each element, even though the system is made up of the elements. Now, analogously, on hypothesis 2, the system as a conscious system can have effects on individual elements, neurons and synapses, even though the system is made up of them. Each molecule in a liquid is affected by the liquidity of the system, even though there are no objects but molecules. Each molecule in a solid is affected by the solidity of the system, even though there are no objects but molecules. Similarly in the conscious brain, each neuron in the conscious portions of the system can be affected by the consciousness of the brain, even though there are no objects but neurons (with glial cells, and the rest).

So if hypothesis 2 is right, we have to suppose that the consciousness of the system has effects on elements of the system, even though the system is composed of the elements, in the same way that the solidity of the wheel has effects on the molecules even though the wheel is composed of molecules. So far so good, but the analogy between the system causation of the wheel and the system causation of the conscious brain breaks down at this point: the behavior of the wheel is totally determined, and the behavior of the conscious brain, on hypothesis 2, is not. How could that be? How exactly would the neurobiology work on such a hypothesis? I do not know the answer to that question, but I am struck by the fact that many of the explanations given in neurobiology do not postulate antecedent causally sufficient conditions. Thus, for example, to take a famous case, the readiness potential discussed by Deecke, Scheid, Kornhuber, and Libet[4] is not causally sufficient to determine the subsequent action, as is emphasized in Libet's discussion of how consciousness might interfere in the operation of the readiness potential. Paradoxically, these experiments are sometimes taken as somehow arguing against the freedom of the will in these cases. This conclusion does not seem to me to be implied by the data and I will now digress briefly to describe the issue.

What happens is this. The subject forms a conscious prior intention to move his finger (or flick his wrist) or some such every so often. That is a free, conscious decision. On the basis of that, he does consciously move his finger every so often, and before each finger movement there is an activation of the brain, in the form of the readiness potential, recordable on the scalp. In these cases the readiness potential precedes the conscious awareness of the intention-in-action by about 350 milliseconds. How is this supposed to be a threat to free will? Libet describes the case somewhat question-beggingly when he says, "The initiation of the free voluntary act appears to begin in the brain unconsciously, well before the person consciously knows he wants to act" (p. 51). The expressions "initiation" and "knows he wants to act" may be misleading. Here is another way to describe the case: the subject consciously adopts a policy of finger movements and consequently knows what sorts of acts he wants to perform when he makes that decision. The brain

---

4. L. Deecke, P. Scheid, H. H. Kornhuber, "Distribution of readiness potential, pre-motion positivity and motor potential of the human cerebral cortex preceding voluntary finger movements," *Experimental Brain Research*, vol. 7, 1969, pp. 158–168; B. Libet, "Do We Have Free Will?" *Journal of Consciousness Studies*, 6, no. 8–9, 1999, pp. 47–57.

unconsciously gets ready for each movement before the conscious initiation of the movement. No one to my knowledge argues that the activation is unrelated to the prior conscious decision; nor does anyone argue that the activation is a sufficient cause to determine the subsequent voluntary finger movement. Libet's description lends itself to interpretation that the readiness potential marks the onset of the action. But that is not true. There are typically about 350 milliseconds between the readiness potential and the onset of the intention-in-action and another 200 milliseconds to the onset of the bodily movement. In any case, as far as we know from the available data, the occurrence of the readiness potential is not causally sufficient for the performance of the action. As far as I can tell we do not know enough about the whole neurobiology of intentional action to have a complete theory of the role of the readiness potential in the causation of action. But it seems clearly premature to assume that the existence of the readiness potential shows in any sense that we do not have free will.

More interesting are cases where the body actually starts to move before the subject is conscious of any intention-in-action to move it. Famous examples are the runner who starts running before he can have consciously heard the gun go off, and the tennis player whose body starts to move toward the oncoming ball before he can have consciously registered the flight of the ball in his visual system. In both cases the body actually starts to move before the subject is consciously aware of the stimulus that triggers the movement. Neither of these cases, however, threatens the idea that in each case we have free voluntary actions. In both cases the subject, as a result of repeated training and practice, has well-established neural pathways that are activated by the perceptual stimuli prior to the onset of consciousness. To put the point crudely, the subject is playing tennis or running a race of his own free will, and if he is going to be any good at these activities his body must be able to move in certain key situations before he is consciously aware of the stimulus that triggers the movement. The temptation is to assimilate all of these—both the readiness potential and the trained athlete—cases to the sorts of "reflex" movements where the agent really does not have free will. Thus, for example, if I accidentally touch a hot stove I will withdraw my hand prior to feeling the pain. Here, it seems to me, the antecedent conditions are sufficient to cause the onset of the action. But the other cases are quite different from this. In both the readiness potential and the trained athlete cases, the movements depend on my having a conscious prior intention—to move my finger, to play tennis, to run a race, etc.—and I can cancel that intention at any time. In the hot stove case there is no prior intention, and I could *not* have *not* moved my hand.

Let us pursue the investigation to the next step. How are we to think of the relations between the microelements and the system feature of consciousness? For the passive forms of consciousness, such as perception, the totality of the features of the microelements at any given point must be sufficient to determine the conscious state at that point. What about volitional consciousness, the sort of consciousness where the gap exists? It seems to me the same principle would hold. The totality of the features at the relevant microlevels—neurons, synapses, microtubules, or whatever—would be sufficient to uniquely fix the conscious state at that point, including volitional consciousness. If we were to give up on this principle it seems to me we would have to accept some form of dualism. We would have to think of consciousness as breaking loose from its neurobiological base. We would have to give up even the most naive forms of supervenience, the idea that any change in consciousness must be matched by a change in neurobiology.[5] The point we have to keep insisting on is that consciousness is not some extra thing in the brain. It is just a state that the system of neurons is in, in the same way that the solidity of the wheel is not an extra element of the wheel in addition to the molecules. It is just a state that the molecules are in.

But when we insist that the system features must be uniquely fixed by the elements of the system we are not thereby giving up on free will, because the gap is across time. The gap is not between the state of my neurons now and my conscious state now; the gap is between what is happening now in the conscious volitional component of the whole brain system and what is going to happen next.

Furthermore, notice that in hypothesizing a causal sequence that is not at every stage manifested by causally sufficient conditions, we are not postulating randomness. Why not? Remember that I said that we should think of consciousness as a unified conscious field; and the experience of conscious volition is a crucial aspect of that conscious field. The hypothesis that is suggested by the discussion so far is that we should think of rational agency as a feature of that total conscious field. We have seen that, at the psychological level, rational agency can offer

5. I am no fan of the concept of supervenience. Its uncritical use is a sign of philosophical confusion, because the concept oscillates between causal supervenience and constitutive supervenience. But we do want to preserve the naïve underlying idea that any change in consciousness must be marked by a change in neurobiology. See my *Rediscovery of the Mind*, Cambridge, MA: MIT Press, 1992, pp. 124–126, for further discussion.

causal explanations of phenomena that are not deterministic in form. If the rational agency is realized in neurobiological structures that have these properties as well, that are themselves the underlying structure of rational agency, then the neurobiological processes would lack causally sufficient conditions, but they would not thereby become random. They would be driven by the same rational agency that operates as a feature of the system.

So the hypothesis of the gap as a neurobiological hypothesis comes down to this: The unified field of consciousness is a biological phenomenon like any other. It is entirely explained by neurobiological processes. Among those processes are those that cause and realize volitional consciousness, the consciousness of deliberating, choosing, deciding, and acting. Given certain assumptions about the nature of those processes, their existence requires a self. The self is not an entity in the field, but it determines a set of formal constraints on the operation of the field (as we saw in chapter 3). Stated in terms of our example, the neurobiological phenomenon of the freedom of the will amounts to three principles:

1. At any given point in time such as t_1 the total conscious state of the brain, including volitional consciousness, is entirely determined by the behavior of the relevant microelements.

2. The state of the brain at t_1 is not causally sufficient to determine the state of the brain at t_2 and t_3.

3. The move from the state at t_1 to the state at t_2 and t_3 can be explained only by features of the whole system, specifically by the operation of the conscious self.

One way to appreciate the difference between these two hypotheses is to apply each to our science fiction fantasy of the imagined robot, the Beast, that we constructed in chapter 5. In that chapter we imagined that we constructed a conscious robot, and that it had experiences of the gap, like our experiences. But now let us ask how we would deal with free will as an engineering problem, as a design problem correlating consciousness and technology. If we build the robot in accord with hypothesis 1, we will build a machine that is completely deterministic; indeed, we might build it according to standard cognitive science models of computational systems, either traditional systems or connectionist. The machine would be designed to receive input data in the form of sensory stimulations, it would process these according to its program and its database, and it would produce outputs in the form of muscle movements. For such a machine, consciousness might exist, but it would play no causal or explanatory role in the behavior of the system. That is, having built a completely deterministic system, we might then arrange it so that by bottom-up causation it has conscious experiences that match the stages of its lower-level operations. It might suffer from anxiety and indecision at the top level, but all of this would be epiphenomenal. The mechanism at the lower level would completely determine the subsequent behavior of the system. Indeed we could have all of these features and the system might not even be predictable, for we might put in some randomizing element in the hardware that would make its behavior unpredictable, even though consciousness was still epiphenomenal. Consciousness would exist but would just go along for the ride.

On hypothesis 2 we have a different sort of engineering task altogether. On hypothesis 2 the whole organization of the unified conscious field functions essentially in the operation of the system. The structure and behavior of the microelements at any given point in time is sufficient to determine the character of the consciousness at that time, but it is not sufficient to determine the next state of the system. The next state of the system is determined only by the conscious decision making that is a feature of the whole system. As an engineering problem I have no idea how we would go about constructing this, but then at present we have no idea about how we could go about constructing a conscious robot anyway.

Granted the psychological reality of a gap, it seems to me these are the two most likely possible forms of an explanation of human behavior. First, psychological indeterminism coexists with neurobiological determinism. If that thesis is true, free rational life is entirely an illusion. The other possibility is that psychological indeterminism is matched by neurobiological indeterminism. I have tried to show that this is at least an empirical possibility. I have no idea which if either of these hypotheses will turn out to be true. Perhaps some third possibility that we cannot even imagine will turn out to be right. These are the two hypotheses I can come up with if I follow relentlessly the lines of investigation suggested by both what we know from our own experience and what we know about the brain.

Frankly, I do not find either hypothesis intellectually attractive. Hypothesis 1 is comforting in that it enables us to treat the brain as we treat any other organ. We treat the brain as a completely deterministic system, like the liver or the heart. But hypothesis 1 does not sit comfortably with what we know about evolution. On this hypothesis there is an enormously elaborate and expensive conscious system, the system of rational decision making, which plays no causal role whatever in the behavior of the organism, because the behavior is entirely fixed at the bottom level. On this view, there would be no selectional advantage whatever to having a conscious, rational, decision-making system, which is the result of a long period of evolution and which is extremely expensive biologically speaking, and which occupies an enormous space in our conscious experiences. Furthermore, the illusion of rational decision making, on this hypothesis, would not be like other illusions, which do indeed have a selectional advantage. So, for example, assuming that color is a systematic illusion, there is nonetheless an enormous selectional advantage in an organism that has the capacity to discriminate objects on the basis of color. But on hypothesis 1 no selectional advantage whatever is conveyed by conscious rational decision making.

But hypothesis 2 does not sit comfortably with our existing conception of biology either. The problem is not that hypothesis 2 asks us to think of consciousness as playing a "top-down" causal role in the behavior of the microelements, because, as a system feature, consciousness functions like any other system feature. In the end when we talk about consciousness affecting other elements, we are really just talking about how the elements affect each other because the consciousness is entirely a function of the behavior of the elements. In the same way, when we talk about the behavior of the wheel affecting the molecules, we are just talking about how the molecules affect each other. So the problem with hypothesis 2 is not that it entails top-down causation of consciousness. That is an easy problem to deal with. The problem is to see how the consciousness of the system could give it a causal efficacy that is not deterministic. And it is not enough help to be told that we could accept the randomness of quantum mechanical accounts that are not deterministic. Conscious rationality is not supposed to inherit the randomness of quantum mechanics. Rather, conscious rationality is supposed to be a causal mechanism that proceeds causally, though not on the basis of antecedently sufficient causal conditions. Indeed, on some accounts, one of the functions of the cell is to overcome the instability of the quantum indeterminacy at subcellular levels.

I have not tried to solve the problem of the freedom of the will, but just tried to state exactly what the problem is, and what the most likely lines of its possible solution are.

Index